THE SPINNER'S ENCYCLOPEDIA

The author cotton spinning using a bracelet distaff and a supported spindle. On the board is a basket of punis

THE SPINNER'S ENCYCLOPEDIA

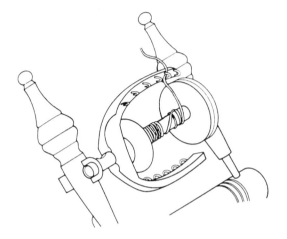

Enid Anderson

A **DAVID & CHARLES** CRAFT BOOK

This book is dedicated to all the Servite Sisters who were at 'St Josephs Priory'. Harrow Road West, Dorking, Surrey, England, with whom I spent so many happy years.

Enid Anderson

British Library Cataloguing in Publication Data

Anderson, Enid
  The spinner's encyclopedia.
  1. Hand spinning – Dictionaries
  I. Title
  746.1'2'0321   TT847

  ISBN 0-7153-8794-4

Typeset by Typesetters (Birmingham) Ltd, Smethwick, West Midlands
and printed in Great Britain
by Butler & Tanner Limited, Frome and London
for David & Charles Publishers plc
Brunel House   Newton Abbot   Devon

Distribution in the United States of America by
Sterling Publishing Co, Ltd., 2 Park Avenue, New York, NY 10016

· CONTENTS ·

The craft of handspinning is part of our history and, whilst we can experiment with many fibres and techniques within the confines of the traditional aspects of the craft, the beauty of the history and traditions make it difficult to improve on what has been produced by spinners for generations. However, sadly, many of the earlier techniques used by our ancestors, together with the tools they used, have been lost in time, therefore it is today's spinners who must create and build information to be passed onto future generations – an exciting project.

◇

Spinning is having a revival. We live in an age of mass production that developed to meet the needs of the people; a worker may only see one part of an item being made and never experience the satisfaction of the finished article. Due to the increased stress of everyday living, spinning as a therapy has much to offer. The spinner can experience the fulfilment of producing an article from start to finish and can enjoy the creativity involved. In earlier times, spinning was performed by cottagers who were often illiterate; it was considered lowly work. Mechanisation and the introduction of Spinning Jennies in one generation destroyed handspinning as a trade. It gradually returned; its image had changed, however, from a trade to a craft. In earlier times traditional skills were passed down through families; today, in many cases, community life and the accompanying craft skills have been destroyed by an economic climate that often dictates that people must leave home to find employment, and by the large new roads built to produce faster travel. Fortunately, many craft associations have been formed which counteract this to a degree.

◇

How does one explain the sensations of spinning – the sounds of the wheel, the movement of the treadle, handling the fibres – cares and tensions melt away and complete relaxation ensues. Add to this the satisfaction of building upon the traditions of the past for the future and the picture is complete. I do hope the reader will join me in making this possible and derive as much pleasure from this craft as I have done.

The Spinners Encyclopedia evolved from an indexed note-book on the history terms and techniques associated with spinning, compiled by the Author from many sources for the benefit of her students. The Author hereby acknowledges her debt to those sources, and sincerely hopes that she has covered them all in the Acknowledgements.

There are many different ways of performing spinning techniques. This is understandable, as earlier methods were not always recorded in detail, so they have evolved often in different ways. During the research and experimentation for the book, many tasks performed in different ways produced a similar result. An example of this is which hand is to the front when spinning – use whichever is more comfortable. Many spinners are ambidextrous, changing hands when necessary. Occasionally within the text is stated which hand is to the front only because it is the more usual hand to use. The Author nearly always uses her right hand to the front, which also makes transferring to a Great Wheel easier.

Clear cross-referencing should enable easy use of the contents. There is as little or as much as one wants to learn in a craft and spinning is no exception. Many students are under the impression that they can spin once they can produce a yarn; the contents of this book should prove otherwise.

INTRODUCTION

ıca · Acc　　*es · Actual weight · Affinity · Alpaca · Angora · Anilı*
Acceler　*Actual weight · Affinity · Alpaca · Angora · Aniline*
ıca · Acc　*es · Actual weight · Affinity · Alpaca · Angora · Anilı*

Abaca or Manila Hemp Abaca or Manila hemp (*Musa textilis* – from the musa plant) is grown in the Philippines and belongs to the plantain or banana family. It has a lustrous fibre with a staple from 91.5cm to 2.742m (3 to 9ft). Cutting commences once the flowers appear. The leaf stalks have a fibrous coating; this is removed and drawn between a block of wood and the fine teeth of a knife. The pulpy matter is discarded. The remaining long white fibres are cured, sorted and baled. The outer leaf fibres are very strong, but not so coarse as *sisal*, and are mainly used for mats, cord and twine. The finer fibres can be made into clothing.

To SPIN: dampen the fibres, tie in hanks and spin like a hanging strick of Line. *Sisal* is spun in the same way.

Accelerant A substance, sometimes a swelling agent, added to a dyebath to accelerate the diffusion of the dye.
See *Dyes and Dyeing*

Acclerating Wheel Head On the great wheel the extra pulley which is used to increase the spindle speed.
See *Minor's Head* .

Accessories See *Carders; Distaff; Lazy Kate; Niddy Noddy; Skein Winders*

Actual Weight The weight of a quantity of wool including scoured, greasy, skin or slipe wool etc, not related in any way to the clean content; a term related to trade returns.

Affinity The quantitive expression of *substantivity*, ie the difference between the potential, chemically, of the dye in its standard state in the fibre, and the corresponding chemical potential of the dyebath.

Allergies Occasionally students of the craft of handspinning find they are allergic to some natural fibres. There are many manmade fibres available in roving or sliver form in a range of colours.

Alpaca The alpaca, llama, guanaco and vicuna are all members of the South American camel family, *Lama pacos*. They are without humps and are approximately 121.9cm (4ft) high. They have been domesticated since ancient times and are related to the camels of the Old World.

Developed from the wild guanaco, today these animals are raised in Southern Peru, Northern Argentina and Bolivia and thrive in high altitudes. They have not been bred in large quantities successfully elsewhere. In earlier times they were used for their flesh and fleece, today purely for their fleece, which can be white, brown, grey or black in colour. The fleece consists of two kinds; coarse, medullated beard hairs and soft, highly lustrous alpaca wool hairs with very little crimp. The staple length varies according to the time allowed for growth – approximately 20.4cm (8in) per year. Commercially purchased alpaca is usually from a two-year growth. The alpaca resembles the llama, although the animal is somewhat smaller with longer hair, which can reach a length of 50.8cm (20in) – occasionally more. Its feet resemble that of the camel. The finest breed is the *suri* whose fleece hangs to the ground and measures up to 60.9cm (2ft) long.

The animals are either clipped once a year or sometimes once every two years, usually around December. The yield varies, approximately 2.5kg (6lb) of hair for a year's growth. Once sheared, the fibres are sorted into seven grades. A single fibre can hardly be seen. The fibres do not have developed scales, therefore the yarn does not have the lightness in volume of wool. It does not felt easily or bleach satisfactorily so it can only be used in the natural colouring, or dyed to a darker shade. It can be purchased scoured and combed, so requires very little preparation. It blends very well with other fibres. There is very little waste, as the fleece may be used in its entirety.

To SPIN: if difficult to handle, add a little oil emulsion before spinning. It can be lightly combed or rolled into rolags and spun as wool of the comparable staple length, since its softness does make it suitable for knitwear. A worsted spin is also suitable, due to its length and lustre. If purchased as long, combed strips spin from a strip laid over the forefinger; the triangle will be long. A very fine thread can be spun. A firm take-up is required on the wheel, unlike camel and cashmere it requires very little twist. Peruvian handspun done on small handspindles produces very fine yarn.

WASHING: skein off, wash and rinse. Hang and weight the skein sufficiently to set the twist. There will be no shrinkage.

Textiles made from Alpaca are often brushed to raise a nap; usually whilst still tensioned on the loom, working along the weft from side to side. Knitting may also be brushed.
See *Salt, Sir Titus*

9

Angora Goat The wild goat, *Capra hircus*, came originally from Asia Minor. The angora goat is now bred in South Africa, United States and Turkey. It yields mohair (from the Arabic *mukhayyar* – a coarse hair cloth). Angora goat has a longer, finer and silkier coat than other goats, and has a fibre length between 10.3cm and 30.5cm (4in to as much as 12in). It is white and lustrous and can produce as much as 2.5kg (6lb) of mohair per one clipping. This is graded into three categories.

1 Tight lock: this includes very fine ringlets.
2 Flat lock: wavy fibres of medium quality.
3 Fluffy: open fleece.

Before spinning mist with warm water. It can be spun by the worsted method, dyes well and, because of its structure, fabrics made from it do not crease. Wash as alpaca.

Angora Rabbit This longhaired breed of rabbit, *Lepus cuniculus*, produces angora hair fibre. It is available in a variety of colours. Best quality obtained from animals aged between 5 and 18 months; earlier than that the hair is rather fine although it can be spun as a combination with wool. After 18 months it becomes coarser in texture and on sorting usually the longest staple may be found on the shoulders and back. The under parts of the animal produce fur which is rather tender, shorter and soft. The upper parts contain long hairs, similar to *kemp*, which it is advisable to remove before clipping or plucking. If the animal is clipped, the staple may be 2.5cm to 7.6cm (1 to 3in) long; when plucked (brushed) 5cm to 10.3cm (2 to 4in) long. The plucked hair is better for spinning. If many animals are kept, then the different parts of the yield, comprising varying lengths of staple, can be sorted. This is impractical if only a few animals are available. It is essential to store the hair, once sorted, very carefully, as it is very fly-away. Laid between layers of tissue paper, in a container, is a satisfactory way of storing.

To Spin: if the fibres are very short, lightly oil before spinning. The correct twist is obtained through trial and error; if overtwisted, the softness of the yarn is lost, with insufficient twist the yarn will break. Some spinners, if spinning without oiling the fibres, sprinkle talcum powder on their hands before spinning. The fibre must be dry; if damp or matted it will not spin.

To join the fibres of the angora to a woollen leader before spinning, first twist the angora fibres with a damp thumb, this makes the attachment easier. The hand movements must be rapid to the rate of the treadling as the fibres are short. The tension should be fairly loose, as a firm twist is required, but only as much as is necessary to hold the fibres together and still keep the yarn fluffy. The skeins should be dipped in water with no additives, as this would reduce the static elasticity and thereby reduce the fluffiness; then they should be lightly weighted to set.

This is a very useful fibre for blending with, for example, wool. The wool should be pre-carded, then layered with the angora fibres; they can then be re-carded to blend. A satisfactory blend is between 30 and 50 per cent angora with wool, the wool producing good elasticity to the resulting yarn.

Aniline Dyes The first synthetic dyes were made from *aniline*, an oily liquid produced from coal tar.

Alizarin is the red colouring matter of madder, but it can also be prepared synthetically.
See *Synthetic Dyes*

Animal Fibres Are made of protein (keratin) and contain carbon, hydrogen, oxygen and sulphur. They are very warm, strong and durable. Each hair has a surface of overlapping imbrications (scales) which catch into those on adjacent hairs so as to maintain the spun position of the bundle. Whilst silk is protein (fibroin) it does not contain sulphur. It is the sulphur in animal fibres that attract moths. See *Alpaca; Camel; Cashmere; Goat; Llama; Mohair; Musk Ox; Silkworm*

Anti-Tetanus It is essential for spinners, especially those who spin 'in the grease', to have antitetanus injections.

Apron By tradition blue, but in any case preferably a plain colour to make tasks, for example teasing, easier to see. When spinning 'in the grease' it is useful to lay a cloth across the apron to absorb the worst of the dirt and grease. If carding indoors it is wise to cover the immediate working area with cloth or paper.

Arra The term used for a loan on the security of the wool clip in the Middle Ages.

Artificial Silks Chardonnet, nitro or collodian silk, which is no longer made as it is unable to command a higher price than manmade fibres developed later. They and other manmade textiles were collectively called *artificial silks*, due to the comparison between the way the silkworm extruded silk from its spinnerets and manmade filaments are produced by extruding a viscous fluid through holes. There the resemblance ended as no direct comparison can be made between real and artificial silk, other than perhaps the cost. See *Sericulture*

11

ales · B̶ 〔A/B〕 at Head · Bezoar · Binders · Black Fleece · Blaze · Ble
· Barill̶ ead · Bezoar · Binders · Black Fleece · Blaze · Blendir
ales · B̶ at Head · Bezoar · Binders · Black Fleece · Blaze · Ble

Asbestos A mineral fibre, which was spun by handspinners for many centuries, now it is recognised as a health hazard, so is no longer spun. In earlier periods it was used for shrouds, possibly to keep the remains of different bodies separate.

Asclepias The North American milkweed family which bear fruit with tufts of silky hairs similar to cotton fibre. Named after the Greek God of Medicine (one variety is called pleurisy root). Similar plants which yield cottonlike fibres are *bombax* and *kapok*.

Babylon Meaning 'Land of Wool'; grew very rich due to her woollen trade.

Back Washer The name given to the machine which washes tops to remove all impurities. It also dries them by passing over steamheated cylinders, or hot air cylinders.

Backwashing The removal of oil during the worsted process.

Badly Bred Wool that has little character.

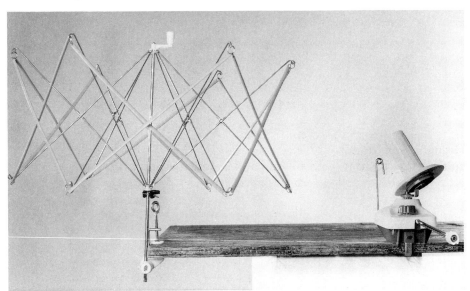

Plate 1 (*left*) SWIFT; (*right*) BALL WINDER

Bales After shearing, the wool is placed in a sack or bag in a square or oblong shape. A bale is a *woolpack* holding between 45.4kg and 454kg (100 and 1,000lb), generally 136.2kg to 158.9kg (300lb to 350lb), the variation occurring according to the country of origin.

Ball Winder An efficient and easy-to-use device for winding wools. When using a ball of wool wound on a ball winder, always start from the inside of the ball. Ball winders can also be used for winding yarn from the wheel (if yarn is already washed and/or dyed). Useful also for plying two yarns.

METHOD: take the two ends from a ball of yarn, ie from the inside and the outside, attach both ends to the bobbin on the wheel, proceed as if plying from a lazy kate.

Barilla A crude soda used as a scouring agent for fleece. Made in earlier times from plant ash.

Bassines Also known as *bassinets* and *basin waste*. A filature waste of lower quality. The remaining last few layers of silk in the inside of the cocoon, where the supply is nearly finished after reeling is completed. It is fairly weak. Also silk from damaged cocoons and double cocoons, often stained as a result of the chrysalis dying in the cocoon.
See *Filature; Sericulture; Silk Reeling*

Bast Fibre The word *bast* means that the fibres are obtained from the stem (*phloem*) of the plant. They are long fibrous strands found between the outer and inner core of the stem. These are vegetable fibres. Examples are *flax; hemp; jute; kenaf; nettle; ramie*

Batching This is the method used to blend the hemp fibres for strength and uniformity after separation. The resulting blend is softened by treating with oil and water and the impurities removed after which it is carded, drawn and spun. See *Hemp*

Bat Head A wooden paddle which is attached to the headpost of a great wheel with a cavity for the spindle shaft which is attached horizontally with leather or corn husk bearings. A drive belt goes directly to a pulley groove on the spindle. This is the simplest great wheel. A primitive accessory to the great wheel and capable only of producing the coarsest yarn. See *Great Wheel*

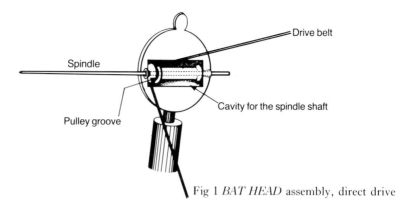

Fig 1 *BAT HEAD* assembly, direct drive

Batt Also referred to as *lap, webb*, and *matt*. Fibres carded on a carding machine. Alternative meanings see *Laps; Matt*

Bave A term used in silk production. A single bave is the result of the fusing together of two single threads called *brins*.
See *Silk Reeling*

Beaver *Castor fiber*, the Old World beaver, and *C canadensis* from North America, have two coats; the grey is silky, the reddish-brown is coarser.

Beeswax Polish For fine antique furniture and spinning wheels.

RECIPE: grate a small block (or more, depending on the amount of polish required) of beeswax into a screw-capped jar. Cover with white spirit or turpentine, shake gently to mix. Sometimes, if the beeswax is stored for a time in its block form it becomes hard, this may require a little more spirit to be added if the polish seems rather too firm.
  Beeswax is also useful to rectify slipping driving bands. Rub a little of the pure beeswax into the cord, not too liberally. Please note: there are varying reasons for a driving band slipping:

  a) the cord was unsuitable
  b) the knot, splice, or whatever means used for joining, may be slipping
  c) the drive band has stretched, so adjust the tension
  d) the wheel and whorl grooves have a build-up of dirt and grease; this will need to be removed.

Beet A bundle or sheaf of tied flax crop or straw. See *Flax*

Bellies Wool that is shorn from the bellies of some sheep. Packed separately from fleece wool.

Belly Wool Wool from a sheep's belly that is discarded in skirting due to its dirty and tangled condition.
See *Fleece – Sorting*

Belt Traction Belt traction is essential for successful spinning. It can be assisted by rubbing a dressing onto the band. The dressing used is very much the personal choice of the individual. Dressing may be obtained from agricultural merchants who deal with belt-driven machinery. Alternatively beeswax may be used in moderation.
See *Beeswax*

Bezoar *Capra hircus* is considered to be the ancestor of the domestic goat. It has short greyish-brown hair with a black line along the back. It still lives wild in the high mountains of Central Asia.

Binders Fibres growing from one staple to another that act to hold the fleece together. The fibres on hoggets, yearling sheep, join at the tip and, as the age of the sheep increases, gradually work down lower until in an old sheep the binders actually join the staples near the skin of the animal. When shorn the staples then fall apart and this is then referred to as a *locky fleece*.
See *Staple*

Bishop Blaise The patron saint of woolcombers and Bishop of Sabaste in Asia Minor in the fourth century. He is said to have invented the wool comb and was tortured with his own device. The festival of St Blaise falls on February 3 when, in early times, the wool-combers had festivities on that day.

Bison The North American buffalo is, in fact, a bison (*Bison bison*), and its European relative is the *Bison bonasus*. The hair is very coarse, dark brown in colour. The undercoat is a soft brown fibre, most enjoyable to spin, and of interest to spinners who enjoy spinning a more unusual fibre.

METHOD: separate the hair and the undercoat by hand. Wash gently to remove any adhering dust. Lightly oil. A similar spin to camel down.

Black Fleece Also known as *black wool*; any coloured fleece in the black, brown, grey, silver or varied range.

Blaze The first waste silk from the thread which the silkworm produces to secure itself to the object on which it develops its cocoon. The thread is filled with sericin and is the least lustrous. It has value as *noil*.
See *Keba; Sericulture*

Bleaching – Chemical Linen soaked in a solution of chloride of lime becomes bleached when exposed to oxygen both in the air and water; the released oxygen destroys the colour of the fibre.

METHOD: boil the linen yarn (or fabric) for an hour in a good quality soap solution. Rinse and repeat. Spinners vary in their choice of bleaching chemicals. Whichever is used, chloride of lime must be present.

LIME ONLY SOLUTION: make a concentrated solution by dissolving the lime in rain water 28g (2oz) to 1*l* (2pt). Fill a container with sufficient liquid to cover the linen when it is put into the container (allowing for any 'soak up' of liquid), to the proportion of 0.25*l* (½pt) of the concentrated solution to 4*l* (8pt) of water. Place the linen into the solution for approximately 2½ to 3hr; turn occasionally with a glass rod. Lift the linen out and expose to the air for several hours. The lime-soaked fibres become bleached and the colour is destroyed as explained above. Wash the bleached linen and dry outdoors. When handling any chemicals great care should be taken; always use in a controlled situation.

Bleaching – Gold – Linen
METHOD: wet the linen. Prepare a solution of 14g (1oz) of soap and 14g (1oz) of soda to 4.5*l* (1 gal) of water. Place the linen into the liquid, bring to the boil slowly and simmer for approximately 2hr. Leave to soak for several hours or overnight. This process may be repeated if necessary.

Bleaching – Grass The oldest, most widely used process and the most natural for bleaching linen. Causes no damage to the fibre structure and is permanent. The skeins of yarn are laid out onto grass for several weeks during which time they must be kept damp and turned occasionally to prevent staining. The colour is removed from the fibre by the oxygen given off by the plants and the atmosphere. Over a period of time the linen will gradually whiten. *Bleachfields* were a common sight in the cotton districts before the discovery of chlorine in the late eighteenth century.

Bleeding When there is a loss of dye due to washing.

Blending Blending of fibres in all fibre preparation is important, otherwise for example, different characteristics in the fibres may show in the finished yarn as streaked, especially where there may be a slight colour variation; this often becomes more apparent in the finished yarn. Fibres can either be blended completely to achieve one colour tone or blended to produce a streaked effect. Great care should be taken to achieve a complete blend when mixing, as however carefully the fibres are teased and sorted into what may appear to be equal quantities, variation in tone can appear between separate cardings, and these will show up even more sharply in the finished yarn. The same applies to partial blending; careful quantity control must be exercised to produce a balanced effect within the yarn.

Blocking Plain garments which are knitted and crocheted require blocking before being stitched together. The purpose is to shape each piece and to remove curled edges or unevenness, and to set the stitches. There are several methods of blocking; three are described below. *Note*: do not block ribbing or bulk designs.

METHOD 1: take several layers of white blotting paper of sufficient size to accommodate the pieces being blocked. Draw the shape of the piece/pieces on the blotting paper to scale using a soft lead pencil. Dampen the layers of the blotting paper and secure them to a board of the same size. Pin the piece/pieces to the pencilled shape and lay aside in a warm place to dry. (The various layers of the blotting paper when dry can be changed to produce a fresh drawing surface for the next pieces.)

METHOD 2: pin the knitted shape to a board; it should be fairly taut without undue stretching. Using a steam iron, go over the surface except for the ribbing, working from top to bottom. The steam should penetrate the piece without pressing. Leave in a warm place to dry, then remove pins.

METHOD 3: the results of this method are often very apparent at craft shows and exhibitions, where overpressed garments are displayed. If it is to be executed correctly and successfully, it requires care. Pin the pieces to the required shape and size. Place a damp cloth over the piece to be blocked and press gently over the surface except for the ribbing. It is difficult to gauge the correct pressure and this can result in overpressing. Once pressed, lay aside to cool.

Blocky Consistent length and diameter of staple.
See *Tippy*, which is the opposite of this term.

Blood Grades USA A system of blood grades based on Merino and Ramboullet sheep to indicate how much fine wool is in the breeding. The higher the blood grade, the finer the fibre. The system incorporates seven standard blood grades: *full blood, half blood, three eighths, one quarter, common, braid* and *britch*. Full blood or half-blood is considered to be quite fine; braid is coarser.

Bloom The visual appeal and brightness of the skin side of the shorn fleece which shows when the fleece is rolled after shearing.

Bloom Dips Usually orange coloured and often applied to the fleeces of sheep before selling. It is considered by some farmers to enhance the appearance of the animal.

Blooming A means of increasing the brightness of the colour during the dyeing process, usually by the addition of tin.
See *Dyeing*

Blue Dutch Similar to *Blue Flemish* flax. Produced in Holland; mainly used in the manufacture of twines because of its strength.

Blue Flemish A dark coloured flax produced in the Bruges and Ypres districts of Belgium.

Bobbin Also called reel. The bobbin on a spinning wheel receives the spun yarn. The bobbin is placed onto the spindle, before the bobbin whorl (bobbin screw), with the bevelled end of the bobbin lying in the 'U' of the flyer. At the opposite end is the bobbin whorl; onto this screws the spindle whorl. This produces two grooves together, the one in the bobbin whorl and the other in the spindle whorl. Variations occur in the circumference of the whorls from one wheel to another. The bobbin must move freely on the spindle shaft, which is usually made of steel, brass or cast iron. The spindle (or needle) must be kept clean at all times.

Occasionally the bobbin may tend to move along the spindle with too much movement; a washer placed on the spindle before the bobbin will resolve this problem. An empty bobbin requires a slacker band when commencing the spinning, then constant adjustment as it fills with spun yarn. Most new wheels are sold complete with several spare bobbins.

To remove a full bobbin will depend on the design of the spinning wheel being used. On a double band for example, it may be necessary to reduce the tension and remove the drive band, then turn the front and back maidens to release the flyer assembly and then unscrew the whorl and remove the bobbin. On a scotch tensioner, the brake band must be released first and then the drive band. Whatever the wheel design, it is advisable always to become conversant with the various wheel parts before starting to spin.
See *Flyer; Whorl*

Bobbin Drag Also called *Flyer Lead, Friction Drag* and *Scotch Tensioner*: the well known Ashford wheels from New Zealand are an

example of this. The flyer is driven only. A single drive band links the driving wheel and the spindle whorl; it should be tight enough to turn the spindle and flyer, but if too tight will make treadling difficult. There is no drive band to the bobbin, so this rotates at the speed of the flyer until the spinning starts. Draw in of the yarn is impossible, therefore a brake is required on the bobbin which is provided by a friction band. This is attached to the mother-of-all (or sometimes on a part of the upright), taken over the bobbin whorl and attached to a peg on the other side. The peg can be turned when tension is required. The friction band should be tightened sufficiently to make the bobbin rotate slower than the flyer and thus cause the spun yarn to wind on. Unlike the double band wheels, on a scotch tensioner the two whorls are tensioned separately. To adjust the tension as the yarn on the bobbin builds up, the peg is turned slightly. There are various designs of bobbin drag, according to the wheel being used.
See *Scotch Tensioner*

Bobbin Holders Also called a *Lazy Kate* in England and a *Whirrie* in Scotland. When a bobbin is full of yarn it is removed from the wheel and set aside with other full bobbins for plying. Storage for the bobbins is provided in the form of racks. The designs vary; often comprising two uprights on a wooden stand with a long rod between, onto which the full bobbins can be placed side by side. Another similar design has taller uprights with several rods between, one above the other, and the bobbins are again placed side by side.

Bobbin Lead Also called *Double Band Drive* and in which one con-tinuous drive band is doubled, and placed twice round the driving wheel and once round the bobbin and the spindle whorls. A cross appears in the band due to it being doubled; this cross adjusts during spinning. When the wheel is turned clockwise the cross will appear between the bottom of the wheel and the whorls (the band coming from the spindle whorl is underneath at this stage to avoid excess friction). When the driving wheel is turned anticlockwise the cross should be between the top of the wheel and the two whorls (the band coming from the bobbin whorl should be underneath).

One rotation of the wheel puts a twist in the yarn and, as the bobbin is rotating faster due to its smaller circumference, the yarn is drawn in. It is desirable when choosing a wheel to take careful note of the whorl circumferences and choose a model which has the greatest difference between the two.

Body A term related to wool when the staple has the appearance of being full and bulky.

Bold The term donating a wool that has been well grown and is of good character and appearance.

Boll See *Cotton*

Bombax A silk cotton tree of West Indian origin. Similar trees are found in Africa, Asia and America. It produces a cotton fibre that can be spun; it feels silky to the touch. Sometimes it is used as a stuffing for a variety of purposes, for example cushions.

Book of Silk A book of silk is forty hanks, some 2.27kg (5lb) in weight. Japanese books weigh approximately 2kg (4½lb) and contain about fifty-five skeins; Chinese books are heavier.
See *Silk Reeling*

Boon Also called *Shoves* and *Shous*; in flax production, after retting and breaking, woody particles remain in the flax bundles, this boon has to be removed by *scutching*.
See *Chenevote; Flax – Linum usitatissimum*, section on *Scutching*

Botany The name given to the 250kg (450lb) soft, plastic-type sack container for fleece into which the sorted fleeces are placed. It measures 152cm×76.2cm×81.3cm (60in×30in×32in).

Botany Wool All wool of 60s quality and over, and the name given to fabrics, tops and yarns made from merino wool. Referred to wool sent from Botany Bay, the penal settlement in Australia.
See *Merino*

Bottoming A term used in natural dyeing when the fibre or yarn is dyed one colour, then top-dyed another colour.

Bottom Wool The short, soft undercoat on some sheep breeds that have a long hairy coat, eg the *Blackface*.

Bourrette A yarn made of low-waste silk.

Boutonne A name given to *knop yarn*.

Bow To make a bow suitable for bowing cotton, cut a piece of 1.3cm to 2cm (½in to ¾in) thick willow to measure approximately 60.9cm to 91.5cm (2 to 3ft) in length. Tie a piece of catgut or smooth cord to each end and pull gently into a softly curved shape. Willow is very supple which allows it to bend easily, however other, similar, woods could be used. The size of the bow is determined by the length of the arm of the manipulator; it should fit comfortably under the curved arm. See *Bowing*

Bowing The whipping up of raw cotton until it resembles a soft cloud of fibre.

METHOD: hold the bow with the left or right arm placed across the top, press to the diaphragm firmly. Lay a small pile of raw cotton onto a table of suitable height. Place the bow so that the cord or catgut lies across the cotton, just touching it. Pluck the catgut with the free hand and the cotton will start to fluff up. Continue until it resembles a soft light mass; when this is achieved treat another pile of cotton in the same way. It is necessary, from time to time, to remove particles of the fibre which have become caught on the catgut. The bowed cotton can be used for spinning in a variety of ways; either with prior carding using hand cards; by making punis; or coiling around a bracelet distaff, to name just a few. In earlier times the bow was large and attached to a wall, then the cord or gut was hit with a wooden mallet to fluff up the cotton, the bower sitting in a crouched position. See *Bow; Punis*

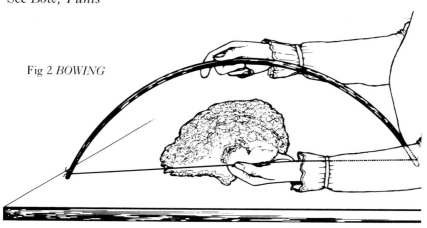

Fig 2 *BOWING*

Bradford Spinning The name given to the English method of spinning worsted yarn. The wool is oiled and combed to produce a smooth lustrous yarn which is woven into worsted suitings. The French do not oil the wool, which is dry spun.

Braid The name given in the blood-grading system for the lowest quality of wool.

Branding Most commonly called *raddle mark*
a) the branding of sheep with a branding fluid for means of identification

b) stencilling on bales of wool to signify the owner, type of wool and serial number.

Break See *Fleece – Preparation Methods*, section on *Choosing a Fleece*.

Breed Family name of sheep having many variations within a breed.

Breed – British Classification As far as British wools are concerned there are three main classifications and eight official grading classifications.

1 Mountain and Hill
2 Longwools and Lustre
3 Shortwool or Down

There are approximately fifty breeds in Great Britain and many hundreds of crosses. Crossbreeding is practised for many purposes, but fleece for spinning is rarely the main consideration. The classification relates very much to the environment of the natural surroundings of the sheep and the fleece they develop as a result to protect themselves from the elements.

GRADING CLASSIFICATIONS
1 *Down wools*
2 *Fine wools*
3 *Medium wools*
4 *Masham cross* and *Leicester*
5 *Lustre wools*
6 *Cheviot, Radnor* and *Welsh*
7 *Swaledale, Blackface* and *Herdwick*
8 *Lamb wools*

Brick of Silk Combed rovings of silk are sold as a *brick*. Before spinning the silk brick should be taken from its bag and the roving shaken very lightly to enable it to breathe.
See *Silk*, section on *Spinning Silk*

Brightening Oiling the silk with an emulsion of olive oil and washing soda, then scrooping.

Brightness A term relating to the finer types of wool to describe the whiteness.

Broad Wool that is stronger and coarser than is usual for that particular type.

Broggers Also called *Staplers*, were the merchants who controlled the raw wool trade in the fourteenth century. They acted as middlemen and dealers.

Broitches Also called *tines*. The teeth on combs used for wool-combing.
See *Combing*

Broken A trade term applied to the best wool of the skirtings, which are similar in characteristics to the fleece wool.

Broker Agent used to execute an order; either he/she sells the wool on behalf of the grower or buys on behalf of the merchant and manu-facturer on a commission basis.

Brown Cotton *Gossypium religiosum* (religious cotton) is also called *nankeen* or *slave cotton*.
The botanical name derives because it was the fibre used in monks' robes in ancient India and China. A beautiful fibre which grows in varying tones of brown to an average length of 1.3cm (½in). When it is inbred, the colour becomes lighter unless crossed with some from another area. It is found wild and also is cultivated on a small scale in Mexico where it is known as *coyuchil*. It is grown too in Central and Southern America, Africa, China and South East Asia. The plant is relatively unproductive. Commercial growers show little interest; possibly they are wary of the fact that, if brown cotton grown near white cotton crosspollinates, their white cotton would be affected. A hardwearing yarn providing sufficient twist is inserted. Spun and woven tightly due to the short staple. Spins well on a cotton spindle, sometimes better than on a wheel.
Much of Mexico's brown cotton is now put through an iron bath; after being woven this is called *reforzado* and the colour bleeds a little. In earlier times brown cotton was ginned on the last day of ginning after all the white cotton had run through.

Bucking Tubs In olden times, after spinning flax, the skeins were thrown into a bucking tub or hollowed out log. The *bucking* or *bleaching* was done with hot water or *lye*. After washing, the linen was spread out in the sun to whiten further.

Builds A term used in the construction of yarn onto the spindle when spinning on a great wheel, referred to as cop or roving builds. The cop build is the method most commonly used for handspindle spinning, the weight is then at the base.
See *Cone; Cop*

23

Bulk Classing When a number of small lots of wool from various owners are graded and combined into standard lines.

Bulky or Dense Wool comprising staples that each carry a great number of fibres and closely packed on the sheep's back.

Bulky Yarns An untrue description of a yarn, often used however to refer to thick yarns. However a bulky yarn can contain less fibre and more air, or could be dense and heavy. A thin yarn can, in fact, be spun with plenty of air and appear lofty and very light but not bulky or thick.

Bullen Dust from the outside of *flax*.

Bump A loosely spun cotton yarn, having the lowest yarn count of cotton.

Burr Plant seeds with hooks that cling to the wool. Very difficult to remove as they tend to bury themselves into the fleece. Avoid burred fleece.

Burring Also called *burling*, is the removal of burrs, vegetable matter, slubs, and any other items that may spoil the quality of cloth.

Burry Wool containing burrs; if only a small percentage, they can be removed by combing or carding; if the burr content is excessive then it is necessary to carbonise before carding.
See *Carbonising*

Butt A parcel of greasy wool in a recognised wool pack weighing less than 90kg (200lb) gross (New South Wales). Weight varies in different states.

Butterfly See *Finger Hank*

Byzantium History states that the European Justinian of Byzantium, in the sixth century AD, persuaded two Persian monks to smuggle silkworm eggs and mulberry seeds out of China, hidden in walking sticks. This was said to be the start of the Western silk industry. Silk textiles of Byzantium became famous.

Combing · Cortes · Cotton · Crimp · Crocking · Cros   things ·
·bing · Cortes · Cotton · Crimp · Crocking · Crossbre   ys · Cabl
Combing · Cortes · Cotton · Crimp · Crocking · Cros   things ·

Cabling Cabled yarns are those where the single strands are respun in the same direction as their initial twist. When plying in the opposite way to the original twist there is, as stated under plying, a loss in the TPI, however, the reverse occurs in cabling, ie a gain occurs.
See *Plying*

Camel *Sp Camelus bactrianus* and *C dromedarius* are found in Mongolia, China and Central Asia. The camel was domesticated by the Babylonians around 1000 BC. The camel fibre used by today's spinners comes from the two-humped Bactrian camel named after *Bactria*, an ancient land that is now Afghanistan.

The Bactrian camel produces two coats, a soft warm inner down resembling *cashmere*, and a rough, outer, hairy layer. The down usually has a staple length of 2.5cm to 7.6cm (1 to 3in) and does not felt easily. Each hair has a double walled *medullary* canal that provides the camel with excellent insulation.

The camel cannot be shorn due to the fact it is required to cover long distances. It may have to adapt, in a day's journey, from sandy deserts to icy windswept mountains. Due to the thermostatic quality of the camel fleece, this is possible. When the temperature increases the coat begins to *rise* and it is shed in great matted lumps of wool and hair mixed. When the caravan sets out on a long trek, baskets are tied to the last camel in the line and a member of the caravan has to follow behind to gather the clumps of fibres and to place them into the baskets. The filled baskets are sold at towns along the route. For commercial use the down is separated from the hair. The coarse hair, ranging in length from 12 to 15.3cm (5 to 6in), is combed (*tops*) and the short soft wool, ranging in length from 2.5cm to 7.6cm (1 to 3in), is usually sold as a loose mass (*noils*).

Spinning methods:
DOWN: tease the fibres. Spin as cashmere; a slightly less silky yarn will result. The down can produce a soft, woollen camel yarn.

HAIR: this is more suitable for worsted spinning, it also mixes well with wool. Combed hair is spun by folding over the forefinger, the draw-out triangle should be long.

Short camelhair requires a firm tension on the wheel. Hold a handful of the hair tightly and join some of the fibres to the leader thread. The draw-out triangle should be short. When spun, wash the yarn and weight sufficiently to stretch, taking into consideration the strong twist that has been imparted into the yarn. Camelhair coats and sweaters are made from the down and not from the hair.

Canary Stain The strong yellow discoloration in many fleece which is impossible to remove by scouring. This may be due to damage caused by suint (sweat) of particularly high alkalinity rather than to bacterial action.

Cantons The name given to Southern Chinese silks produced in the province of Kwang-Tung. The fibre is very fine, but it is not as white as *Chinas*.

Capped The opening of some bales in big lots by the removal of the cap to enable buyers to inspect the entire contents of the bale. Other bales have the front flaps dropped to expose only a portion of the bale.

Carbonised Rag Fibre Animal fibre recovered by wet or dry carbonising process. Wool or hair recovered by the wet process is referred to as *extract*.

Carbonising Commercial processes used after scouring in order to remove organic matter, eg burrs etc, from wool. In the wet process, the wool is passed through a weak solution of sulphuric acid. As the acid does not evaporate, it concentrates in the organic matter and eats it away, leaving the wool intact. The wool is then dried in an oven and sometimes crushed; this reduces the organic matter to dust, which is then drawn out by suction fans or by mechanical shaking. The fibres are neutralised, rinsed and dried. In the alternative dry process, the rags are treated with a dry gas (hydrochloric acid) in an enclosed chamber heated to 90°C (194°F). After several hours they are removed, then shaken to remove any cotton etc, from the wool.

Carbonising Types Wools with a large amount of vegetable matter that cannot be economically mechanically removed.

Card Clothing Also called *carder furnishing*. Goes back to the thirteenth century. Card clothing is the name given to the wire covered surface attached to the card and which is used to work on fibre preparation. The foundation, into which the wires are set, varies. Some are of leather, in others, the clothing may comprise layers of woven cloth sometimes laminated with rubber. There are two distinct types of card clothing:
a) *sheet*: mainly found on flat carders; the wires are set in a plain overlapping pattern or a twilled pattern

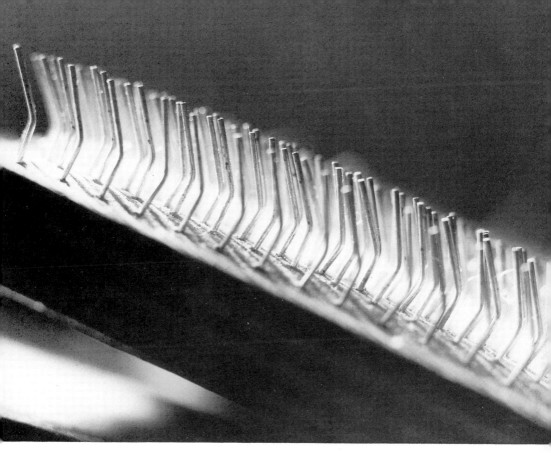

Plate 2 *CARD CLOTHING ON HAND CARD*

b *fillet*: a continuous strip of clothing suitable for machine cylinder carders. The wires are arranged in longitudinal ribs.

Both sheet and fillet can be obtained in differing sizes. When the carding process starts, the teeth should be coarser; when the carding process is well advanced the teeth should be finer as the carding at this stage will be easier.

Card clothing is chosen with various considerations in mind:

1 The wire size
2 The type of foundation into which the wires are set
3 The function of the carders, ie what they are required to do
4 The number of wires per inch across both the length and the width of the foundation
5 The pattern of insertion of the wires in the foundation.

It is not always practical or possible for a spinner to have several different pairs of carders, in which case a medium grade is chosen.
See *Crocheux; Doubleur; Dresseur; Fendoir; Fourchette; Goutiere; Noggs*

Carding – Hand

DEVELOPMENT: for two millenia, and possibly longer, carding, the preparation of fibres before spinning, depended on the thistle-like *Dipsacus fullonum* (teasel). The prickly head has flexible bristles with a hook at each tip to seize and teaze the wool out. Dried teasels were selected and set in a square or rectangular wooden frame having a handle. This was called a *card* from the popular Latin, *cardar*-tease, comb. It was also known as *strikers*. The Spanish who first went to Southwest America used towcards of teasels comparable to those used in England.

The first evidence of metal toothed cards was in the thirteenth century AD; these replaced the strikers. The carders had hooked metal teeth similar to those of today. Late in the seventeenth century carding benches or stock cards were developed. A further development attached one card to the bench in slots and someone called a *stock carder* sat astride the bench and worked the second card by hand. In an alternative design, the person, known as a *knee carder*, sat on a stool incorporated with a bench with his knees together facing the stock and the fixed card. One card was attached to a bench in a sloping position towards the worker, the second card was suspended from the ceiling against a counterweight, this card had a cord running through a pulley.

TODAY: a spinner has a choice of carders; some have flat backs, others have curved. Each carder is a rectangular wood (sometimes metal) piece with a handle. Attached to one side of the carder is card clothing, traditionally leather, although also available in strong cardboard composition and rubber, into which is set hundreds of wire teeth that incline slightly towards the handle. The carders are used in pairs. The teeth vary in their setting; some cards have finely spaced teeth suitable for carding fine fibres, others have much coarser, widely spaced teeth, suitable for coarser fibres. The usual size of hand carders is 22.9cm × 10.3cm (9in × 4in); if too large, they tend to make the carding process very tiring.

When choosing a pair of carders make sure that the teeth are flexible and that the handles are comfortable to hold. The carders should be stored with their teeth placed together as protection. Before using the carders, mark on the back of each carder one for the left hand and one for the right hand and always use them thus. Beeswax polish applied to the backs and handles before use is beneficial. (See *Beeswax*)

CLEANING: carders can become very dirty. Leather card clothing cannot be washed, although teeth set in rubber can be dipped in water to clean providing they are dried quickly and carefully. Carders can be cleaned with a metal comb and brush. A metal knitting needle can be useful for removing fibres from the teeth, or one card can be used to comb another and loosen the fibres which can then be removed easily by hand.

To produce a true woollen spin, hand carders are essential equipment for the spinner.

See *Card Clothing; Flick Carder*

Carding To card is to open up the wool fibres, straighten and space them by using hand cards, or a drum carder or machine. This process introduces air in the wool and removes dirt, seeds and tangles. It is a most important process and greatly affects the yarn produced. A spinner may be required to spin large quantities of yarn which must be consistent (see *Twists Per Inch*). Inadequately prepared fibres will produce thick and thin places in the yarn. Carding is also used for blending fibres for colour and texture.

See *plates 3; 4a; 4b; 5a; 5b.*

Plate 3 *HAND CARDING*: place the fibres previously teased, onto the left hand carder; any overlap of the fibres should be at the base of the carder

Plates 4a and b *HAND CARDING*: start stroking the left hand carder with the right hand carder, commencing halfway up the left hand carder, and gradually work up towards the top of the left hand carder (see below)

Plates 5a and b *HAND CARDING*: when carded sufficiently, transfer the fibre by brushing the right hand carder down the left hand carder, thus transferring the fibre from the right hand carder to the left hand carder. Continue carding as before until necessary to transfer again, this time from left hand carder to right hand carder. See below, again sweeping one carder against the other from top to base. When sufficiently carded refer to 'rolags' for next stage

CARDING PROBLEMS, GENERAL: these are often due to poor preparation of the fibres, inadequate teasing for example. Some fleece require more work before carding than others.

a) *the student's arms ache profusely*: this is due to the carding pressure being too heavy and tearing the fibres apart. The movement is too heavy if one carder 'rasps' against the other. The teeth on both carders should lightly brush the fibre – see *fig 3*.

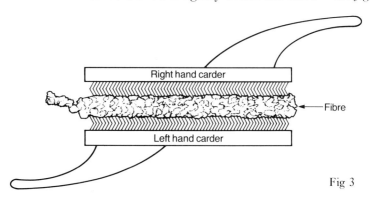

Fig 3

b) *the fringe of the fibres protruding at the bottom of the card becomes folded*: this can be avoided if, at the end of each stroke movement, the fringe is lifted with the carder stroking the fibre – see *fig 4*.

c) *the rolags are uneven and fall apart*: this is due to uneven placing of the fibres onto the card resulting in a patchy construction, followed by rolling the fibres too loosely into the rolag.

d) *uncarded sections in the rolag*: come about because too much fibre is placed on the card, or there is insufficient teasing of the fibres.

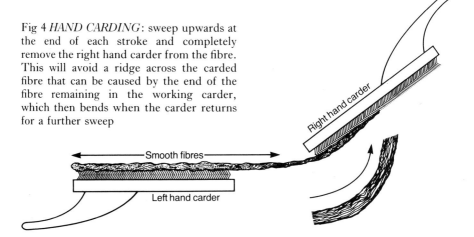

Fig 4 *HAND CARDING*: sweep upwards at the end of each stroke and completely remove the right hand carder from the fibre. This will avoid a ridge across the carded fibre that can be caused by the end of the fibre remaining in the working carder, which then bends when the carder returns for a further sweep

Carding – Drum The first drum carder was patented in 1784 by Lewis Paul of Birmingham, England. It was very similar in design to today's drum carders, which consist of a large and small drum, surfaced with wire teeth and turned by a crank which cards the fibres into *batts* (also called *laps* or *web*). These do save considerable time, although many spinners prefer to use hand carders.

To produce well combed fibres from a drum carder it is necessary to prepare the fibre well first. It is a mistaken idea that the fleece can be fed into a drum carder in an haphazard fashion and the carder will produce smooth sorted batts of fibre in a short while.

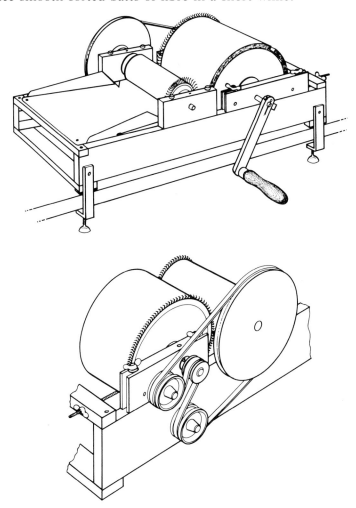

Fig 5 *DRUM CARDER*: this shows the Home Style, swift change drum carder made by Patrick Green in British Columbia. The main drum can be easily changed and replaced with finer or coarser clothing. Easy to clean; weight 16lb. There are many different makers of drum carders who cover a range of styles and prices

METHOD, WOOL: some spinners prefer to wash and completely dry the fleece first. They tease, comb or flick card. Others do not wash or card, they simply tease the fibres.

Fig 6, 1 Feed the prepared fibre into the machine whilst turning the handle. The teeth of the front roller, called the *licker-in*, start to do the job of carding. During the fleece feed-in, do not retard, otherwise it will wrap around the front roller. Throughout the process the front roller should stay almost free from fibre. Do not overfeed the rollers – 28g (1oz) wool will be sufficient for two batts. During feeding, the

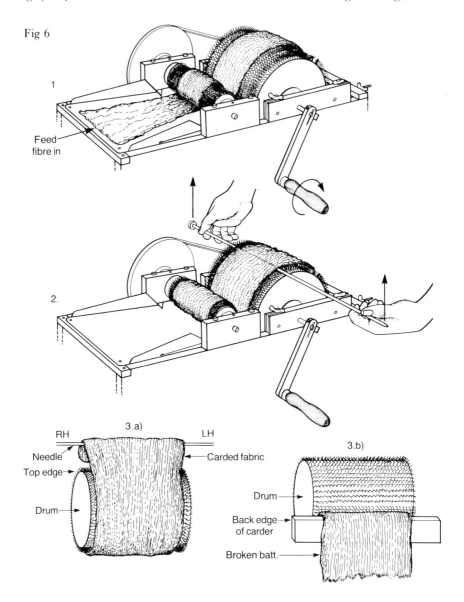

Fig 6

1

Feed fibre in

2.

3.a)

RH   LH

Needle   Carded fabric

Top edge

Drum

3.b)

Drum

Back edge of carder

Broken batt.

back roller carding cloth should be clearly seen through the fibre; once all the wool is fed in, stop turning the handle.

TO REMOVE (DOFF) THE BATT: *Fig 6, 2* stand behind the carder and turn the handle (this will be in reverse now) until the seam of the carding cloth is seen at the top of the large cylinder. Slip a steel needle in under the fibre and to the opposite side and lift the needle until the batt breaks.
Fig 6, 3a: holding the needle and fibres, reverse the drum and lift the wool which lies over the back of the carder (see *fig 6, 3b*) off backwards. If the batt does not come off easily and cleanly, use the needle to loosen. From time to time it may be necessary to lift the batt from the carding cloth with the needle; this will assist the removal in one piece rather than tearing the batt where it may be tighter on the card. As with testing a rolag, hold the batt to the light, the fibres should be even; if there are too many patches of light and shade, card a second time. Continuing to turn the rollers once the fleece has been fed in will not produce a better carded batt; this will tear the fibres that have already been carded and placed on the card clothing.

The easiest method, if a second carding is necessary, is to tear the batt into thin strips and feed in; this will place the fibres in different positions to the earlier carding. Remove the batt after carding, and test as before. Either place the batts in a pile or roll them up. Depending on the type of spin required either roll them up as rolags and spin in the same way which will produce a lighter textured yarn, or tear into strips and spin lengthways for a finer spin.

The overlapping pattern as the fibres are carded on the drum cards affects the way fibres are drawn out at the spinning stage. If difficult to spin in strip form, turn the strip around and spin from the opposite end – the draw out may be easier this way. As with hand carders, different coloured fleece can be mixed on a drum carder. The mix may either be complete to produce an overall colour, or in such a way that the colours are more distinctive. Practice is necessary to obtain the second result; students discover very quickly that it is easy to obtain a complete mix, whereas great care must be taken to avoid overmixing if definite individual colouring in the batt is required.

METHOD, INDIVIDUAL COLOURING IN A BATT: first produce batts in each colour to be mixed. At the second carding feed in strips from each coloured batt; colours can be laid on top of one another or they can be fed into the roller a colour at a time in a continuous 'thread'. Practice is the key word; it is useful to keep a notebook in which to record the results obtained from various methods of insertion and the resulting colour mix in the yarn produced. Careful colour mixing can impart great depth to a yarn. The drum carder must be kept clean and well oiled, follow the maker's instructions carefully; these will also state how to adjust the distance between the two drums.

Carding Machines In the cotton industry, carding was the first textile process to be mechanised. In 1748 patents for cylinder machines were taken out by Daniel Bourne of Leominster and Lewis Day of Birmingham. In 1775 Richard Arkwright brought together the basic features of the modern carding engine.

Today, cans of sliver are produced by high-speed carding engines. In the 1830s there was a continual haze of dust ever present in the card rooms, a common complaint was the *carder's cough*. Today's regulations ensure that all dust in cotton factories is removed by underfloor ducting. Commercial carding can be executed on a machine called a *scribbler* which passes the wool between a series of revolving cylinders covered in cardclothing.

Plate 6 Original carding engine 1775 (Arkwright)

Plate 7 Kay's wire card-making machine 1790

Card Makers In earlier times card making was done entirely by hand; the wires were bent and set individually into a leather backing. METHOD USED: first, the skin was stretched on the *panteur* then pricked with a fork and the pins set. Another worker made the wooden pads onto which the skin containing the wires was mounted.

In 1790 John Kay invented a wire cardmaking machine and card makers became obsolete. In 1797 Amos Whitemore invented a machine that bent and set the teeth.
See *Card Clothing*

Carding – Mill Mill carders produce the excellent fibres available to the spinner by passing the fibres, first over a serrated metal blade, then over large cylinders which have coarse teeth. The fibres are removed by doffer cylinders, which pass them onto more carding cylinders each covered with finer teeth. The process continues from carding to doffing until the finest teeth produce the satisfactory high standard, end product.

Carding Schools From 1780 these schools existed where women and children were used as cheap labour to piece together the cardings to keep the *slubber* supplied.
See *Slubbings*

Carding Wool Wool suitable for the woollen trade, but shorter than that required for combing in the worsted trade.

Card Yarn Yarn that has been spun from wool prepared by carding.

Carpet Beetles These eat silk and any protein fibre.

Carrier Rod Reeling Waste During the automatic reeling process in silk, a certain percentage of the silk filament is taken up on the steel rod carrier. At varying times, when too much accumulates, it is slashed and removed. The resulting 2.5cm (1in)-wide raw tubes are then cut into 15.3cm (6in) lengths. To prepare for use, they must be first placed in hot soapy water and soaked for 2 to 3 days; the cocoon remains must be carefully removed and the remaining silk degummed. Overhandling should be avoided until the silk is dry. The resulting reeled silk spins a lustrous, noilfree, yarn.
See *Sericulture; Silk*

Carroting The treatment of fur fibre by chemicals to improve their felting capacity. Reagents most commonly used are mercury in nitric acid, and mixtures of oxidizing and hydrolysing agents. In earlier times 'felted' cloth was usually beaver on the outside and rabbit in the inside. See *Felting*

Cashmere The Tibetan or Cashmere (sometimes spelt *Kashmir*) goat is domesticated and found in the mountains of Iran and in the high plateaux of Mongolia, China and India. The animal is usually associated with the Himalayan region of Kashmir, where once the beautiful Kashmir shawls were made together with their derivations, the Paisley shawls. The goat thrives in altitudes between 3,660m and 4,575m (12,000ft and 15,000ft), the higher the altitude, the finer and softer the cashmere. Attempts have been made to raise these animals in different parts of the world; as soon as they are moved, they cease to produce cashmere down.
    The Cashmere goat has a long outer protective covering of hair with a staple length of up to 12.5cm (5in), and an undercoat of down with a

staple length of 3.8cm to 7.6cm (1½ to 3in), the colouring in varying shades of white, grey, brown and black. The undercoat is the true cashmere of commerce which is obtained by plucking or combing. The yield is low; this accounts for the fibre being very expensive.

SPINNING: control with oil lightly sprayed onto the fibre. Release the tension on the wheel to add a firm twist; it should only just tug to wind on. Tease gently to fluff it up. The drawing out triangle will be small. The fibres are so 'fly-away' that they are difficult to control; use the tips of the thumb and first finger to control the down. Once spun, wind into skeins, dip in warm water and weight to set the twist. Ply if required.

Cashmere Yarns Often misleading as *cashmere* yarns may not necessarily be made wholly or in part from cashmere fibre. This can refer to any fine yarn produced on the Continental system from any high-grade wool.

Cast Poor, low quality wool, often the result of bad breeding; it does not reach the grade standard.

Castle Wheel It is also known as a *cottage wheel*. This is an upright wheel with the driving wheel above the flyer mechanism.

Catalogue A list prepared by the selling broker showing the lot number, owner's brand, wool description and the number of bales in each lot. Used by buyers for valuing purposes and by growers for wool inspection.

Cat Hair It is possible to spin with the longer-haired varieties, for example Persian and Angora. Not easy to obtain the fibres in sufficient quantities. Short-haired varieties are very difficult to control.

Cedar Bark A vegetable fibre widely used with success for spinning in earlier times.

Cellulose Fibres Natural plant fibres consisting mainly of carbon, hydrogen and oxygen. Cellulose fibres feel cool because they readily conduct body heat.

Character A wool term denoting the regularity of the crimp.

Charka A spinning wheel designed to fit into a hinged box, the spindle uprights are collapsible and the wheels fit into the lid for ease of transporting. Used extensively in India. When Gandhi was the

CLASSIFICATION OF TEXTILE FIBRES

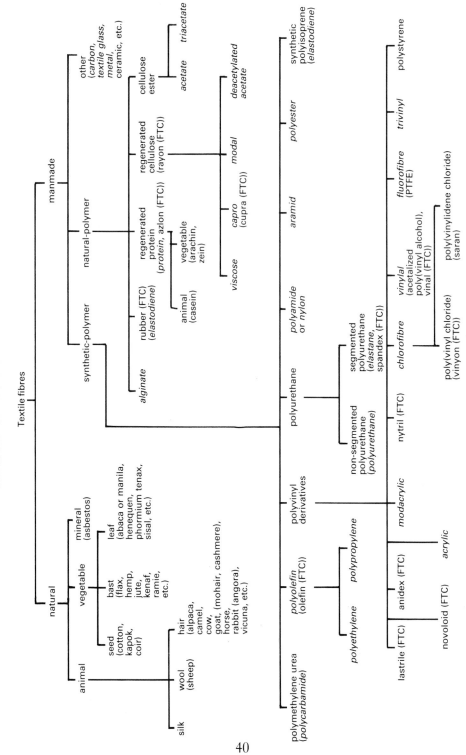

Hindu Nationalist leader, he encouraged, through competitions, the design of a wheel suitable for spinning cotton, a fibre available throughout India. The wheel was to be inexpensive.

Gandhi spun each day, as he felt that spinning was good for the soul and for the economy. He referred to spinning as a sacrament. The *charka* was thought to have evolved from the reel used by the Chinese for unwinding raw silk from cocoons. From this, in turn, evolved the great wheel. Native-reeled silk in India is also called *charka*.

Chenevote In earlier times flax fibres were spread to dry over fires made of chenevote or boon.
See *Flax – Linum usitatissimum*

Cheque (Wool) The amount, in total, from wool auctions in one season.

Chinas The name given to silks produced in the Northern provinces of Chei-Kiang, Kiang-Su and An-Hwei in China. They have an excellent lustre and the fibres are of the purest white.
See *Cantons; Tsatlees*

Chinchilla Rabbit: treat as *angora* rabbit when spinning.

Churka Known in Italy as *manganello*. A handturned mangle, commonly used throughout South East Asia, to remove the seeds from cotton. It let the cotton through but not the seeds.

Classification Of textile fibres – See *Table*

Classing – Wool After shearing, and before being sorted, the fleeces have to be divided into classes according to their character for *quality, soundness, length, colour* and *type*. In each class must be the maximum degree of uniformity possible; in the wool trade this is known as *classing* and is a highly skilled job. The wool classer classifies the fleece considered as a whole. He removes fringes of the wool from the upper parts of the leg and also the underbelly; this is called *skirting*. Badly marked places are also removed. No breed produces absolute uniformity; variations can occur between fibres in a single lock, and from one part of the fleece to another, so classing can only be done to a practical degree.

Points considered:
QUALITY The classer judges the degree of fineness, often helped by the number of crimps, the greater crimps per inch the finer the yarn.

SOUNDNESS He tests for any weaknesses that would show up in the stress imposed by manufacturing. He must also take into consideration, during the classing, the percentage of impurities in the fleece.

LENGTH It is desirable to have fibres as uniform in length as possible.

COLOUR AND TYPE The general colour quality related to a particular type.
The classed fleece are placed into bins. When a bin is full, the wool is pressed into bales, each averaging about 135kg (300lb). These bales are then branded, weighed and the number, weight and description entered into the wool book. The wool is then ready to be marketed.

Clean Basis The final price of scoured wool after deductions and scouring charges.

Clean Content The weight of wool after scouring.

Clock Reel Also called *click reel, wrap reel, yarn reel*. A device that registers the yardage of the yarn wound onto it. Often with four to six arms, not unlike a windmill in appearance, and worked by a handle. On most clock reels the arms measure approximately two yards (nearly 2m). The reel clicks loudly after forty revolutions, indicating to the person winding that one *knot* (73m – 80yd) has been wound. Seven knots make a skein or hank. Variations exist between different designs and sizes of reels producing different thread quantities; each unit, according to size, producing *a lea, a cut, a wrap* or *a knot*.

Closing of the Band A term related to quill-type wheels – eg the great wheel – the band is crossed when plying.

Cloth Fairs Craft fairs held in cities throughout Europe in the Middle Ages, not unlike our craft markets of today. Here retailers sold their yarns, dyes and fleeces.

Clothing Wool Wool which is classed as suitable for carding but not for combing. It is a term used in carding wool indicating the length of the staple. The length is not standardised, as it varies according to the count of the wool, ie into fineness.

Cochineal A red dye made from the dried bodies of female *Coccus cacti* insects. Native to Mexico, they feed mainly on the cactus, *Opuntia cochinellifera*.
See *Dyes and Dyeing*

Cocoon Produced by the silkworm. A cocoon may yield anything from 450 to 1830m (500 to 2,000yd) of silk. See *Sericulture; Silk*

Codilla From the Latin for tail; collected after the scutching stage of flax preparation and of a lower grade than tow.
See *Flax – Linum usitatissimum*

Coir Available from tropical areas including Sri Lanka. A red-brown seed fibre taken from the husk of the coconut, *Cocos nucifera*. The fibres, which are stiff and brittle, grow around the coconut and are held together at one end by a woody covering which has to be removed. The fibre is extracted by soaking the husks in water for long periods, sometimes as long as nine months. The fibre is then removed by tearing off, either by hand or mechanically. The fibre obtained is up to 30.5cm (12in) long with moderate strength; it is spun into yarn for making ropes, mats etc. A coarser grade, known as *bristle fibre*, is used for brushes, and the remaining short fibre is used for upholstery, mattresses etc; this is mainly obtained from Sri Lanka whilst yarn fibre comes from Continental India.

SPINNING: The fibres can be combed with a dog comb. Dampen, then spin by folding a strip over the forefinger. Spins a crude, stiff cord that does not take the twist easily, so a heavy tension is required on the wheel. After skeining soak, then weight heavily. Suitable for mats and baskets, resistant to rot.

Collage The craft of constructing pictures or designs by glueing a variety of material types to a background. It is an excellent way of using yarn oddments, even those which have been a mistake; all yarns can be used for one purpose or another in collage. Yarn oddments may also be used to make fabric pictures, ie those assembled by stitching.

Colour Mixtures Any natural coloured fleece, of beige, browns, black and greys or white, can be mixed to produce alternative attractive colours. A black sheep may appear to be brown if the tips of the fibres have been bleached by the sun. Beige wool may be a blend of brown and white fibres or, in some cases, different colour fibres may grow on one sheep. This does not refer to *kemp* in the fleece.

Combing – Wool See pp 44–53

Combings The undercoat that can be combed from various types of animals.

Combing Wools Wools considered to be suitable for the *worsted* industry, and for worsted handspinning.

Combing – Wool The process for combing long wool fibres into a parallel arrangement suitable for worsted spinning. It removes all the short fibres (*noils*) and leaves remaining long parallel fibres; this arrangement is referred to as *tops*. Woolcombing tools are being made today based on earlier designs, to enable the craft of woolcombing to be developed once more. Wool can be prepared for worsted spinning using a more simplified method. Historical and modern methods are described to give the spinner a choice.

BRIEF HISTORICAL DETAILS OF WOOLCOMBING: this craft as a trade became obsolete in the nineteenth century by the introduction of machinery and was one of the last textile occupations to be mechanized by the Industrial Revolution. Edmund Cartwright took out a patent in 1789 for the first machine comb. However, combers continued manually until about 1856.

In England were two classes of combers: –

The basketeer was a small farmer who lived outside the town and employed several combers. They lived with him, he paid them a weekly wage and they all worked together. If there were four combers, then there would be four sets of combs etc, and they shared the stove. They became known as 'a pot of four' named after their stove which catered for four combs at a time. See *fig 6a*. The basketeer obtained his wool from the mill. He had to wash and wring it in his home for which he was paid.

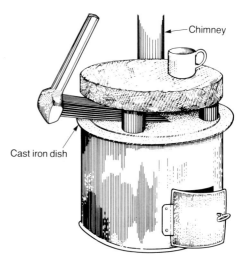

Fig 6a Iron stove or 'pot'

The independent comber: he also worked in his own home but obtained the fleece from the mill, washing and wringing it at the mill then taking it home in a sheet to comb.

Woolcombing as practised in earlier times: variations in the precise methods used in woolcombing occurred from locality to locality, no two were exactly the same; however, the purpose was the same, ie to align the fibres and remove the noils.

Equipment Used in the Comber's Workshop: a vertical post, iron pad, a bench, an oil can, combs, an oil lamp, a broitch straightener and a stove.

The pad: this was screwed into the post with the projecting end slightly raised.

The combs: each weighed approximately 3.2kg (7lb) and measured 17.8cm (7in) wide (variations did occur). The heads were embedded with long iron or steel teeth set at between 60° and 80° to the handle. The teeth were referred to as 'two pitch', 'three pitch' etc, for example 'three to eight pitched' meant it had three to eight rows of teeth (*broitches; tines*). Usually combs were three to five pitched, but they varied according to the wool type being combed. The longer teeth measuring approximately 30.5cm (12in) were furthest away from the

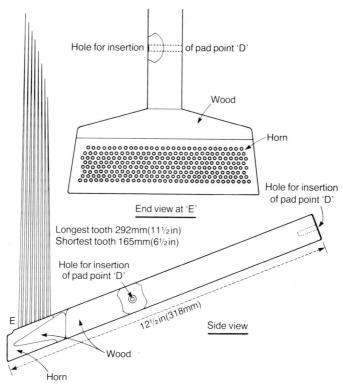

Hole for insertion of pad point 'D'

Wood

Horn

End view at 'E'

Hole for insertion of pad point 'D'

Longest tooth 292mm(11½in)
Shortest tooth 165mm(6½in)

Hole for insertion of pad point 'D'

E

12½in(318mm)

Side view

Wood

Horn

Fig 7 Eight 'pitch' comb

handle and became shorter, approximately 17.8cm (7in), towards the handle. Each tooth was tapered from base to tip. The heads of the combs were often capped with horn which helped to combat the shock of combing. As the corners became worn they were repaired with small iron plates. The handles were usually made of ash and were 25.4cm to 30.5cm (10 to 12in) long. They had iron-lined holes, usually one in the side and one at the end which corresponded with the spikes in the post to hold the combs in a horizontal position. The teeth often became soft and bent by constantly being inserted into the stove; they were straightened by using a tubelike tool that fitted onto one tooth at a time and which, when pressed down to the base, straightened the tooth.

Oil: this was added to the fleece when necessary. Whilst an olive oil and water emulsion is used today, in the past woolcombers used pig oil, fish oil and olive oil. One can imagine the problems encountered when the final washing stage was reached.

The stove: earlier-styled stoves burned charcoal and when it was heated the combs were placed directly onto it. Later stoves had a cast iron dish, a stone cap on a support, and a chimney. On this was burned coal to heat the combs (and the embedded wool on them) without burning. Whatever the design, the purpose was to heat the combs so that the lanolin in the wool, or the added oil, became soft and thus was easier to work with.

Process: when starting work, the combs were placed on the dish of the stove until they were heated. A heated comb was put onto the *jenny*, a ledge attached to the vertical post; this held the comb with the handle horizontal and the teeth pointing upwards – this process was called *lashing on* or *donning on*. (Early references state that combers sat with the combs on their knees with the teeth facing upwards for the lashing-on and combing, then they stood at posts to pull the slivers from a comb attached to the post.) The washed wool was then thrown onto the comber's bench and lashed to the comb by using sweeping controlled movements onto the teeth. When the locks were lashed on, the comb was transferred to an iron pad (metal bar) with the teeth pointing sideways, the rows lying parallel to the ground.

Jigging, also called *fetching-off*, is the combing process. The pad comb was then combed or *jigged* with the free comb. The comber took it in both hands and swung from up to down in a circular movement,

Plates 8–9 *WOOLCOMBING BY HAND*: (*top*) at the mill door. Centre: workman leaving with the wool for combing, and a jug of oil – work to be done at home. In some cases the wool would be washed before leaving the mill, using company's soap and mechanically-driven squeeze rollers. Right: workman returning finished work, the top and the noils. Left: out-of-work labourer turning in combs and woolsack. (*below*) washing wool

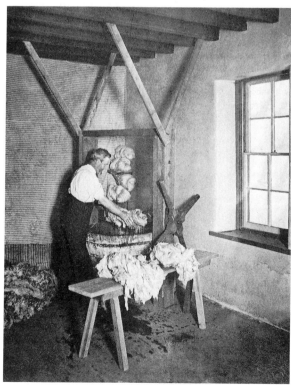

Plates 10–14 *WOOLCOMBING BY HAND*: (*above left*) putting the wool onto the comb. The comber's 'pot' can be seen on the right with a 'full' comb being heated. The steel pins rested on the stone cover and did not reach the fire. The wool was allowed to fall away from the stove. Note the diz hanging below the fixed comb (*centre*) combing or 'lashing' wool. The fixed comb with the teeth in a horizontal position being combed by the second heated comb, using long strokes starting at the top of the staple and moving towards the first comb, removing the wool to the second comb, until only a fringe was left, this being removed as noil. The wool was then combed from the now fixed second comb back to the first comb until the comber was satisfied with the work

(*above right*) drawing off the sliver – the second combing operation. The wool is worked by both palms of the hands to the centre of the steel pins and then the fringe of wool is grasped between thumb and fingers of both hands (thumbs facing the comber) to gradually be drawn off into a sliver. Care is taken to 'nip' the wool at a uniform distance from the pins, approximately every 12.7cm (5in). The remaining fringe on the comb is noil

(*right*) drawing off the sliver – also part of the second combing operation. The sliver is examined carefully on the bench for foreign matter or 'neps' – the latter are often bitten out by the teeth. If the sliver was dry it was the custom to fill the mouth with water and eject as required, leaving both hands free. The sliver was then broken into 22.9cm to 25.4cm (9 to 10in) lengths and re-combed. When drawing off, the sliver is passed through a diz to give uniform thickness; the drawn sliver is folded up in the left hand to avoid dirt on the floor. It was again examined, then wound into a neat bundle called a 'top'

(*far right*) the finished work, combed sliver (*right*); tops in balls (*left*)

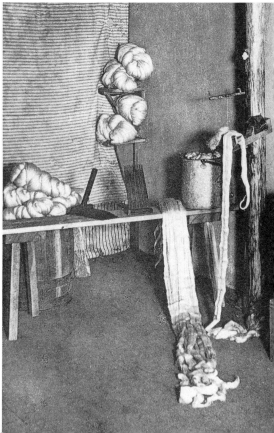

first only engaging the fringe of the fibres and gradually working inwards, the wool being kept right up to the bed of the teeth. The wool was gradually drawn from the fixed comb. The newly filled comb was either transferred to the post, or the wool was worked back onto the fixed comb by working now from right to left in a circular movement. At all times the combs were kept warm. If they became cool when fibres were on, then only the teeth of the combs were inserted into the heat. Once sufficiently jigged, the wool was pushed to the middle of the comb, where there was more spring than at the roots of the teeth, and drawn off into 1.83m (2yd) lengths called *sleevers* (also called *fingers*). These were laid on a bench, side by side with the ends overlapping, to mix the longer ones that came off first with the shorter ones which came off last. The sleevers were then broken into 25.4cm (10in) lengths, oiled and jigged a second time. Finally, the wool was drawn off the filled combs with both hands and through a horn or leather oval disc (*diz*) with a hole in the centre; through this hole the fibres were drawn to smooth and to produce an overall consistency of size. These, rolled into balls, were known as *tops*. Any remaining wool in the combs was removed. Those fibres left on the front of the comb were known generally as *noils* and in various areas as *nilkings*, and those fibres left on the back of the comb were called *backings*.

This completed the process, although variations occurred, one in particular. If not drawn through a *diz*, the sleevers were laid in 1.83m (2yd) lengths on a bench a dozen at a time. Each batch was twisted into a ball; once all the fibre was combed and formed into balls it was taken to the mill for *back-washing*, ie a second washing and was brought home for the *straightening*, ie second combing. The sleevers were split into 20.4cm to 25.4cm (8 to 10in) long pieces, placed on a bench side by side and each layer (*layter*) was oiled, combed and then put through a *diz*. The wool was kept moist by the comber squirting water from his mouth over it. The combing process was followed by *picking*, a careful examination for any faults. The comber bit out any knots with his teeth and spat the knots out when his mouth was full. The tops were taken in a box to the mill at the end of each week. The receiver (*tekker-in*) examined the contents of each box, carefully testing for cracks (*pushes*) and finding out whether the tops were damp with water (to add weight) or oil. If satisfactory the comber was paid for the work done. See *Bishop Blaise; Tines*

WOOLCOMBING TODAY: whilst the combing techniques used today are readily identifiable with those of the past, substitutes or alterations have to be made in line with availability of equipment.
Requirements: a pair of wool combs, a pad, a diz, fibre supply, heating, an oil emulsion. A pair of accurate scales.

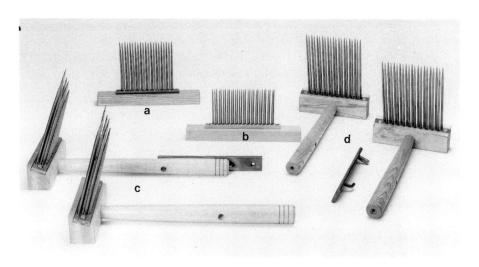

Plate 15 *WOOL TOOLS*: a) heavy duty wool hackle; b) fine wool hackle; c) four row combs and mount; d) two row combs and mount

THE FLEECE: to produce a smooth yarn to a high standard with a good lustre, careful selection of a suitable fleece is necessary. Avoid extremes, ie a very coarse long fleece type or a fine highly crimped one. A staple length of approximately 15.3cm (6in) is easy to work with, although any staple length between 10.3cm and 25.4cm (4 to 10in) can be used, preferably with a pronounced lustre. The selected fleece should be carefully sorted into various qualities, then washed (avoid disturbing the lock distribution and still keep the qualities separate). When the fleece is completely dry, lay on a flat surface and separate the locks. This is a simple task; if the fleece is gently parted, the locks will show clearly. The separated locks should be placed in a line on a bench or table lying parallel to one another with the butt (root) ends lined up. Spray evenly with oil emulsion (see weight control for the exact amount to use). This spraying will assist in the combing process, and the moisture content will help to control static electricity (a problem that can cause difficulty to the hand comber). During the combing process the fibre can be sprayed lightly with water from time to time as a means of control.

HEATING THE COMBS: never place the combs directly onto a hot plate, gas ring or into an open fire. The combs need only to be warmed sufficiently to make the lanolin or oil flow, and thus permit the comb to work easily through the fibres. The easiest and safest methods of warming the teeth on the combs are:

a) place the teeth only into a container of boiling water

b) place the teeth only in a large saucepan filled with water and then heat on the stove or

c) the combs can be laid in the grate of a fire near the heat.

Whatever the method used, at all times protect the head and the handle of the combs from the direct heat. Unless this is done the teeth could, eventually, drop out. Unlike combers in the past who could heat combs with fibre on them, methods a) and b) make this impossible; with method c) it is possible if great care is taken.

WEIGHT CONTROL: to produce a consistent yarn, it is necessary to carefully weigh and use the same quantities of fibre, and to measure the oil and water used for each batch being combed.

PROCESS: *lashing-on*, also referred to as *donning-on*. Heat the combs, secure one comb to a pad or bench with the teeth facing upwards. Place a lock at a time, butt end (root) on, to the front row of teeth to a depth of approximately 1.3cm (½in) on each lock (the pointed tip of each lock hangs freely at the front). Build up across these teeth. When loaded with the previously weighed amount, turn the comb onto its side and secure to hold. Take the second warmed comb with the teeth facing downwards, and using a circular movement (combined with up and down movements) move deeper at each swing into the fibre. When the fibres have been transferred from the fixed to the free comb, it is necessary to transfer them back onto the fixed comb. This can be done in two ways; either exchange the combs, ie fix the free comb and release the fixed comb, or use a swinging horizontal anticlockwise circular movement (in the opposite direction to the first transference) until all the fibres have gradually latched on to the fixed comb. The degree of combing varies according to the fibres used and to the expertise of the comber.

When the desired appearance of the fibre is obtained where they are nicely evened out and free from noils, the process should be halted at a point where both combs have an equal quantity of fibre. Place both combs in a vertical position (teeth facing upwards). Secure one comb and, stroking the fibres gently, form into a point. Draw out about 5cm (2in) of fibre, then pinch again. Continue hand over hand, each time pulling out another amount of fibre from the mass and pinching. Continue drafting, pulling out the sliver into a continuous ropelike form; break off after approximately 91.5cm (3ft) each time that length is obtained.

PLANKING: as the 91.5cm (3ft) lengths are drafted, lay them side by side on a table or bench, flowing in one continuous direction. Planking will even out the difference that will occur between the first fibres (the longer ones) and the last fibres, the shorter ones.

Treat the second comb in the same way producing an even sliver and plank as before, remove the noils from the combs.

Warm the combs. Secure one comb to the pad, teeth uppermost; take the planked skeins and lash the tips onto the comb using all the teeth this time, not just the front row as before. As the comb is loaded allow the sliver to break off each time a protruding piece reaches approximately 25.4cm (10in) in length. Turn the comb onto its side and using the warmed second comb start to comb again, working from the tips to start with. Continue as before, including the transference of fibre from one comb to the other. When both combs hold equal amounts, draw off as before, only this time pass the fibre through the diz.

USE OF THE DIZ: place the pointed end of the fibre through the diz in one of two ways, whichever is preferred.

a) gently pull the combed fibre through the diz or
b) push the diz tightly onto the fibre. This method makes the process harder, but does make quantity control easier. Pinch as before when pulling off and continue until only the noils remain.

THE FINAL STAGES: the choice is made whether *top* or *roving* is required. Either wind a collection of slivers into a top or form a roving by softly twisting the sliver. To spin from a top (sliver) tends to produce a slightly more hairy yarn. Roving produces a smoother yarn as there is more control because of the imparted twist.

FORMING A ROVING: a roving is made by inserting twist into sliver after it has been planked.

METHODS OF INSERTING TWIST: if a great wheel is available, this is an excellent means of forming a roving, but this facility may not be available to many spinners; an alternative is a handspindle with a long shaft. Feed the sliver onto the handspindle and holding the spindle in a horizontal position, gently impart twist then wind on to the shaft. A hand- or grasped-spindle is necessary; the sliver would part if weight was added to it. Whatever method is used make sure, when turning a sliver into a top or roving, that the fibre is arranged so that the end that was pulled off first will be at the point where spinning commences. It will then flow in the same direction as it was drawn from the comb. The twist must be slight and even throughout. Roving twist should be the opposite to that of the finished yarn, ie roving S for spindle Z. Spinning can be direct from the spindle shaft or from a ball wound from the shaft. A wooden knitting needle or a piece of dowelling could be substituted for the spindle. See *Doffing; Donning-on; Fingers; Noils*

Combing with a Dog Comb This method is suitable for small quantities of fibre and produces a semi-worsted yarn. Teasing will produce something similar. Keep in mind the purpose for which the yarn is to be spun when choosing the fleece. A lustre type is suitable. Do not choose a fibre which is too fine and crimped or one which is too coarse.

METHOD:

a) clamp a dog stripping comb (or similar) securely to the edge of a table or bench

b) select and separate locks of equal size and quality from the fleece

c) hold several locks with the tips away from you. Place onto the teeth of the comb near the tips; pull gently to open the tips of the locks. Repeat the combing, working further down the locks each time. Reverse, and comb the butt ends previously held in the hand. Turn the locks over the comb on the underside. When combing is satisfactorily executed, the fibres should be open and aligned.

d) the combed fibres should be placed in a container with all the tip ends facing one way and the butt ends the other. They are ready for spinning in this form.

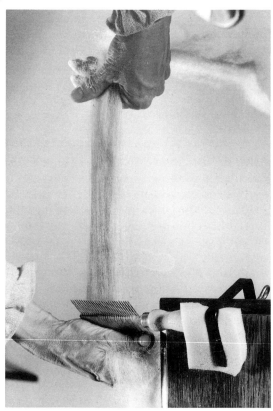

Plate 16 *COMBING WOOL*:
using a dog comb

Some spinners prefer a top to spin from; this can be formed by placing the combed locks one on top of the other overlapping each other by approximately half the staple length in sequence.

Using both hands, lightly draft the length; if executed too vigorously the fibres will tear apart. The completed length can be coiled into a basket. A slight twist added to the length before coiling will make storage more compact and controlled. After spinning a worsted yarn, ply; this helps to even out any irregularities between the singles yarn sizes.

Comeback Sheep obtained as a result of crossing merino sheep with fine crossbred sheep, then crossing of the progeny with a merino. The progency from this cross is known as a *comeback*.

Common Mallow Fibre Has been spun and woven into cloth since Rome's classical period, about 600 AD. The plants are grown today as far north as latitude 56° in West Siberia.

Compatible Dyes Dyes that when mixed behave in dyeing as an homogeneous dye.

Condensing The placing of fibres into a more compact size.

Condition Comparative part of water present in wool.

Conditioning Wool Testing wools, whether greasy or scoured, to ascertain the moisture content.

Cone Also referred to as *builds*. Yarn that has been wound onto a paper container to form a cone-shaped package.

Continuous Filament Manmade or synthetic yarn, in which the filaments continue the full length of the yarn produced. Yarn of one or more filaments is usually referred to as *monofilament* or *multifilament* respectively.

Cop Also referred to as *builds*. Yarn wound so that its body is built up and its ends are conical.

To facilitate spinning on a spindle wheel it is necessary to build a cop of the yarn near to the front bearing. A well constructed cop shape keeps the yarn back against the flange and away from the spindle point. If poorly wound onto the spindle, the yarn will fall towards the point and hamper spinning. Zigzagging assists a satisfactory build-up. When complete, ease the cop off from the bottom and place onto a vertical spike and reel off. The traditional way to start the spinning was to place a damp corn husk around the spindle shaft and secure, leaving the spindle top exposed; this makes it easy to start, as the fibres quickly catch on to the husk. Other spinners use a leader cord to start spinning.

Cortes, Hernando First took the silkworm to Mexico in 1531, but the silk industry did not thrive and had died out by the seventeenth century.

Cotted or cotty wool. Fleece that has become matted or felted before shearing. Can be caused by damp, crowded conditions. The skin sheds fibres that remain in the fleece and then, because of moisture or perhaps movement of the sheep, the fibres become matted into entanglements called *cotts*. Some breeds are more inclined to cotting than others.

Cottering Entanglements occurring of either fibres or filaments of a yarn, or one yarn with another during the movement of winding during spinning, or warping during weaving.

Cotton-Bombast Historical references state that knights used raw cotton padding to protect their skins from the friction caused by chainmail; it was also used as padded jerkins under their *hauberks*. Tudor dandies quilted their doublets with it, hence the adjective *bombastic* which developed from those times.

Cotton – Count Number of hanks containing 840yd required for 1lb. The ply number follows the size number for example 8s/2 = 8 × 840yd has been made into a 2 ply yarn, yardage per 1lb=8 × 840 ÷ 2.

$$Tex = \frac{590.5}{\text{cotton count}}$$

See *Bump*

Cotton – Dead See *Cotton – Gossypium Family*

Cotton – Fustian In past days this referred to cloth woven with a cotton weft on a linen warp. Early imported cotton was used as a stuffing and probably was not spun into yarn until the making of English fustians.

Cotton Gin A machine used for separating the seeds from the cotton fibres. Many varieties were used; one, the *saw-gin* was patented in America by Eli Whitney in the eighteenth century. It was mainly for short stapled cotton. MacCarthy's *roller gin* ginned the longer staple. The *churka* used in India and China was a more primitive type.

Plate 17 *CROMPTON'S MULE*:
replica of early machine

Plate 18 *COTTON BALLS*

Cotton Gossypium Family The word cotton is thought to have derived from the Arabic – *qutun*.

TYPES: Egyptian; Peruvian; Sea Island; Pima; and Upland. Sea Island is considered the best for handspinning; it is the finest and most costly. Pima cotton is produced by crossing Sea Island with Egyptian; it is cream in colour, long and lustrous.

Historical details: Mohenjo Daro in Sind is where fragments of cotton cloth were discovered. Historical facts indicate that cotton was known and used in India as far back as 2700 BC. It has been cultivated by man for thousands of years in many parts of the world. Possibly the earliest details of cotton to reach England were brought by Sir John Mandeville on returning from India in 1350.

According to some authorities, Thomas Highs claimed to have invented the *spinning jenny* (named after his daughter) in 1764 and John Hargreaves produced an improved version in 1767. Other authorities award Hargreaves the sole credit.

Richard Arkwright developed the *spinning frame* to spin cotton warps, around 1769, and put the first water-powered spinning mill into production.

Samuel Crompton in 1779 perfected his spinning mule (invented first in 1773), which could spin warp and weft.

Edmund Cartright added the power loom in 1785 and in 1793 the Cotton Gin by Eli Whitney completed the modernisation.

COTTON: thrives best in subtropical conditions and is mainly cultivated in the belt bounded by latitudes 40°N and 30°S. It requires moisture and sun during the growth period, and can be obtained from annual or perennial plants. Annuals supply the bulk of the world's needs, the plants reaching, on maturity, heights between 45.5cm and 135cm (1½–4½ft). Perennials, given perfect growing conditions, can grow 4.5m to 6m (15 to 20ft) high. Whatever the type being grown, it is much affected by environment, soil and climate. The climate, in particular, needs to be right for each stage of the development.

FIBRE DEVELOPMENT: cotton contains about 96 per cent cellulose and, as with similar fibres, it is stronger when wet – up to 30 per cent stronger. When approaching maturity, flowers appear on the plants, their colouring according to the type. There is a succession of flowers, each bloom dying after a few days. When the petals fall they expose the embryonic *bolls* (seed pods) which will be the eventual fibre source. Each boll has up to six compartments; these contain seeds covered with small hairy down fibres over the surface that collect moisture for the seed. These fibres start to grow once the flower has opened, although the seeds at this stage are immature. Each tiny cotton cell consists of a thin primary wall of cellulose protected by the cuticle and a central cavity (*lumen*) containing the *nucleus, protoplasm* and *cell sap*. These vegetable cells start to grow outwards extending the skin (*cuticle*) of the seed. These cells, when mature, will be the cotton fibres. They extend during the first growth stage and then the wall thickens in a process whereby layer on layer of cellulose is added to the inside of the primary wall. Each layer comprises tiny fibrils of cellulose in a spiral formation around the wall in differing degrees at irregular intervals. After the boll opens, the cell contents dry and the wall collapses, but, due to the spirals around the wall, it becomes convoluted. The convolutions allow the fibres to adhere to one another during spinning although they appear smooth. The boll bursts open when the pod, seed and a downy mass of fibre reach maturity; see plate 18. The shell becomes brown and hard and the locks of fibre-covered seeds (which may be white, cream or brown) are exposed ready to be harvested (picked). The staple length of the fibre is approximately 5cm (2in) long, soft and silky in texture. Shorter fibres tend to be coarser. The thickening already mentioned should be to the degree of from one quarter to one third of the original diameter; if it fails to develop thus, the fibre is termed *immature*. If no development occurs, it is referred to as *dead*. If too many cells are affected, it will greatly reduce the value of the cotton. Cotton which forms *neps* may be from this category, also cotton that has been dyed and woven may show light patches that have resisted the dye.

HARVESTING: the cotton must be harvested at exactly the right time; over-ripe fibres are less pliable. When picked, the fibre comprises about two-third seed and one third fibre. The seed cotton is placed in bags and taken to the *ginnery* (see under ginning) where it is processed to separate the seeds from the fibres (*lint*) and the very short fibres from the longer ones. The short fibres known as cotton linters are used in the manufacture of certain types of rayon.

This is not the end to the potential of this plant; the hulls are removed from the kernels and used as carbohydrate roughage for livestock. The kernels are crushed to obtain the oil, which is used in cooking fats and margarine. The remainder is used for non-edible items, for example soap. The oil residue from the press provides concentrated protein foods for livestock.
See *Churka; Fuzz Hairs; Trash*

TERMINOLOGY Cotton is not referred to as a thread; the correct word is *end*, whatever the length. When these ends are twisted together the process is called *doubling* even though the number may be uneven. The number is referred to as *fold*, never 'ply'; for example *two-fold, three-fold*. The thickness is the *count*. The length the *staple* – this term was inherited from the wool trade.

Cotton Ginning The removing of the fibres from the cotton seeds.

Cotton Gossypium Family See pp 58–9.

Cotton Hair The hair on the seed of the cotton plant.

Cotton Linters See *Cotton – Gossypium Family*.

Cotton – Quality A truly spinnable cotton should comprise length, fineness, maturity and uniformity. Sadly, however, whilst these are the desirable requirements, they are not always possible. Not only do variations occur because of the time of harvest, between one field and another, and between individual plants, but a bale of cotton may contain fibres from different areas. Today, in many cotton growing regions, growers are trying to eliminate the discrepancies by using a pure seed strain that, it is hoped, will in future produce a more uniform crop; this is obviously more advantageous than using mixed seed of unknown pedigree.

Count International numerical system for classifying fleece according to the diameter of the fibre (ie, the degree of fineness). A low count (20s and 30s) indicates coarseness, medium wools are in the scale 50s and 60s. A count in the 70s and above is considered superfine. The number of hanks of yarn each 560yd long (512m) that can be spun from 1lb of clean wool. For example a 64s would be expected to make 64 hanks of yarn each 560yd long.

It would be a wrong assumption on the part of a spinner to consider wools within a recommended count range as the only ones suitable. Wide variations occur within breeds as for example, wool spinning counts in the range 48s to 56s. The spinner should become conversant with the various qualities so that a careful choice can be made. Some spinners do not wish to know the count number, preferring to rely on the feel and quality of the fleece by using their own judgement. Others rely on their suppliers to choose the right fleece for a particular project.

SPINNING. COUNT LOW: spinning a yarn with a low count fibre can produce problems. Heavy yarns have a tendency to resist the twist and to want to return to their untwisted state, especially if spindle spinning, when the strength in the yarn will cause the spindle to reverse in direction. Until the twist is set, the problem persists. Use a spindle sufficiently weighted to assist with the spinning. On a flyer wheel increase the tension and thus the pull on rate, but make sure that sufficient twist has been inserted. The Navajo spindle is useful for spinning low count yarns.

COUNT – HIGH: the handspindle or great wheel are excellent tools for spinning fine yarns (high count). When spinning a high count yarn on a flyer wheel, great care must be taken to avoid overtwist. Whilst overtwist can occur in low count yarns due to the difficulty of wind on, where the yarn will begin to kink rather than break, in high count yarns overtwist causes breakage. Once the spinner has adjusted to the type of yarn being spun, whether from low count or high count fibres, problems will be kept at a minimum or obliterated entirely.

Cow Hair Hair from cows and horses can be used for spinning. It tends to be coarse and hardwearing and can be used for making rugs. An emulsion of oil and water will assist in the spinning.

Coyuchil See *Brown Cotton*

Crimp The waviness throughout the length of a wool fibre. Fine wools have small wavy lines (crimps); coarser wools have well spaced crimps. The crimps indicate the diameter of the fibres; the closer the crimps per inch, the finer the fibre and reverse wise. Whatever the crimps exhibited, they should be consistent in the staple length. Regularity of crimps is a criterion in determining wool quality.*
A down wool, with crimps spaced closely together, will produce a warm, light yarn as the spongey texture (close crimps) will prevent the individual fibres laying close together; this forms many air pockets and thereby warmth and loftiness. A longwool, with the crimps well spaced in the staple, will produce a smoother yarn as the well spaced crimps will permit closer relation of the staple and therefore fewer air pockets.
*Irregular crimps may indicate a fleece of lesser quality. The waviness of the crimp can be all in one direction or in many directions.
Not all wools show a simple *uniplanar* wave formation, as seen in merino types. Some have waves in which there may occur twisting; others have helices or ringlets, eg in the Wensleydale. Curls to flat spirals occur in some Devon wools.
See *'Doggy' Wool*

Crocheux A metal plate in a triangle construction used in 1750, France. Its purpose was the bending of the wire staples in carders to their required shape.

Crocking The term used in industry whereby the dyed fibres either fade or are rubbed off. Because of the structure of wool, and its absorbency, wool fibres retain the dye to a greater level than many other fibres, therefore crocking is less likely.

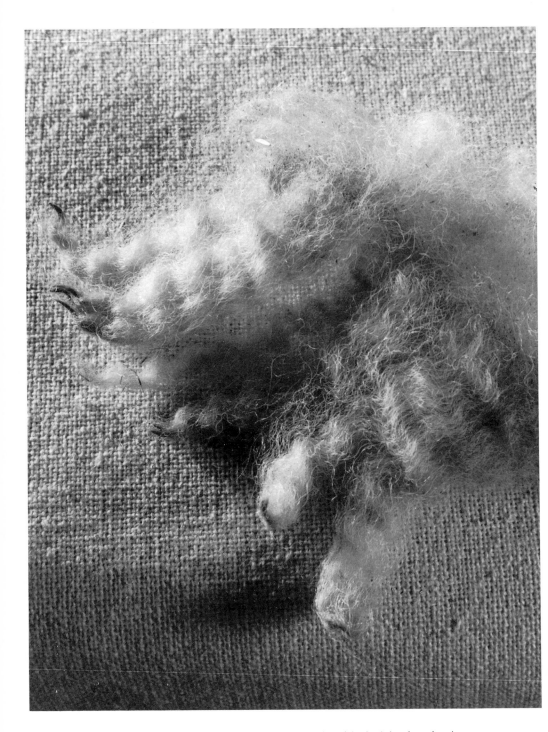

Plate 19 Showing crimp in the wool and locks joined at the tip

Croisure A term used during the reeling of silk when the reeled silk must form a crossing (*croisure*) to help the gum (*sericin*) fuse the threads into one and to remove the adhering water before the silk is wound onto the *creels*.

Cross-Band Yarn One with a Z-twist, ie looking up the thread, the twist is seen to run from right to left. It is made by reversing the direction of the spinning wheel. The opposite of *open-band* yarn. See *Z-Twist; S-Twist*

Crossbred – Sheep Sheep obtained by crossing one breed with another. Sheep provide wool, meat and hides; one single breed will not provide all these elements to a high standard.

The merino produce the best wool, but their meat is poor. Meat-producing breeds often have poor fleece. Crossbreeding has produced sheep which provide meat and passable wool. With crossbreeding it is possible to develop a particularly desirable characteristic, for example to improve the wool quality on meat-producing animals. Further crossbreeding can swing the type in the direction of the original parents.

Crossbreeding can produce a wide range of crossbred qualities.

Crossbred Wools Wools that are coarser than those from merino sheep but not coarse wools suitable for carpets. Qualities usually around the 36s to 58s. Originally this term related to wools obtained from a cross between a Spanish merino and an English ram. Today, however, the term has no connection with any particular breed of sheep.

Crutching Also known as *dagging*. The shearing around the tail of ewes, leaving the ewes clean for the ram. Usually carried out twice a year, in early autumn and midway through the year. The later crutching is done from two months, to as little as one week, before lambing. Heavy crutching should be discouraged as it can spoil a fleece for shearing time. The crutching should be just enough to keep the ewe clean and to enable the lamb to find the teats easily.

Crutchings, Clarts The dried lumps of dung and earth which encrust the staples in the britch area. See *Daggings; Doddings; Shirlings; Muck Lumps*

acca M | D | n · Denier · Devil's Grip · Distaff · Diz · Doggy Woo
a Musli | | Denier · Devil's Grip · Distaff · Diz · Doggy Wool · D
acca M | | n · Denier · Devil's Grip · Distaff · Diz · Doggy Woo

Dacca Muslins The famous Dacca muslins produced in India; their cotton yarn, spun at 407.14km (253 miles) per pound, was a world record. The threads were spun on miniature supported handspindles, and were so fine they were said to drape 'like air'.

Dead Wool Wool pulled from sheep that have died, but have not been slaughtered. A term also used to describe hairy fibres, eg *kemp*.

Decortication A process for removing fibres from the stalks of *ramie*, which cannot be retted as other bast fibres. Decortication is a means of peeling the fibres from the stalk. These fibres are then degummed by soaking or scraping or by boiling in caustic alkali solution. There are several different decortication processes. See *Ramie*

Deep Grown A term used to describe a wool that is considered to be rather long for the quality; also used in relation to a long, sound, deep staple about half as thick as a shafty wool.

Degreasing The removal of suint, grease and any foreign matter from wool by an aqueous or solvent process. Also the removal of grease, oil, fat and dirt from textile materials by using an organic solvent.

Degumming Is also referred to as *boil-off, boiling-off* and *stripping*. It is the removal of sericin from silk yarns, fabrics or silk waste before spinning by using a hot, mild alkaline treatment that does not affect the underlying fibroin. The silk available to handspinners usually has been processed and therefore is free from sericin (gum). If it is necessary to remove sericin, the following method is simple to execute.

The skeins of silk should be tied loosely with ribbon to prevent tangling and they should be soaked overnight in a warm soapy solution of either soft water or rain water (soap flakes are suitable) with approximately 40g (1½oz) soap to 4.5l (1 gal) water. Pour off the solution and rinse in warm water. Prepare a second soap solution, immerse the silk in it, and bring gradually to just below boiling point. This is a very important factor, as silk boiled in too high a temperature will lose its natural lustre and become dull. Simmer gently for about ¾ to 1 hr; the time will vary according to the type of silk. Pour into a colander and rinse in hot water. The process can be repeated until all the gum is removed and the silk feels clean and soft; add a dash of white vinegar to the final rinse. Weak alkalis, eg soap and ammonia will affect silk very little.

Fallbrook House (see stockists) removes the sericin by thoroughly dissolving soap and washing soda (for .45kg [1lb] of thrown silk waste, use 113.4kg [4oz] soap powder or flakes to 113.4g [4oz] washing soda), add sufficient warm water to dissolve the soap and washing soda and to just float the silk. Bring to simmer, gently cook until the fugitive colour disappears and the silk shines. Check after ½hr, remove a sample and rinse. If a second simmering is necessary, use only soap, less of it, and reduce the time. Rinse in hot water and hang to dry. Dry the silk naturally, away from direct sunlight. Degumming is often done after thrown silk has been woven. It is placed in canvas bags and 'boiled' in a strong soap solution for several hours and then thoroughly washed. This is called *discharging*.

The loss of weight caused by degumming varies from silk to silk. Boil-off ranges from eighteen to about twenty-four per cent and is usually greater for the yellow kinds than for white silks. Japanese and Chinese silks are white; most European silks are yellow.

Denier A denier is the unit to express the count of net silk. It is a standard weight of a given length of filament yarn. In Britain it is the weight, in grams, of 9000m of yarn; the higher the number the thicker the yarn. This measurement originated in the silk industry.

Density A wool term used to describe the related closeness of the fibres in the staple.

Depth of Staple A term denoting the length of staple on the body of a sheep.

Detwisted The description applied to a strand of fibres or filaments from which the twist has been removed.

Development The capacity of the merino for growing more skin than it requires to cover the body when smooth, thus producing folds of skin. Varies according to the merino type.

Devil's Grip A very serious defect in conformation which appears as a depression behind the withers and often is associated with poor character wool which is short and yolk stained.

Dewlap The upper fold under the neck of a merino sheep.

Diesse Fibres ready for spinning (from the German).

Dimensional Stability The extent to which a yarn can resist any distortion from its original state.

Dingy Wool of very poor colour often with excessive yolk and not likely to scour white.

Dipping – Sheep This is necessary to remove and kill any ticks, maggots, lice, etc. Sheep dipping started around 1850, before that sheep were smeared with a variety of mixtures including tar and whale oil; this was called *smearing* or *salving*. Scouring of fleece was a problem, it was usual to use water, urine and seaweed ashes.

Direct Drive The drive belt runs directly to the spindle shaft.
See the *Great Wheel*

Dis Means bunch of flax in Old English (Anglo-Saxon).

Discharging The use of chemicals to destroy a dye or mordant already present in a material and so leave it white or of a differently coloured pattern. A term also used in relation to removing gum from silk.

Distaff See pp 68–75

Diz Thought to have derived from the word *dizen* related to the Low German *Diesse*. The horn disc may be Continental. A component of woolcombers' tools, this is a small disc, usually made of horn or leather, with a hole in it. Its purpose during *jigging* was to smooth the fibres, keep the sliver to a uniform size and to act as a check for short ends. The resulting smoother fibres were then wound into a ball and called *top*.

Docking Lambs' tails are often docked to prevent them getting dirty. Dirt attracts flies which lay eggs that hatch into maggots that burrow into the flesh of the animal for sustenance.

Doffing See *Combing – Wool*

Dog *Canis familiaris*: dog fur can be spun; some breeds are more suitable than others, for example, *Chow; Samoyed; Husky; Collie; Afghan; sheepdog; retriever*. Some breeds have an undercoat that can be brushed out; others have undercoats suitable for spinning.

Dog Combings Those breeds with a longer coat are suitable, although it can be a while before sufficient hair has been collected; in the meantime the hair must be carefully stored in an airtight tin as a guard against moths. The addition of a little oil before carding or combing makes spinning easier. Odour in the yarn can be a problem however much it is washed. A dog shampoo may be the answer or using a pleasant-smelling fabric softener in the final rinse.

'Doggy' Wool A term given to shiny wool that has a very indistinct crimp, lacks breeding and has greatly reduced felting capacity.

Donning – On See *Combing – Wool*

Double Band Drive See *Bobbin Lead*

Double Band Wheel Sometimes referred to as a *Saxony wheel*. A double band flyer wheel where the flyer whorl and the bobbin whorl are side by side on the spindle. Whilst this type of wheel is referred to as 'double band' normally the drive band is a continuous one which is crossed into a figure of eight and folded over until it has the appearance of two bands. This folded band drives the spindle whorl, which should be V-shaped to give the necessary traction. The band also drives the bobbin whorl, which should have a U-shaped groove to allow for slippage, and also the drive wheel. The size of the spindle whorl governs the number of revolutions it makes for one turn of the wheel and is one factor that influences the tpi; another factor is the spindle pulley diameter in relation to the bobbin diameter which, in a good wheel, produces an efficient drawing- and winding-on. If the difference is very small and the twist is excessive, wind-on will be slow. The bobbin on a double band wheel should have a deeper groove than those on the spindle (and thus smaller), resulting in the bobbin turning faster than the spindle flyer and thus causing wind-on of the spun yarn. The wind-on is increased if the tension is also increased, thus preventing slippage. An empty bobbin requires less tension; as the bobbin fills, the tension should be increased. The flyer pulley is often a double one, consisting of two different-sized whorls, sometimes referred to as warp and weft, which thus enables the spinner to select the more appropriate whorl for the yarn being spun. The flyer whorl is usually connected by a left hand screw (but sometimes by other means of firm attachment), enabling it to be removed when necessary to remove the full bobbin.
See *Bobbin Lead; U-Flyer*

Double Flax Wheel Also called a *gossip wheel* and a *lover's wheel*. An earlier wheel design which had two spindles and flyers to enable two people to spin at one time.

Distaff The word derives from the Anglo-Saxon *dis* for flax and *staef* a stick. A Scandinavian word for distaff is *rock*. In earlier times the *distaff* or *spindle* side of the family referred to the female side; the *spear* was the male side. The word 'distaff' was also sometimes used in relation to woman's work. In North America, by tradition, distaffs were tied with a green ribbon for those who were married and red for the unmarried – the spinster – hence the derivation of the word used today.

The distaff, which is an upright pole, is designed to hold the prepared and arranged flax for spinning and to provide a constant fibre supply. Some spinning wheels have a distaff incorporated in their design; others do not and therefore a free-standing distaff is used. Some earlier wheels, still preserved today, may have a hole on the table indicating that at some time a distaff was secured into it. Today, due to the decline in flax spinning, modern wheels tend not to have a built-in distaff. Earlier free-standing distaffs were often elaborately decorated or hand turned; the pole was set into a base, or small stool with three legs, to hold it in an upright position. There were many designs; tapered, lantern shaped, prong shaped and others made from branches. The height of the distaff is important in relation to the spinner; it must be easily accessible without the need for the spinner to overextend, which would cause tiredness. The spinner also requires a small cup or pot to hold water with which to moisten the fingers whilst spinning to produce a smooth linen thread. Some earlier wheel designs had an extension arm incorporating a pot. When spinning long fibres, for example flax *line* on the great wheel, many spinners tied the fibres to their waists.

DRESSING THE DISTAFF, also called *dressing the dolly* is constructing and attaching the flax strick to a distaff with ribbon.

There are several methods and, as distaffs vary considerably in their design and height, one dressing method may be more suitable than another to a particular type. Sometimes it may be necessary to add bulk and shape to the flax when dressing a distaff. To achieve this, wrap some crushed tissue paper around the top part of the distaff and then cover it with plain, uncrushed, tissue paper. This base will be used as the central core to add the necessary 'body'. Lantern-shaped distaffs produce their own shaping. Flax types vary, some fibres are better suited to a particular method of dressing on the distaff. Practice and experience will show the spinner how to gain the necessary expertise. It is pleasurable to satisfactorily dress a distaff, and the finished work is most attractive, with the coloured ribbon and the fibres producing contrast.

METHOD 1: possibly the oldest known method; the distaff is dressed by hanging the flax sticks with the fibres parallel.

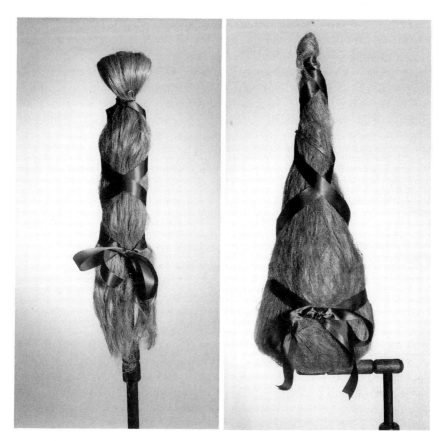

Plates 20–1 Dressed Distaff: (*left*) method without cross-combing; (*right*) using the cross-combing method

a) shake the strick gently to ensure parallel fibres
b) tie at the top with string
c) fold a length of ribbon, approximately 183cm (2yd) in half and secure the strick to the top of the distaff, tying at the centre of the ribbon, about 5cm (2in) from the top. The fibres can be held in place around the distaff by lightly crossing the ribbon ends and finally tying a bow or knot.

METHOD 2: cross layering the fibres.
- 1 The strick must be held by the root end and shaken to untwist the fibres. If the strick is rather large reduce it in size to between 55 and 70gm (2 to 2½oz) of fibre; this quantity will be sufficient to work with.
- 2 Using approximately 274cm (3yd) length of narrow ribbon (or string), tie at the centre point of the ribbon about 6.4cm to 7.6cm (2½ to 3in) from the top of the strick, below the root end.

- 3 Either tie the string around your waist (this is the traditional method), with the flax hanging from the centre front of the body, and work the process on the lap, or tie the flax at the waist as described and lay the fibres on a table at a suitable height. Some spinners prefer a third alternative, ie to work the flax on the floor without attaching to the waist. Whatever method is used, the knotted end of the strick must be facing the body and the fibres at the commencement of process laying straight ahead.
- 4 The purpose and main requirement of preparing the flax is to produce a film of fibres which crisscross upon themselves layer on layer, none should be parallel. Facing the tied strick at the knot end, as described in 3, take and hold the strick with the right hand at its bottom untied edge on the left hand side. Take the fibres from the strick and start to fan out a thin film, holding at the same time with the palm of the left hand the thin layer of fibres coming from the right hand. Start moving the right hand from the left side across towards the right, fanning out a film of fibres. Follow closely behind with the palm of the left hand containing and holding the layer of the film. When the right hand reaches across to the right side, transfer the remaining fibres to the left hand (the left hand should be at the right side having followed the right hand across). With the remaining fibres in the left hand, reverse the process, this time fanning out a film of fibres across to the left side, with the right hand palm following to control the layers. Continue reversing this process until there are no more fibres to fan out. There should now be a fan of crisscrossed fibres with none lying parallel.

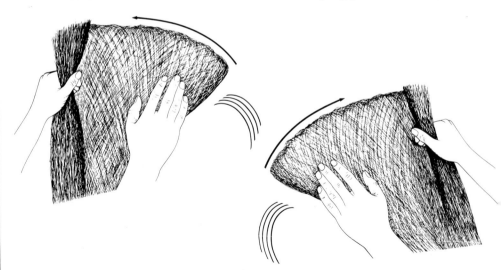

Fig 8 Fanning out flax prior to dressing a distaff: cross-combed

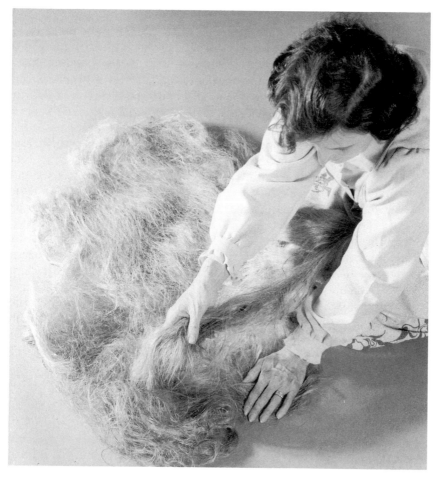

Plate 22 Dressed Distaff: fanning out flax stick

- 5 If the strick was tied to the waist, untie it and go round to the other side of the table, or if on the floor, move to the bottom of the fan. Likewise, if you have been working on your lap, the prepared fibres must be transferred to a table or firm surface. Turn up the lower edge of the fibre fan, approximately 3.8cm (1½in) and lay onto the fanned fibres; this will tidy the bottom edge.
- 6 There are two ways to do the following:–
  a) lay the top part of the distaff along the centre part of the prepared fan of flax and secure it very firmly to the top of the distaff at the centre with the ribbon or string, then wrap the fan of flax around the distaff allowing a small overlap then place the distaff into its holder and holding a ribbon strand in each hand wrap it lightly but firmly around the cone of flax, crossing from

side to side and tie with a bow at the base of the fibres. Tuck up any stray fibres around the base of the cone. If the flax has not been firmly tied it will be difficult to handle whilst spinning; or

b) when attaching the fan of fibres to the distaff some spinners prefer to lay the distaff on the left hand side of the fibre fan, with the distaff touching the tied top. The distaff is then rolled across the fan, making sure the top of the distaff and the top tied part of the fan remain together as the fan and distaff are rolled to produce a cone shape. The cone is then attached and dressed with ribbon as method a).

Spinning is a craft where the techniques can be adjusted to find the most convenient and comfortable method best suited to the individual and the task in hand. Here is an example of this: – some spinners prefer to use narrow ribbon, about 1.3cm to 2cm (½in to ¾in) for tying the strick; others prefer to use string for the securing and attaching to the distaff, then they cut the ends of the string short and apply the ribbon as a top dressing. The advantages of the latter method are that the strick can be, in most cases, more securely tied with string, and the ribbon that is added as top dressing will be pristine and not creased in any way, providing a more professional finish.

METHOD 3; U OF FLAX: separate between 40g and 50g (1½oz to 2oz) of flax from the strick, and loop it into a U-shape. Lay onto a table with the U curve on the left side. Place the distaff at right angles to the U shape at the open end of the curve. Pull the fibres out very carefully from the centre of the U whilst keeping its shape and at the same time roll the fibres onto the distaff. Gradually ease out more fibres and roll as described until all the fibres are wrapped around the distaff in a light cloud effect. The applied fibres may be top dressed with ribbon if required to look visually attractive, or else, with dampened hands gently shape the fibres tucking in, where necessary, to neaten.
See *Flax; Ribbons; Saint Distaff's Day*

Distaff – Hand Held distaffs are used with handspindles in many parts of the world. Short hand-held distaffs are used for spinning short-stapled fibres. Longer distaffs held under the arm or in the belt are used for longer fibres. In the past, they were beautifully decorated with carving, the menfolk of the family making them for their wives and daughters. In addition to various forms of decoration, music was often added in the form of bells. Held distaffs have retained popularity due to the fact that they are portable. Distaffs, whilst traditionally used for flax spinning, can also be used with other fibre types when spindle spinning.

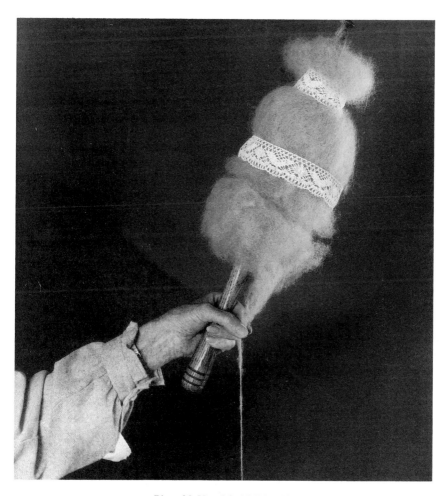

Plate 23 Hand-held Distaff

METHODS
a) make several rolags. Tie one end of each to the top of the distaff and leave them hanging like lambs' tails, use one at a time; alternatively
b) build a base of crushed tissue paper and secure to the top of the distaff. Tie the rolags at one end to the top of the distaff with a ribbon (at the centre of the ribbon length) then crisscross the ribbon to the bottom of the rolags and tie. To attach the distaff and permit maximum freedom attach a second ribbon to just below the rolags then pin to the spinner's shoulder (see Plate 24). Either place the distaff under the left arm or on the left side of the body under a belt; or
c) prepare several batts of wool using either hand cards or drum

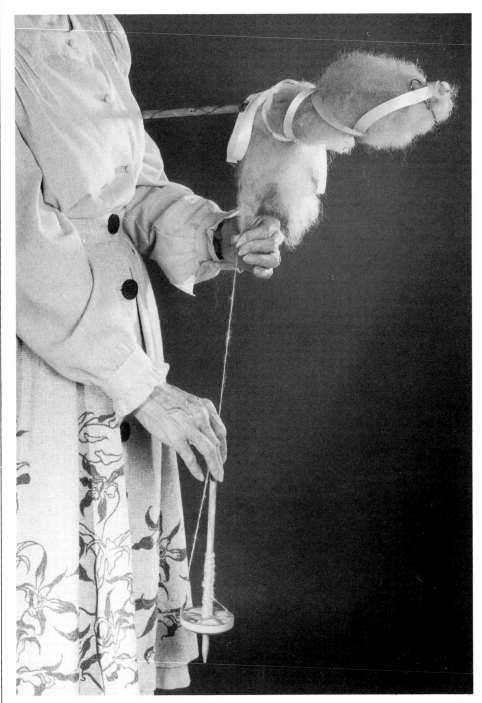

Plate 24 Matching distaff and drop (suspended) spindle: the distaff is attached to the spinner's shoulder by a ribbon pinned in place

carder. Layer one on top of the other onto a flat surface. Lay the end of the distaff onto the left hand side of the fibre mass, and roll it across to the right hand side at the same time wrapping the batts around it firmly. Using approximately 1.83m (2yd) of narrow ribbon, secure the batt construction at the top of the distaff tying at the centre of the ribbon leaving two equal sized 'tails' of ribbon. Crisscross the ribbons as for dressing flax on a distaff and tie about three-quarters of the way down the fibre mass. The wool can then be drawn out easily when spinning.

Practice is required to produce ease of spinning using a spindle and distaff combination. Once the technique has been mastered, it is a more satisfactory way than holding the fibre supply in the hand. Less tangling occurs, the fibre supply is more constant and the yarn produced far superior.

The visual interest of spinning especially when demonstrating the craft, can be enhanced by using a matching distaff and spindle. See Plate 24.

INSTRUCTIONS FOR DESIGNING A MATCHING DISTAFF AND DROP SPINDLE
Materials Required: a 91.5cm (36in) length of 1.3cm (½in) diameter dowel rod; one small cuphook; various coloured enamel paints suitable for the chosen design; clear polyurethane varnish; fine grade glass paper; an inexpensive plain wood drop spindle.

Distaff: carefully rub down the rod using glass paper that has been slightly dampened. Brush away any surplus dust. Choose a suitable simple design, for example convolvulus, which is a climbing plant. Draw onto the rod very lightly in pencil, then paint. If using a convolvulus design, mix red and white and green and white to obtain varying colour tones. Allow the enamel to dry thoroughly. Apply a thin coat of varnish and ensure that no runs occur. Dry, and rub down very lightly with the glass paper. Remove any dust. Apply a second coat of the varnish. When dry, insert the cuphook in one end at the top, taking into consideration the direction of the design.
Drop spindle: rub with the glass paper if necessary. Remove any dust. Decorate the spindle, using matching design to the distaff, down the stem and on top of the whorl. Using matching colours, paint the underneath of the whorl completely plain. Dry and then apply two thin coats of the varnish; dry thoroughly between each application and, if necessary, rub down with dampened glass paper. If there is no notch at the top of the spindle, insert a small cup hook. When dressing the distaff use narrow ribbons to tone with the colours in the design. See *Saint Distaff's Day*

Double Fleece A sheep's fleece consisting of two years' growth.

Double Treadle Wheel See *Occupational Therapy; Stockists*

Doubleur The brass teeth to be used for cards (carders) were bent on a *doubleur* which was an upright implement, part wood, part metal, into which the teeth were partly inserted and then bent to the required shape. France, 1750.

Doubling The combination of two or more tops or rovings and drawing them at the same time into a single end. Doublings promote regularity at each stage.

Doppione Also called *doupione; douppioni; dupion; dupionni*, etc, which is a breeding term used in silk, meaning double cocoon. It arises from a situation where two silkworms have spun close together and the cocoons have joined into a 'single' cocoon composed of two *baves*. The monovoltines are more likely to show this abnormality than the polyvoltine breeds. Produces an irregular rough, coarse silk which has been reeled from the double cocoons. The name also given to a silk fabric made from these irregular threads (slubs).

Down Is the undercoat of various animals that have a coat of mixed wool, down and hair.

Draft/Drafting The drawing out of fibres to decrease the mass per unit length. The rolag, roving or fibre is attenuated to produce a yarn to the required thickness whilst spinning. The drawing out is called *drafting*, and the amount drawn is the *draft*. When learning to spin, students find the main difficulty is their inability to draft quickly enough; this is caused, in most cases, by the fact that they tend to clutch the rolag or fibre supply firmly, restricting the release of the fibres. The resulting yarn is disappointing and either breaks or is lumpy. Most of the attention of the spinner is on the front hand and the wheel, rather than concentrating also on holding the fibre supply lightly, thus releasing the overlapping fibres evenly. The front hand should always be at the point of the spun yarn, not on the unspun fibres.

Drafting Roller Roller drafting was first mentioned in 1738 in a patent taken out by Lewis Paul.

Drafting Zone Also called *drafting area*: the area between the hands containing the fibres that have been drawn out during drafting.

Draw The attenuation of the fibres from the fibre supply.

Draw – Cotton CHOOSING THE FIBRE: the fibre chosen should be free from dirt and have a reasonable fibre length. Carded fibres will produce a less compact yarn and combed fibres a sleeker yarn. Cotton is available as a roving or sliver, also ginned. If ginned, washing may be necessary. Slivers may be broken into uniform lengths then divided to make rovings. These will require a long draw.

Some cottons are compressed in bales, so will require bowing or carding before spinning. When carding, use carders that have finer teeth more closely set – the teeth are often longer than those on wool cards; use only the tips of the teeth (wool carders are not suitable). If a clear white is required cotton can be bleached, it can also be dyed and will not matt.

SPINNING: *for a loose mass of short fibres*, hold loosely in the right hand with the thumb and forefinger holding the cotton junction firmly. The drawing-out triangle will be very short, the hands will be close together. Use a short draw-spin with rapid treadling. Insert plenty of twist, but avoid overtwisting. Spin a Z-spin; if S-spun it tends to come apart.

For a combed strip of short fibres, hold the junction of the fibre supply with the thumb and first finger just firmly enough to enable the wheel to draw the fibres out of the strip. Due to the length of the fibres the drawing-out triangle will be minute. A long draw is suitable.

SHORT DRAW: the spinner works close to the orifice, using a twisting movement with the drafting hand to assist the drawing-out. The hands can be worked together or the back hand can move away. A high amount of twist should be inserted to hold the short cotton fibres together, therefore the wheel tension should be loose and the wind-on not too rapid. If overtwisting occurs, increase the tension. If the thread is pulled from the hand and disintegrates (a common problem when learning to spin cotton), insert more twist. Spin cotton finely, ply if a thicker yarn is required. If too thick a singles yarn is spun, fibres can be pulled off the surface and the yarn will become weak.

LONG DRAW: a controlled long draw can be used when spinning cotton, the right hand drawing back (as for woollen long draw) but just keeping ahead of the twist and releasing a constant fibre supply. Practice will produce co-ordination between the treadling (which should be fairly rapid) and all movements. The wheel should just tug the fibres from the supply; if sections along the draw are thicker than others, use a jerking action to even them out.

METHOD: join the rolag. Treadle to impart twist. Place the finger and thumb of the left hand on the yarn in an overhand position. Take hold of the rolag about 2.5cm to 3.8cm (1 to 1½in) from the junction and draft out with the right hand and at the same time roll the yarn with the left hand (an untwisting action); when required, release the left hand and allow more twist through. When sufficient twist has been inserted, wind on rapidly to prevent overtwist. If a thicker yarn is required, ply two singles together. Cotton is sometimes treated with a solution of caustic soda, while the fibres are under tension, to give it a permanent sheen (*mercerised*).
See *Bowing; Bump; Cotton; Mercerisation; Punis*

Draw – Long Using a spinning wheel, reduce the tension on the wheel for this spin. Hold the rolag in the right hand and join to the leader; the left hand works about 22.9cm (9in) from the orifice in an overhand position holding back the twist. Lightly hold the rolag, with the thumb and index finger of the right hand about 5cm (2in) from the rolag junction, *Fig 9a*. It is these 5cm (2in) which will make the

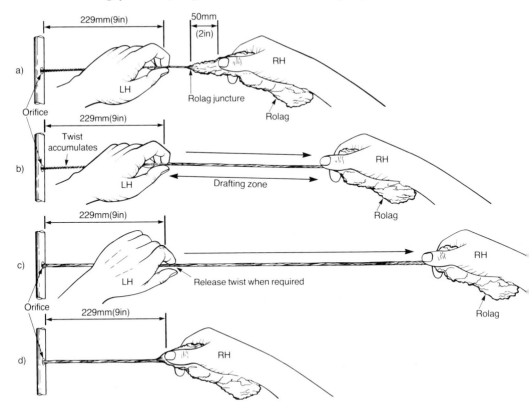

Fig 9 *DRAW – LONG*: the hands can be reversed if more comfortable and yarn drawn to the opposite side

thread; no fibre should be permitted to escape from the fingers. Start to treadle. As the twist builds up between the orifice and the left hand, move the right hand across the body and draw out the fibres, *Fig 9b*. The left hand allows sufficient twist through at this stage to add some strength to the fibres to prevent disintegration. Sweep the right arm until it is fully extended, attenuating the fibres as the twist enters them, *Fig 9c*. When an area in the drafting zone has been attentuated sufficiently, then the twist should be inserted by letting more twist build up, then open the left hand and release this twist into the thread. When sufficient twist has been inserted feed the spun yarn towards the orifice and wind onto the bobbin. As the yarn is swept in and wound onto the bobbin, additional twist will have been inserted, so this should be taken into consideration in determining the original twist quantity. Hold the right hand about 22.9cm (9in) from the orifice, *Fig 9d*. Build up extra twist then replace the left hand about halfway between the orifice and right hand, ready to start the process again. Move the right hand 5cm (2in) up the rolag as before.

With a scotch tension wheel, unlike a double band wheel, very little twist is inserted during the wind-on, therefore to compensate for this, the right hand should be kept fully extended until the required twist is obtained and then wind on.

The long draw enables faster yarn production. It requires practice to become proficient in, for instance, the attenuation of the fibres together with (when necessary) the opening and closing of the fingers of the left hand to release or control the twist. Twist will only travel up a taut thread, so the correct tension and pull must be gauged also. Once this spin is mastered it can be most satisfying.

Draw – Short Using a spinning wheel for *semi–woollen spin*.
METHOD: tie the leader onto the bobbin and place over the hooks (*hecks*) and out through the orifice. Hold the fibre supply lightly in the left hand and attach a few fibres to the leader to start. Begin to treadle, turning the wheel clockwise. The thumb and index finger of the right hand should be used to guide the twist into the fibres, the hand between 12.7cm and 15.3cm (5 to 6in) from the orifice. The left hand drafts back, distance between the hands 7.6cm to 10.3cm (3 to 4in). The yarn should be fed in regularly onto the bobbin and the treadling kept as smooth as possible. The wheel should not be permitted to draft the fibres by pulling, this is incorrect. Move the yarn on the hooks as the bobbin fills and thus provide an even build-up.

This type of spin can be used for both woollen and worsted spins, as it is suitable for long and short staple wool fibres. The hand movements determine the type of yarn produced.

a) *a light woollen spin*: the hand controlling the twist should release

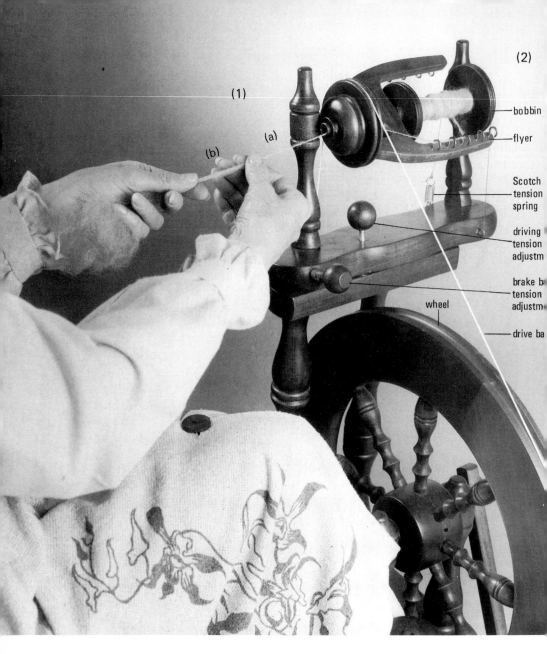

(1)

(2)

(a)

(b)

bobbin

flyer

Scotch tension spring

driving tension adjustm

brake b tension adjustm

wheel

drive ba

Plate 25 *DRAW-SHORT*: 1) in section a) twist is inserted, section b) drafting area. The hands should be at least 7.6cm (3in) apart, and the front hand at least 12.7cm (5in) from the orifice

2) nomenclature of an Ashford scotch tension wheel, which has a positive drive on the spindle and a braking action on the bobbin

the yarn and not smooth backwards during spinning

b) *a semi-worsted spin*: can be achieved by using the rolling movements of a worsted spin.

Drawing The process by which slivers are blended (or doubled) drafted and levelled to the roving stage.

Drawing-Out Triangle The triangle formed in the area where the fibres slip past one another as they are drawn out of the fibre supply into the twist by the pull from the hands and wheel, and the fibres already caught in the twist. Whatever the fibre being spun, the end result will be determined by

a) the triangle formed of the unspun fibres
b) the amount of fibres released
c) the type of fibre and
d) the method of preparation; all these will influence the spun yarn.

The number of fibres in the triangle at a given time will determine the thickness of the yarn produced. Fewer fibres in the triangle will result in a thin yarn and vice-versa. It is necessary to control the amount of fibre in the triangle; any sudden increase in the bulk in the triangle will form a lump. The fibres must be consistent in the triangle to form a consistent yarn, any irregularities in the triangle will alter this. The back hand should control the amount of fibres released; the hold on the fibre supply should be relaxed, if held too tightly, especially if the hand becomes moist, this will make drafting difficult. Whatever fibre is being used, the triangle will vary according to the fibre length; it should be long enough to permit the fibres to slide past one another as they are drawn into the twist. If the twist is permitted to run into the triangle, it becomes reduced in size and drafting will cease as the spinner will no longer be able to draft out. It will then be necessary to untwist the yarn and return the triangle to its original size.

Dresseur A tool with a metal tube and wooden handle used in France in 1750 for correcting wrong angled teeth in the construction process of cards (*carders*).

Dressing Flax A combing process, usually by hand, whereby the stricks or pieces of fine flax are made parallel and the naps or bunches of entangled fibres are removed. The ends are squared off by pulling out or breaking the fibre strands that protrude from the ends.

Drive Band Also referred to as *drive cord* or *drive belt*. The type of drive band varies according to the design of the spinning wheel.

CHOICE OF CORD: the main criterion is that it must be strong and pliable. If it has too much elasticity, it will stretch; if there is no elasticity, it will be difficult to spin with. Spun plied cotton is suitable; linen and twine are not always elastic in use. Some synthetic cords are a possibility. The cord should be to the required thickness to fit the spindle whorl, and it must also slip in the bobbin groove.

JOINING METHODS: whatever the method chosen, the two ends of the cord should be joined as neatly and as flat as possible.

a) *joining with a reef knot*: after tying the ends together, they should be clipped closely. Dangling ends can cause the wheel to throw the drive band

b) *joining by stitching*: open the cord ends and fuse one into the other for about 5cm (2in). Stitch firmly together using strong thread

c) *joining by fusion*: nylon cords can be joined by applying a lighted match to each end to fuse them into a continuous band. After the fusion of the butt ends, they should be held under running cold water and the melted ends smoothed together.

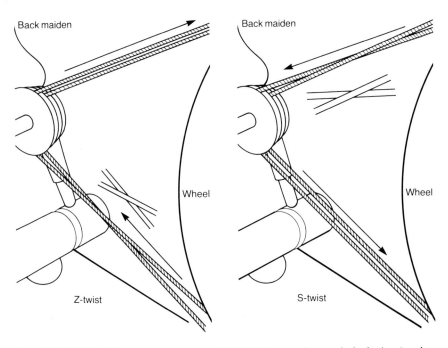

Fig 10 *DRIVE BAND*: correct crossing. Z-TWIST, wheel turned clockwise (to the right), cross in band set at the bottom. S-TWIST, wheel turned anitclockwise (to the left), cross in band set at the top

REPLACEMENT OF A DOUBLE BAND
1 Remove and measure the old band.
2 Move the mother-of-all close to the wheel using the tension screw. (If using a nylon cord that does not have the elasticity of cotton, move the mother-of-all only about halfway to the wheel.)
3 Pass the cord (one continuous band) twice around the wheel; the first time around the bobbin pulley (whorl) and the second time around the flyer pulley (whorl) to form a crossover on the band below the wheel, then join the ends together.

The tension should be held firmly without being too taut, as this can be adjusted, after the join has been completed, by the tension screw. The bobbin pulley (whorl) has a smaller diameter than the flyer pulley (whorl) so that the bobbin turns faster than the flyer and this results in the yarn being wound onto the bobbin. If the flyer pulley (whorl) has two grooves, place the band around the groove with the smaller diameter, the larger diameter will provide less twist on the yarn; these are sometimes referred to as the warp and weft whorls.

SCOTCH TENSION BRAKE CORD: this requires a smooth fine cord for the brake band. When measuring, to replace, allow extra length for at least two or three turns around the peg. A driving band is also required, capable of a neat fit around the large wheel and the flyer whorl.
The Great Wheel has a continuous belt or band, which is sewn or spliced to join. Belt dressing can be rubbed well into the band to provide good belt traction if necessary. If a belt jumps, it may indicate that the alignment between drive wheel and pulleys (whorls) is not true, therefore adjustment is necessary.

Drive Ratio To ascertain the drive ratio of a spinning wheel, first mark one of the spokes of the wheel, then count the number of revolutions of the flyer to one turn of the wheel, this will tell you how many twists are being put into the yarn to one turn of the wheel. This is written: – 5:1; 6:1; 7:1 or whatever is applicable.

Drum Carder See *Carders*

Dual-Purpose Sheep Sheep produced for both wool and mutton.

Dumped Wool Wool that is compressed tightly into a package for shipment and held together by metal bands.

Dyes and Dyeing There are many beautiful natural coloured fibres available to the handspinner and capable of producing a range of design possibilities. It is therefore sad that most students, when they become capable of producing a yarn, immediately want to dye it. Dyeing should be considered as an extension to what is possible from natural fibres. If dyeing is necessary, then the decision must be made whether to use natural or synthetic (chemical) means of dyeing.

Wool is an excellent fibre to start with, as it readily accepts most dyes to some degree or another; it will vary however, not only breed to breed, but sheep to sheep. Dipping chemicals can also affect the dyeing.

NATURAL DYEING: consists of using vegetable and animal substances. Do not leave out of consideration such items as copper piping, soot, tea leaves etc; many things are capable of producing colour.

There are two main groups of natural dyes: –

SUBSTANTIVE (*non-mordant dyes*): these will become fixed on some fibres, for example wool, by the single act of boiling the plant material with the fibres and, without any other chemical being present, a fast colour will result. Walnuts and lichens produce substantive dyes.

NATURAL INDIGO (*Indigofera tinctoria*) is classed as a substantive dye because no mordant is required. Instead an oxidising process takes place and the most successful colours are obtained by repeated dippings and exposure to air.

TO MAKE STOCK FOR VAT-DYEING INDIGO

Ingredients:
56.8g (2oz) powdered indigo
85g (3oz) caustic soda
56.8g (2oz) hydrosulphite of soda
  (sodium dithionite)
Approx 1.13*l* (2pt) hot (55°C/
  130°F) water

Utensils:
two 0.5*l* (1pt) pyrex or glass jugs
one large glass jar with screw lid
  (7lb pickle/jam jar)
saucepan
glass stirring rod
pestle & mortar
water thermometer
rubber gloves

METHOD
- 1 Grind the powder with a little warm water to smooth paste – there must be no lumps.
- 2 Add caustic soda, gradually, to 0.5*l* (1pt) warm water in a jug. Stir well.
- 3 Add hydrosulphite of soda to the other pint of water in second jug. Stir gently.
- 4 Put indigo paste into saucepan, add *nearly* all caustic soda then *nearly* all hydrosulphite solution. Warm to 50°C (120°F), not exceeding 60°C (140°F), and leave for 1 hr in a warm place.

Note: if this temperature is exceeded the whole vat will be ruined, *140°* is the absolute maximum.

Dip the glass rod into the solution to test, it should be a clear yellow, any dark spots indicate the Indigo has not disolved properly, add remainder of the hydrosulphite solution but do no reheat: if white spots show add a drop of the caustic solution.

The dye is now ready to follow any natural indigo dye recipe or can be stored in a glass jar until required. Try not to make too many bubbles during the dyeing process; bubbles contain oxygen.

ADJECTIVE DYES (*mordant dyes*): these require that the fleece or yarn be impregnated by boiling with a chemical first. The name given to these chemicals is *mordants* derived from the French *mordre* (to bite). These chemicals prepare the fibres so that they will receive the dyestuff, otherwise the dye would wash out. The mordants (metal salts) are boiled into the wool; they attract the colour in the dyebath and this in turn fixes to the chemical.

CONSERVATION: it is vital not to overpick an area; always leave sufficient growth to continue. Many plants will produce a similar colour (90 per cent yellows and brown), therefore choose the plant which is more prolific and less rare. Garden plants are readily available; use these in preference to wild ones. Spinners with gardens can grow their own dye material, suppliers of dyebath seeds make it possible to grow suitable plants. Lists are available of protected plants. Lichens grow so slowly that they should be avoided, unless found in quantities.

COLOUR FACTORS: many factors have a bearing on the colour obtained from vegetable matter: −

a) where the plant or tree was grown; for example, if on farmland where fertiliser or spraying had been used
b) the soil type; this can vary considerably in a given area
c) the time of year harvested
d) whether there had been rain or sun
e) time of day harvested.

The dyer will learn by experience which part of the plant to use, for example, flower; leaves; root, etc; also whether to put the whole plant in the dyebath or only a certain part. In some plants the same chemicals may exist throughout the plant, in others they may be concentrated in a particular part. Some plants will produce a different colour from the leaves than from the flowers. The brightest flowers do not always produce the strongest colour, quite the reverse in fact.

It is essential to keep a record of each dyeing and to retain such information as: – plant name, where collected, time of year, mordant (if any) used, colour obtained. This will, over a period of time, build a valuable reference source. A small sample of yarn test dyed before a whole batch could prevent wastage, if the results obtained are disappointing. The great variation that exists in books concerning methods of dyeing is very noticeable; one reason is the vast potential of what can be achieved and therefore each author develops an individual system. With natural dyeing, the writer/teacher can only present processes and techniques for students to try. Because of variations in the colour obtained in different areas, no one can say that a particular plant and mordant will produce a certain colour in every part of the country. Apart from all the conditions already mentioned, the variation in water from one area to another may bring about a completely different result.

EQUIPMENT: most items are readily available and substitutions can be made where necessary.

- 1 *Saucepans*: enamel (not chipped); ovenproof glass; or stainless steel. The latter material is most useful, as other metals can react with the dyes and mordants. The actual size of the saucepan/s is determined by the amount of fibre or yarn. As a guide, complete movement of the fibre should be possible. A separate saucepan is useful to be kept for mordanting with iron.
- 2 *Teaspoons*: small plastic or stainless steel for the chemicals.
- 3 *Rods*: stainless steel; glass; cane; or sticks (must be smooth) – used for stirring and lifting.
- 4 *Protective apron*
- 5 *Rubber gloves*
- 6 *Small accurate scales*: for weighing exact quantities of chemical.
- 7 *Larger scales*: for weighing dyestuffs and fibres/yarns.
- 8 *A4 size ring binder*: to record test details, ie date; plant name; where collected; time of day; quantities used; mordants; boiling time; colours obtained, etc.
- 9 *Muslin bags*: suitable for holding plant material in a dye bath to avoid tangling of plant material into the fibre/yarn. The bags may be made out of well washed old net curtains, provided they are sound with no holes.
- 10 *Hammer and board*: for bruising roots, etc.
- 11 *Small containers*: for mixing mordants.
- 12 *Thermometer*: which records boiling point.
- 13 *Heating*: this can be electricity; gas; coal; or camp-type fire, etc.

WATER REQUIREMENT: soft water is the best. Water that has a high iron content will *sadden* (darken) natural dye colours and make it difficult to obtain bright colours. Rain water can be used.

BEFORE DYEING: the fibre or yarn must be thoroughly washed and rinsed; this will greatly affect the end result. If a fleece is to be dyed, it should be scoured in the normal way. It can be placed in a pillowcase and spun dry. Fleece is easier for the beginner to start dyeing with at each stage of the dyeing, as it is not so compact as a spun yarn. If using

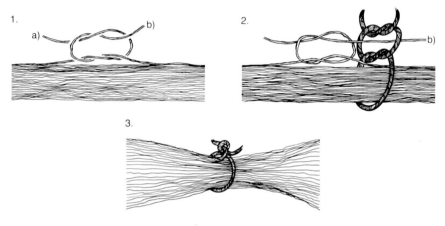

Fig 11 Skeining prior to dyeing yarn: 1) tie the beginning and ends a) and b) securely together 2) put a strong, undyed piece of yarn around the skein and tie to secure around end b) (the skein will require securing in several places, see *Fig 14*) 3) do not tie the yarn tightly, unless an undyed area is required

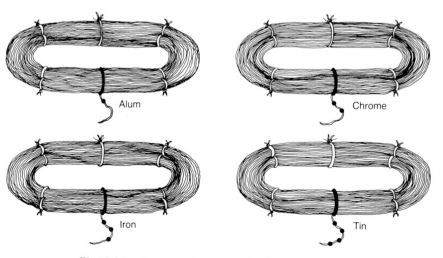

Fig 12 Identification of mordants by knotting string ties

spun yarn, wind it into hanks – 15g (½oz) are a useful size. Tie carefully (see *Figs 11* and *22*) and securely, but fairly loose to facilitate easy penetration of both the mordants and the dyes. Make sure the yarn that has been used for tying when skeining is undyed, and of a different thickness, so that it is easy to identify when removal is necessary. (Dyed wool may run [bleed] during the dyeing process.) When tying for skeining it assists with identification of the mordant if you knot the end of the attaching thread, eg one knot – *alum*; two knots – *chrome*; three knots – *iron*; four knots – *tin*, etc (see *Fig 12*). After washing, dry over a rod and weight the skein to avoid crinkling.

COLOUR EXTRACTION METHODS: to extract the dye from the plant may require different approaches: –

a) *soaking*: soaking some plant matter before cooking assists the colour extraction; do not soak too long, otherwise fermentation will result and a different colour is produced

b) *pounding and crushing*: when using this method, please note that the matter that has been pounded may separate into layers during the soaking, and sometimes the top and bottom layer may be capable of producing separate dye colouring

c) *chopping*: the material is chopped before soaking and cooking.

PLANT COLLECTION, PREPARATION AND BOILING TIMES: this is a general guide only, as variations occur. Use at least equal quantities of dyestuff to wool eg .45kg (1lb) dyestuff to .45g (1lb) wool. Additional dyestuff will produce, in most cases, a stronger colour. Some plants give off *toxins* when boiled so take care.

Plant material should be placed in water, either in a muslin bag or loose (if loose it will be necessary to strain off before immersing the wool in the dyebath). Bring to the boil then reduce the heat slightly for the required time.

After boiling, the dye may be used immediately, or bottled and labelled carefully and stored in a dark place until required. The colour of the dye liquid obtained after boiling the plant material is not necessarily the colour of the wool when dyed; often it is the reverse, dark liquids producing pale colours and vice versa.

DRYING OF PLANT MATERIAL: many different types of natural dyestuffs can be dried and stored until required. Natural drying is preferable. During storage, no damp should be permitted to penetrate the dried material.

IMPORTED DYESTUFFS: these produce, on the whole, more consistent and stronger colours because of the climate in which they are grown. They provide an exciting extension to British dyes.

Plant collection, preparation and boiling times

Type	Time	Preparation
BARK	Spring or early autumn due to resinous content	Pound; break; place in boiling water. Soak overnight. Boil 1¼ to 1½ hr or longer
BERRIES	When ripe	Pound and crush. Boil for 15 min upwards
FLOWERS	Prior to seeding; preferably in full bloom	Chop. Do not boil too long as flowers produce their dyes quickly. Approximately 15 to 45 min
LEAVES	Full growth	Chop; boil 30 min and upwards. Chop up hard leaves and soak overnight, then boil in the same water
LICHEN	Collect after rain or damp weather which causes the lichen to swell. Avoid collection entirely, unless quantities are growing	Can be boiled or fermented then boiled
ROOTS	Winter (root removal will destroy a plant unless leaving remaining plants in a clump. Take this into consideration.)	Wash; chop and soak 24 hr or longer. Boil for 1¼ hr. Some roots do not respond to boiling, eg madder
SEEDS	When ripe	Pound and crush

DYES AND DYEING

GENERAL NOTES CONCERNING DYEING
a) the liquid in the dyebath should be left to cool before immersing the wool
b) the wool should always be thoroughly *wetted-out* before being immersed in the dyebath. Wetting-out cannot be thoroughly executed by holding the wool under a running tap. A drop of detergent in the water will assist in complete water penetration.
c) the wetted-out wool should be at the same temperature as the cooled dyebath
d) the wool should be immersed in the dyebath and the temperature gradually raised to boiling, then reduced to a simmer. Wool should never be kept at the boil for too long, as undue agitation will cause felting
e) the wool should not rest on the bottom of the dyebath. Some dyers leave a quantity of the dyestuff in the base of the saucepan and place more dyestuff (in a bag) on the top to keep the wool under the surface of the water
f) if the dyebath is brought to the boil too quickly, the colour obtained from the dye material will be weaker. When actually dyeing wool, a sustained simmer is desirable
g) when rinsing the wool after dyeing, it should be rinsed in water of the same temperature as the dyebath, with a gradual reduction in temperature through subsequent rinsings
h) if chemicals are to be added to the dyebath, always lift the yarn out first, remove the dyebath from the heat, then add the chemicals, replace wool in the dyebath and return both to the heat and continue the process
i) the amount of water required in a dyebath should be sufficient to cover the wool and permit plenty of movement of the water. This must also be sufficient to take into consideration the water absorbed by the wool (this should be slight if the wool is thoroughly wetted-out). A rough guide is 1*l* (1.75 pt) liquid per 25g (1oz) of wool.

MORDANTS
● 1 *Alum – potassium aluminium sulphate* is a white crystalline powder, and the most generally used of all mordants since ancient times. It is available from chemists and safe. Too much alum will make the wool feel sticky.
● 2 *Chrome – potassium dichromate* or *bichromate of potash* is an orange crystalline substance that is poisonous. Store in the dark. It is a useful mordant for wool, producing a soft feel.
● 3 *Tin – tin salt, stannous chloride*: off-white crystals that are poisonous and should be stored in a glass jar. Tends to make wool feel stiff. Cream of tartar is, in most cases, used with tin. Tin tends

to produce bright tones and is sometimes referred to as *blooms* due to this. Tin can be added after alum to brighten.

Alum, chrome and tin are called *the brightening mordants*.

- 4 *Iron – ferrous sulphate* or *copperas*: green crystals, and also poisonous. Can harden wool if too much is used. Often used as a *saddening agent*; walnut shells and copper sulphates are also used as saddening agents.
- 5 *Copper – copper (cupric) sulphate*, also called *blue vitriol*, is a poison. It is not very reliable with the colour it produces. Iron and copper are also referred to as *dulling mordants*.

To combat the harsh feel produced by some mordants, cream of tartar (potassium bitartrate) is used in some recipes to keep the wool softer. See *Blending*

METHODS OF MORDANTING

Mordanting can be carried out: –

a) *Before dyeing – Premordanting*: the wool is mordanted, then either used immediately or dried and stored to use at a later date. The mordanted wool is added to the dyebath after the dyestuff has been removed.

b) *During dyeing*: the wool (unmordanted) is removed from the dyebath after a given time. The mordant (which has been dissolved in hot water) is added to the dyebath and the wool replaced. Simmer 15–20 min approximately. Rinse thoroughly. Mordanting with iron after dyeing is called *saddening*.

c) *Simultaneous dyeing*: involving mordant, plant and yarn in the dyebath as one process saves time, but tends to produce paler colours. Alternatively, place mordanted wool into the dyebath containing the dyestuff; first a layer of plant stuff, then a layer of wool, until sufficiently full. Bring to the boil slowly, simmer approximately 30 min or until the desired colour is obtained. Either leave to cool in dyebath, or remove and drain. Rinse in clean water. Lay out to dry or spin dry.

MORDANTING: a mordant (metal salt) fixes the dye to the wool by creating an affinity between the pigment and the fibre. The mordant attaches itself to the fibre, then the dye fixes itself to the mordant. This allows colours, which may have no affinity for the fibre, to be fixed.

PROPORTIONS: to 0.45kg (1lb) of wool (dry weight). Accuracy in measuring mordants is essential. Wool is usually mordanted before dyeing, although it can be added to the dyebath.

- 1 *Alum – potassium aluminium sulphate*: to 85g (3oz) and 28.4g (1oz) cream of tartar. Increase to 113.4g (4oz) of alum if the wool is coarse.
  a) weigh the clean dry wool
  b) dissolve the alum and cream of tartar in a little boiling water and add to the dyebath that already contains sufficient hand-hot water to completely cover the wool. Sir well
  c) immerse the thoroughly wetted wool (the same temperature as the bath)
  d) raise the liquid very slowly to boiling point
  e) during this period turn the wool over once or twice very gently to obtain even penetration of the mordant
  f) lower the heat and simmer gently for approximately 1 hr. Turn during this time
  g) either: leave the wool in the water until it has cooled, then lift the mordanted wool out and drain. Squeeze gently to remove excess water. Do not wash. The wool may be stored damp for a day or two or dried and stored. Be sure to label carefully.
  Or: leave the wool in the liquor throughout the night, then squeeze to remove excess liquid and use immediately.
  Alum usually gives the colour of the dye with a tendency to yellowing.

- 2 *Chrome-potassium dichromate*: use 14.2g (½oz) per 0.45kg (1lb) of wool.
  Treat as for alum. Chrome is sensitive to the light, so keep the pan covered during mordanting. Gradually bring to the boil. When turning the wool keep away from the light. Simmer for ¾ to 1 hr, increase to 1½ hr if the wool is coarse. Cool the wool in the liquid. Rinse in water of the same temperature. Squeeze out excess water. Keep the wool covered (away from the light) and dye immediately. Chrome must be handled very carefully otherwise uneven dyeing could result. Chrome gives a somewhat deeper colour however.
  Wool mordanted with alum may have some chrome added to the dyebath towards the end; this will add depth to the colour.

- 3 *Iron – ferrous sulphate* or *copperas* or *green vitriol*: to 7.1g (¼oz) add 28.4g (1oz) cream of tartar per 0.45kg (1lb) of wool.
  Iron can make wool feel harsh; whilst it can be used in the same way as alum and chrome, it is advisable to first cook the wool in the dyebath for 45 min, then remove with a rod, add the iron and cream of tartar (previously mixed in hot water), replace the wool in the dyebath and finish the process in the normal way. When adding wool to the mordanting liquid solution, it is necessary to immerse all at one time, otherwise parts will absorb the mordant more quickly than others. Iron 'saddens' colours, ie makes them dull. It is essential to rinse

thoroughly otherwise the wool will become tender. It is advisable to keep a pan especially for iron.

- 4 *Tin – stannous chloride*: to 14.2g (½oz) add 56.8g (2oz) cream of tartar per 0.45kg (1lb) of wool.

  It can make the wool very harsh and brittle. Heat the water to hand hot. Dissolve the cream of tartar in boiling water, and the tin crystals in warm water. Add both to the dyebath. Stir well. Add the thoroughly wetted wool, which should be at the same temperature. Bring gradually to the boil. Gently simmer for 1 hr. Cool the wool in the liquid. Remove the wool and place in soapy water at the same temperature. Rinse well. After dyeing place the wool in a soapy solution and rinse again. Iron produces similar results to alum, only brighter.

- 5 *Copper sulphate*: to 28.4g (1oz) add 14.2g (½oz) cream of tartar per 0.45kg (1lb) of wool.

  This is similar to chrome, but makes it faster.

Chemicals vary in the time they take to become attached to the wool; tin and iron may be treated as alum and chrome, but should be added towards the end of dyeing.

Different chemicals and mordants will produce different colours from various parts of many plants. If a dye fixes to a wool too quickly, then reduce the strength for the next dyeing session; a yarn requires a certain time to really fix the dye and produce fastness.

Mordants may be used with substantive dyes, although they are not required to fix the dye, they can be used to alter the colour.

Storage

Chemical storage: this is a most important consideration. All chemicals must be stored where they cannot be reached by children, or where they can never be mistaken for something else.

Material storage: all mordanted materials must be clearly labelled and stored until required. A horse chestnut (conker) placed in each container will help to discourage moths.

Utensil storage: these should be stored in a place where they cannot be used by mistake for any other purpose. Any item to be stored relating to the dyeing process must be in a situation where there is no risk of misuse, and kept only for that purpose.

Additives and alternatives: many substances can be added to the dyebath to increase the success of the dyeing.

- 1 *Ammonia*: a chemical used for purposes of neutralising.

- 2 *Cream of tartar – tartaric acid*: a white soluble crystaline substance that adds brightness to alum or iron when used in the dyebath in conjunction with the mordant. Used also with alum, tin and iron to add softness to the yarn and even out the colour. Amount to use approximately 28.4g (1oz) to 0.45kg (1lb) of wool.

- 3 *Glauber's salts – sodium sulphate*: used to assist in the colour take-up when added to the dyebath, especially one containing a natural dye. Causes even colour distribution and prevents 'bleeding' during washing.
  METHOD: about halfway through the dyeing, remove the pan from the heat. Lift the wool out of the dyebath with a rod. Dissolve approximately ½ cup salts in 570ml (1 pt) hot water, stir well. Replace the wool and continue cooking as before.

- 4 *Oxalic acid*: can produce a blue colour from berries and fruit. After mordanting, store for a while before dyeing.

- 5 *Salt – sodium chloride*: common salt assists in exhausting the dyebath. Can fix some colours and brighten others.

- 6 *Tannic acid*, ie *oak galls*: darkens colours, giving browns.

- 7 *Vinegar* (weak solution of acetic acid): white vinegar is preferable. It is useful for neutralizing soap when rinsing wool. About 1¾ cups to 0.45kg (1lb) wool).

DYEING OTHER FIBRES: many fibre types are suitable for dyeing, although some accept dye more readily than others. The choice often has to be made whether to use natural or synthetic dyes.

Linen and cotton: because they are not porous, linen and cotton often produce weak colours if natural dyestuffs are used, therefore it is preferable to use synthetic dyes. Whichever type, it is essential to carefully prepare the fibre, ie scouring, mordanting, sometimes bleaching followed by a second scouring. Alum, chrome, iron, tin and copper can be used. Tannin (tannic acid) assists cotton to take the dyestuff.

Silk: must be thoroughly degummed to remove the sericin (gum) and then mordanted. Alum is particularly suitable, although others can be used. The same mordant quantities used for wool are suitable, but as silk is so lightweight (also, smaller amounts may be dyed at one time), use ½ tsp of alum for 1oz of dry silk; if the colour is not setting, add a further ¼ tsp after 15 min. If dyeing rovings, break into about 3.658m (4yd) lengths and tape each end with masking tape. Fold back and forth, approximately 4 lengths to the yard and tie loosely in three places. This keeps control of the silk during handling and the dyeing process. Avoid high temperatures at all times. Heat dyebaths to

67.5°C (150°F) and keep under 80°C (175°F) for 10–15 min, on mawata, cocoons and rovings; thick yarns may require longer.

Mawatas: dye before separating. Squares should be tied in 14.2g to 28.4g (½oz to 1oz) sections through two corners.

Always weigh all silk fibres in their dry weight, then thoroughly soak in warm water before dyeing. When the dyebath is ready, gently remove water by squeezing, then open up the silk and place in the warm dyebath. Stir as little as possible. Allow the dyebath to cool. Place silk in a colander for support whilst transferring to cooling down rinses. Once fully rinsed, gently squeeze and hang up to dry; hang rovings by the taped ends and mawata by snap clothes pegs onto a plastic covered line. Cocoons, if not adhering to one another, can be laid in a piece of smooth cotton or nylon curtain net and the net hung up to dry. Silk can be dyed brilliantly using chemical dyes.

To Test For Colour Fastness Whatever The Yarn Type

The main criterion, whatever method is used, is to expose some of the yarn to sunlight for a period of time then compare the result with yarn that has been covered in some way to shield from sunlight. Repeated washing adds to the end results.

Method 1

a) make several equal size hanks of mordanted yarn and dye same. Divide into three amounts

b) place one part in direct sunlight; the second part put away in a cupboard or drawer away from light; the third amount wash from time to time

Over a period of time compare the results and keep a record of any differences.

Method 2

Mordant and dye yarns. Then wrap them around a piece of card. Place the card into the lid of a box, which must be a tight fit. Expose one side to sunlight, and the lid of the box will mask the other side. Remove the card from time to time to compare. A further quantity of the same yarn can be repeatedly washed, and by comparison results obtained.

Test Dyeing: many fibre types are suitable for dyeing; without exception wool is the most useful fibre to start with. Fleece, homespun, or manufactured wool, can be used. With a fleece the problems most likely to be encountered are if the sheep had recently been dipped in a chemical bath. Often the least expensive manufactured wools will take the dye more satisfactorily, since they are less likely to have been treated for moth resistance, etc.

Some terms used in dyeing

BLENDING	Used to 'soften' a fibre that may have a harsh feel after dyeing. Natural fibre is blended with the harsh fibre. Blending can also be used to reduce a strong colour to a softer tone. Blending should be carefully controlled; uneven blending may appear 'patchy'. Carefully weigh the fibres to be blended and treat a batch at a time.
BLOOMING	The use of tin to brighten colours; usually done before the end of dyeing and before a soap bath.
DYE BATH	The container with the liquor produced by boiling the dyestuff in water. The yarn/fibre to be dyed will be placed in this.
DYEING 'IN THE GREASE'	The result is similar to tie-dyeing; due to the grease content, the wool absorbs the colour unevenly.
DYE PAN	The pan used to boil the dyestuff in.
DYE PIGMENT	The colouring obtained from plants.
DYE SOURCE	Plant, mineral or animal source that can produce a natural dye.
EXHAUSTED	When the colour in the dyebath has been completely exhausted. With natural dyestuffs the liquor can be used for increasingly lighter tones.
FAST	The colour remains in the yarn, whether washed repeatedly, or exposed to light.
FUGITIVE DYES	Dye colours that fade – they are non permanent.
GREENING	When copper sulphate is added to a yellow dye during dyeing, thus bringing out the green tones.
LEVELLING	When the dyeing is patchy it requires evening out to the same depth all over the yarn. Glauber's salts can be used for levelling.
OVERDYEING, also called TOP DYEING and BOTTOMING	The dyeing of one colour onto another. Used for a variety of effects, similar to blending paints to obtain a colour. Can be done using separate dye baths; place the yarn in the lighter colour first, dye as normal. Rinse and place in the second dyebath and repeat the process. Blue on top of yellow produces green. 'Bottoming' refers to the yellow which is the first colour (the bottom colour) with blue on top. Overdyeing can be useful to lighten or tone down a coloured yarn, or to cover staining.
PRE-MORDANTING	Wool that has been mordanted before dyeing.
STUFFING	Mixing the mordant in the dyebath.
WETTING OUT	Wool must be thoroughly wetted before immersion in the dyebath. Never place under a running tap; this will not permit complete absorption. A drop of liquid detergent in the water will assist absorption.
WORKING THE WOOL	Gently moving, or turning, the wool in the liquid using a rod. Never stir.

CHOICE OF MORDANT: it is not always easy, especially when starting to dye, to know which mordant is most likely to produce the best result from a plant; even an established dyer cannot take into consideration all the factors relating to each plant. Many books provide recipes that will act as guides to the mordant best suited for a particular purpose. On the whole, it is easier to ascertain what is best for an individual area because of environmental factors. Mordant several small skeins of wool, each with a different mordant, then dye accordingly. This will produce for the dyer some of the variations possible and give a guide to the most suitable mordant.

A dyer should keep careful records of dyeing results from the onset; these will prove invaluable when comparisons are required or a particular colour is needed. No author can generalise on all aspects of natural dyeing because of the reasons already stated; it is up to the individual to discover what can be produced from a particular area.

Anne Dyer, in her book *Dyes From Natural Sources*, describes how she uses a thermos flask for test dyeing; this is an excellent method. Obtain a jar and thermos flask with the same liquid capacity. Cut up the dyestuff into small pieces, place in the jar and fill with water. Soak for several hours. Empty into a saucepan with the previously mordanted samples (clearly marked with knotting) and bring slowly to the boil. Empty the contents of the saucepan into the thermos flask (which has been previously warmed by filling with warm water, then emptied). Cork and leave for a few hours, or a few days, depending on the colour required. Empty the contents of the thermos flask into a sieve, remove the dyestuff, rinse and dry the samples. Using the knotted strings to identify the mordants used, place a label on each giving relevant details (plant material etc). Store.

A very interesting test-dyeing exercise is to select a plant likely to be easily available for some time, then test as many parts of the plant as possible, eg flowers; seeds; stem; leaves; roots, etc – whatever is applicable. Over a period of a year, for example, repeat the tests, recording time of year plant material was collected; weather conditions; which side of the plant the material was collected from, etc. To obtain comparisons, vary the soaking and boiling times and the preparation, ie whether chopped, etc. Produce as many variations as possible including the type of water used (tapwater, rainwater or water obtained from another area). The fastness of the dyed material should also be taken into consideration. At the end of the test period the dyer should have valuable information for future dyeing. Whilst tests may be carried out on several plants over a period of time, these can be time consuming and incomplete testing and many unfinished tests will result in no conclusive information.

SOLAR DYEING: dyeing by fermentation, which takes time.

METHOD
a) prepare wool in normal way
b) place the wool into a clear glass containing the dye liquor
c) cover the jar top
d) stand in full sunlight; stir occasionally. When dyeing is complete, empty the jar outdoors (because of the smell of the fermentation)
e) rinse well in clean water and dry.

SPRINKLE DYEING is the use of chemical dyes, eg Dylon hot water dyes to produce a random streak effect in fleece.

Materials required: 0.45kg (1lb) fleece; salt; brown or white vinegar; washing-up liquid; rubber gloves; stainless steel or enamel container; Dylon or similar dye powders.

METHOD: soak the fleece in cold water overnight and rinse; the grease remaining in the fleece will assist in producing the required effect. Pour approximately 20.4cm (8in) of water into the container. Add to this a cup of vinegar, 4tbsp (level) of salt and a generous squirt of washing-up liquid. Place the fleece, tips facing downwards, into the container; it should not be able to move freely. Heat slightly to thoroughly wet the fleece. The Dylon tins are sealed; make a small hole in each of the colours to be used, and sprinkle over the fleece; an uneven distribution is required. Heat the container very gradually and simmer for approximately ¾ hr, or longer, until the colour has reached the base of the container. Do not permit boiling as this will spoil the effect. When coloured sufficiently, remove from the heat and rinse the fleece in clean hot water at the same temperature as the dyebath. Dry thoroughly.

SYNTHETIC DYES: chemical dyes can be controlled, the mordants and presoaked material all react to one another. The dyes are obtained as concentrated powders from chemical companies.
Within natural and synthetic dyes, are those more suitable for protein fibres, eg wool, hair and silk; others are more suitable for cellulose fibres, ie cotton, linen, hemp and jute. Some dyestuffs are effective on both protein and cellulose, although the colours vary in intensity, but the associated chemicals can harm certain fibres. Protein fibres tend to withstand a slightly acid solution, but are destroyed by alkali. Cellulose fibres withstand alkaline substances rather than acid ones.
The technique is the same as for natural dyeing, ie

a) skein yarn (cotton, silk and linen, as they are finer, require firmer ties)
b) scour and rinse

c) if the yarn is dried after scouring, it should be wetted out in water to the same temperature as the dyebath
d) immerse in dyebath.

Some synthetic dyes are best suited to protein fibres:

ACID DYES are particularly good for bright colours on silk and wool.

DIRECT DYES: cotton; linen; some are suitable for silk and wool.

FIBRE-REACTIVE DYES: there are two types; some are good for silk and wool, others for cotton, linen and other cellulose fibres. The dyes react chemically on the fibre.

MULTI-PURPOSE DYES: are a mixture of dyestuffs, so are not really as successful as the dyes mentioned which are for particular types. Follow the maker's instructions carefully.

VAT DYES: organic dyes which are insoluble in water, eg *indigo*.
See *Galls; Indigo; Oxidation; Rock Salt*

Dyed in the Wool Fabrics comprising wool that was dyed before being spun.

Dyed in the Yarn Fabrics in which the yarn has been dyed before being woven.

Dyed Slubbings Worsted tops, dyed whilst in top form, then recombed. After that it is spun.

fect Ya
Yarns
fect Ya

E F

calyptus Oil · Extra Lustre · Fadge · Fellmongering
ptus Oil · Extra Lustre · Fadge · Fellmongering · Fel
calyptus Oil · Extra Lustre · Fadge · Fellmongering

Effect Yarns Yarns that have been designed to produce a particular effect, for example, textured; fancy (with slubs, patterns, etc); coloured in various ways. See *Embroidery Threads*

Elastic Recovery The ability of a stretched fibre to return to its unstretched length is called *elastic recovery*. This will affect the shape of garments. Stretch may be desired in some cases, but not in others.

Elm *Ulmus campestris*: a bast fibre used for cording and mats.

Embroidery Threads The creation of threads for embroidery can be both exciting and challenging for a spinner. Great variety may be requested by the embroiderer and it is often necessary to use both animal and vegetable fibres in a particular design. When couching, an embroiderer may use hard spun yarn.

Emulsion – Dressing Use this to spray a fleece that seems dry to handle; it is especially applicable to a scoured fleece; it can be applied while working or overnight.

Type a) put into a bottle with a sprinkle top equal parts of olive oil and water, shake thoroughly; if desired a quarter part of ammonia can be added

Type b) dissolve 28.4g (1oz) of washing soda in a pint of water. Add neatsfoot oil until the emulsion turns milky.

Some spinners prefer to use three parts of olive oil with one part of water. When mixing any emulsion, it can be shaken to mix or whisked with a hand or machine mixer.

End An individual strand in spinning.

Epinetron An unglazed tile, shaped to fit around the thigh and knee and used in former times. On this a spinner would roll a piece of fleece into a roving.

Eucalyptus Oil Some spinners include eucalyptus oil in the final scouring rinses of the fibre to improve its feel. Others use fabric softener or lemon juice, which improves the handle of the wool.

Ewe Female sheep more than one year old.

Extract The name given to materials derived from fabrics containing a proportion of vegetable fibre. The fibre is removed by an acid treatment; this destroys the vegetable content leaving the wool unaffected. This treatment makes it easier for the pulling process and keeps the staple length well preserved.
See *Mungo; Re-manufactured Materials; Shoddy*

Extra Lustre The heightened sheen on a skein of silk, the result of being stretched whilst steamed.

Eye – Wigging Some sheep have become wool-blind, caused by breeding to achieve as much wool as possible. The result is that the wool grows over their eyes and they cannot see. At crutching time these sheep may be ear-wigged also, which is the removal of the top knot that grows down over the eyes. Wool growing *under* the eyes can be left as it tends to hang down away from the eyes, causing no problems. See *Crutching*

Fadge A woolpack, partly filled with wool, or several bags that have been sewn together; weight between 27.2kg and 68kg (60 to 150lb).

Fairs Also known as *staples* were fairs where wool workers met to celebrate the prosperity during the late Medieval period.

Fancy Yarn Includes *knops; curls; slubs; loops.* A yarn that has deliberately introduced irregularities in its construction, as opposed to the normal appearance of a single or folded yarn.

Fastness The resistance to washing, light, etc. Various grades exist on the standard scale; No 1 has no change, No 5 is greatly changed. For light-fastness, eight grades are used, No 8 is the highest degree of fastness.

Fellmongering *fallen/fell wool, skin wool* is sometimes referred to as *slipe wool* before scouring, or in America as *pulled wool.* The removing of wool from the skins of slaughtered sheep by chemical processes. Skin wool is inferior to fleece wool. The names vary according to the methods used to remove the wool. Some skins are de-wooled before shipment from eg New Zealand but are often dewooled in the importing countries, eg Australia and Argentina. Large

101

establishments for dewoolling exist in many sheep-rearing countries, often near to the meat packing stations. Some skins are shipped to European countries for treatment – mainly to the French fellmongering industry at Mazamet, which is world famous. Other than wool, pelts are a product of fellmongering, dependent on the origin, type and quality The skin consists of five layers: –

1 The *epidermis*
2 The *basal* layer
3 The *thermostatic* layer, sometimes called 'the grain' of the *dermis*, which is rich in blood vessels and in which the wool follicles are found
4 A fatty layer beneath this
5 The *reticular* layer consisting of a thick network of *collagen* fibres.

With some forms of skin treatment, splitting occurs along the fatty layer, which is not desirable unless for wash leathers. Other than the fat, two main proteins are involved in fellmongering, the *keratin* and *prekeratin* of wool, and the chemically similar *epidermis* and *collagen* that make up the structure of the pelt. The main processes used, ie the sweating method and the painting method, act in different ways on these. Both methods require a moist pelt.

Sweating Method: the skins are placed in pits of water to remove the dirt; fresh skins stay for only a few hours, dry skins for longer. The skins are then passed through a deburring machine in which the wool is agitated with beaters and fluted rollers, then doused with jets of water, which partially scour the fleece. The skins are then drained and placed in a warm and moist chamber where either they are hung over rods, flesh side out, or from hooks, flesh sides together. The temperature and humidity are then raised. Putrification sets in, which loosens the fibres so that they can be pulled from the skin. What, in fact, happens is that the multiplying bacteria have digested the *bulb* and *prekeratinous* regions of the fibre in the follicle and in the *basal* layer. They do not attack the keratinised fibre or the epidermis. The temperature during this part of the process is crucial; it must not be permitted to become too high. When ready for the wool to be pulled, the skins begin to smell of ammonia and take on a shiny appearance. The skins are then lifted down, and the wool is either pulled manually, or pushed off with a blade. The sweating time varies slightly according to the temperature used – approximately 2 to 7 days. Care is taken not to reduce the fat content to too high a degree, as this will affect the quality of the pelt; overtreatment can cause splitting. The term given to wool obtained by this method is *skin wool*, sometimes referred to as *pied wool* and *pie wool*. This method is used in the fellmongering industry in France.

SULPHIDE METHOD: the fleece are cleaned in the same way as for the sweating method. The flesh sides are then coated with a paste of sodium sulphide mixed with lime and hung overnight in a warm room. The paste gradually penetrates the skin and dissolves the cuticle surrounding the roots of the wool. This loosens them and they can then be pulled by hand. This method is largely practised in England.

LIME METHOD: a paste is made of lime only and applied as for the sulphide method. The fleece are piled skin to skin in a pit filled with water; this method is not so satisfactory because the lime also soaks into the wool, which can produce problems at the scouring stage. After soaking, the lime is washed off the fleece and the water drained away. The fleeces are then folded and piled thickly; this sets up the required bacterial action, after which the wool is then pulled. Wool obtained by this method is known as *slipe wool*. Wool thus obtained is available for hand spinning; it is inexpensive but weak to spin and very dry.

Felt This is a non-woven wool textile comprised of wool fibres matted together by shrinkage and pounding. Short fibres unsuitable for spinning are generally used with some longer fibres as binding. Used for thousands of years in many parts of the world. In Scandinavian countries archaeologists have found samples of well preserved embroidered felts. In parts of Asia, the same felting techniques have been used for several thousand years. In Medieval times, felt clothing was much in evidence in Western Europe. It is still used by nomadic peoples as a strong material for their tents. The craft became industrialised and died as a craft, although in some Scandinavian countries it survived as a cottage industry. It is having a revival as a handcraft in the west, possibly due to the interest shown in natural processes. Industrially produced lighter weight felts are known as *coloured* and are available for toymakers and display work. The heavy felt, known as *industrial*, is used in industry for a variety of purposes.
See *Felting*

Felting See pp 104–8

Fendoir An implement used in France in 1750 for re-aligning the teeth in the carders during construction.

Fettling When carding mechanically, a build-up of material occurs in the wire covered rollers. This material is manually removed – *fettled*.

Fibre Any material, whether natural or synthetic that can be attenuated (or extended) and spun into a yarn.

Felting Is the process of making felt.

STRUCTURE OF THE WOOL FIBRE: the wool follicle is built up of tiny scales which, when subjected to quick changes in temperature, and vibration, lift and lock down onto their neighbouring fibres, and felting occurs. Some wool fibres felt more easily than others; the amount of crimp in the fibre has a bearing on the felting quality of the wool.

INDUSTRIALLY PRODUCED FELT: is made by using heat, moisture, alkalinity, pressure and agitation. Wet fleece, with its natural tendency to form a mass when subjected even to normal heat and agitation, can be exploited using mechanical means. A machine beats the material with heavy wooden mallets whilst it is immersed in water. This process, known as *fulling* or *milling*, compacts the fibres, reducing in size the width and the length of the piece. Pulling the cloth into shape after it comes out of the soap bath is called *waulking*.

FELTMAKING IN A DOMESTIC SITUATION: it is not practicable to make felt at home if a large quantity is required, however, for smaller projects, eg mittens; hats; boots; waistcoats; bags; place mats, etc, it can be a very satisfying exercise.

Equipment required:

hand or drum carders
kitchen scales
plastic or stainless steel jug
scissors
tablespoon

felting board – Ashford Handicrafts (see *Stockists*), or an old fashioned washboard
plastic sheeting
tape measure

Materials required: greasy wool, soap flakes or alkaline soap and washing soda.

CHOICE OF FLEECE SUITABLE FOR FELTING: some wools felt better than others. It can be disappointing to work on a fibre and find it is unsuitable for the project in hand; this is both a waste of time and material. As with dyeing, it is useful to build up a folder containing test details of each fibre. For example, the type of fibre used; the amount; the liquid quantities; the original size of the piece and the shrinkage that occurred; and the length of time spent on the fulling. This will provide a complete working analysis of a particular fleece and its suitability, and will enable a choice to be made if a strong hard felt is required, or alternatively, a softer, more flexible type.

Opinions vary considerably as to the suitability of types of fleece for felting and, as fleece vary so in their content, testing is the only sure way of knowing what a particular fleece will produce. It is a mistaken assumption that feltmaking will provide a useful means of using up all the old and poor quality fleece. As with any other technique related to spinning, good quality materials assist in providing a satisfactory end result. As a general guide, the fleece should be clean and free from vegetable matter and have a good fine crimp with a staple length of not more than 10.3cm (4in). Down breeds tend to have a spiral crimp, which is not desirable for feltmaking. When a suitable fleece has been chosen, it is necessary to sort it carefully, as different parts of the fleece may well react differently within the felt.

PROCESS, TEST PIECE:

- 1 Card the fibres well. Feltmaking requires both long and short fibres, so avoid flick carding, which removes the shorter fibres. Always carefully weigh the quantities and keep this a controlled situation throughout.
- 2 Prepare several batts not more than 25.4cm (10in) square and lay one on top of the other, in a crossways formation of approximately three to four layers. This will place the fibres in several directions, which assists in locking the fibres together. Obtain as even a distribution of the batts as possible; care should be taken at this stage as it will affect the quality of the end product; there should be no weak areas (*fig 13a*).
- 3 To 1*l* of hot water, add 2tbsp of soap flakes and stir, or whisk, in the jug, until completely dissolved.

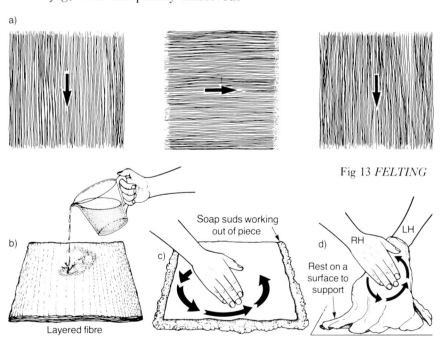

a)

Fig 13 *FELTING*

b)
Layered fibre

c)
Soap suds working out of piece

d)
LH
RH
Rest on a surface to support

- 4 Pour the soap solution over the batt arrangement, starting at the middle and working outwards (*fig 13b*). Aim for an even distribution of the soap solution until the whole area is wetted; if overwet, the fibres will come apart. Wetting the batts will open up the scales. Keep the remainder of the solution for later use.
- 5 Using moist hands, press down on the fibre mass very lightly (*fig 13c*); this will remove any air bubbles that have formed. Using one hand only, continue pressing until the entire surface is flattened; this will also remove dirty water. Using circular movements, starting at the outside edges and working inwards, lightly work over the surface (if the pressure is too hard at this stage it will disturb the fibres and move them away from one another). Gradually increase the pressure. When necessary, add more of the soap solution to keep the piece hot and wet. When sufficiently worked it should be possible to pick the piece up by catching hold of a few fibres at the centre; if the fibres and the piece part company this is an indication that more work is required. Turn the piece over and treat the opposite side, adding more soap solution if necessary. At this stage no shrinkage will appear. Some students at this stage, prefer to slightly raise the piece from the working surface and lay it over one hand and with the other hand work over the surface in a circular movement (*fig 13d*). Throughout the process add more soap solution when necessary.

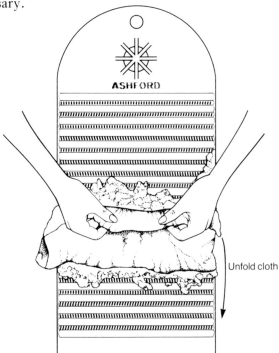

Unfold cloth

Fig 14 *FELTING*

- 6 The felt piece requires strength, and this is achieved by fulling. Lay the board against the front of your body. The piece is then rubbed vigorously, in all directions, on the felting board (*fig 14*); this will cause the scales to lock tightly together. The felt will shrink in the direction of the rubbing, so change rubbing direction from time to time. Considerable shrinkage takes place at this stage. Fold over the cloth and rub on the board and onto itself unfolding it towards the bottom of the felting board. Take time and care over the fulling process, as the quality of the felt is determined by this. Fulling is complete when the felt piece ceases to shrink, it will then retain its shape.
- 7 Rinse well, remove excess water and dry. The piece can be spun dry, and then hung in a warm place until completely dry.

    Record all details. Once a detailed reference is available, whilst no two fleeces react and produce exactly the same results, it will be a useful guideline. Coloured and dyed fleece can be used for felting.

PATTERNS: these are cut to the size required, always allowing for shrinkage, in plastic sheeting. Use only basic outline shapes as they will be easier to work with, then top decoration can be applied to the finished article.

FIBRE QUANTITIES: if careful quantity control is exercised at the test stage, then amounts can be multiplied for a particular project. As an indication only, the fibre quantities for average sizes are as follows: –

Pair of mittens	90–100g (3.2–3.5oz)
Bag	100g (3.5oz)
Pair of boots	250g (8.75oz)
Waistcoat	500g (17.5oz)

The working method is the same as for the test piece. With articles comprising two items, eg the mittens, the fibre quantities must first be divided into half for each mitten, then in half again for each side of each mitten. For each side quantities should be further divided into two for the alternate layering directions. The division of the amounts must be accurate.

MITTENS

To work: take the fibres for one side of a mitten, and layer. Cut an outline pattern shape by laying the hand on a piece of paper, draw round, allowing 2.5cm (1in) extra for seams and hand movement, then cut the pattern in the plastic sheeting (allowing for shrinkage which can be determined by the test piece), see *fig 15a*. Mix 1*l* of hot water with 2tbsp soap flakes (carefully control the quantity of the soap flakes; too little and the fibres will adhere to the hand; too much and it

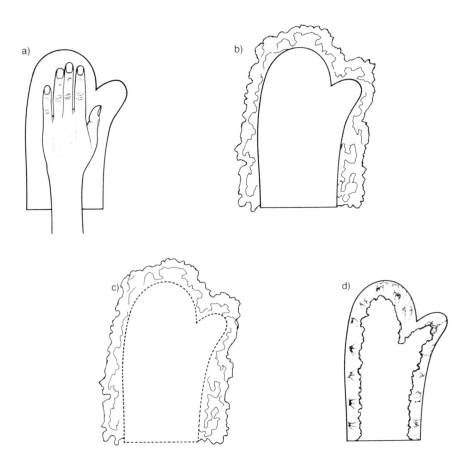

Fig 15 *FELTING*: mittens

will not felt). Work as for the test piece, but this time to the pattern shape, keeping the outline edges dry at this stage, *fig 15b*. Lay on the plastic pattern and fold over the outline edges of the fibres on the felt piece, to the front of the plastic pattern, *figs 15c* and *d*. Lay on top the two fibre layers for the second side of the mitten, making sure that the two second side fibre layers are going in alternate directions. Add more soap solution and work over the surface and the edges. Remove the pattern and, with one hand working in a circular movement, work all over the surface and join the edges. Then work on the felting board to shrink to the desired size. Make a second mitten in the same way to produce a matching pair. At the final stage the mittens may be placed on the student's hand and immersed in a soap solution and rubbed gently one against the other.

Feltmaking can be a useful activity much enjoyed by children.

Fibre Arrangement The way fibres relate to one another, for example in prepared tops the fibres are parallel to one another.

Fibres – Carded For a *woollen spin*, the rolag is formed by rolling from top to bottom of the carder, therefore the fibres are not aligned so produce an air filled light yarn.

Fibres – Carded For a *worsted spin*, the fibres are aligned by rolling from one side of the carder to the other and they flow into the yarn in this formation. This will produce a smooth yarn with very little air.

Fibre Divisions Fibres from plants and vegetables are mainly composed of *cellulose*:

a) *Bast Fibres*	obtained from within the stem of the plant	*flax; hemp; jute; ramie; nettle*
b) *Leaf Fibres*	from the leaves of the plants	*abaca; henequen; sisal*
c) *Seed and Fruit Fibres*	hairy substances that surround the seed and fruit of some plants	*cotton; kapok*

Fibres from animals, based on *protein*:

a) *Wool*	fleece	*sheep*
b) *Hair*	coat	*alpaca; Anglora rabbit; Angora goat (mohair); camel; cashmere goat; cat; cattle (buffalo); cow; musk-ox; yak); dog; llama; vicuna*
c) *Silk*	silk extrusion	*silkworm*

See also *Manmade Fibres*

Fibre Flax Flax cultivated for fibre production differs from that cultivated for linseed-oil production.
See *Irish Linen*

Fibre Length *Crimped length*: is the measurement taken of the unstretched fibre.
Staple length, wool: is the length of the longest fibres in its naturally wavy condition.
Staple length, cotton: the staple length is measured in a straightened condition.
Straightened length: is the length of fibres when measured under sufficient tension to remove crimp.

Fibre Mass Also termed *fibre supply*: the term used for the fibre supply held in the hand during spinning.

Fibre – Mineral *Asbestos* is the only mineral fibre.
See *Asbestos*

Fibres – Intrinsic Qualities

1 Length
2 Fineness
3 Thickness
4 Elasticity
5 Spinnability
6 Strength

7 Colour
8 Lustre
9 Durability
10 Dyeing potential
11 Warmth
12 Felting capacity (or capability).

Fibres – Natural Products from animal and vegetable sources. Natural fibres, eg from an animal, plant, or animal extrusion (the silkworm) that can be spun. Unlike manmade fibres, natural fibres are not consistent. Variations occur, for example, not only between fleeces from the same breed of sheep but also within an individual fleece. During the process of silkthrowing variations occur, likewise in the production of silk.

Fibroin A protein, the main component of silk, produced in the silk glands.
See *Sericulture*

Filament The name derives from the Latin for 'thread'.

Filamentium A continuous single thread formed by an animal, eg silk from the silkworm; also applicable to a manmade thread.

Filature A silk reeling house.

Fine Counts A term used to describe a fine quality flax yarn (used for fine fabrics).

Fineness (Degree of) The diameter of the wool fibre. The fineness will dictate the use of the wool. Wool is given a quality number; the higher the number, the finer the fibres, merino being the finest.

Finger Hank Also called *butterfly*. The name given to a small skein of yarn when wound in a figure of eight on one hand as for spindle spinning.
See *Spindle Spinning*

Fingering Yarn Worsted knitting yarn; the lower qualities are not combed, the noil content remains, which gives fullness to the yarn.

Fingers During the woolcombing process the sliver is drawn off by the comber into 121.9cm (4ft) lengths; these are known as fingers.

Fir *abies alba* is similar to Manilla hemp and is available from Scotland, Germany, Sweden, Scandinavia, USSR.

Flannel Act In England, in 1667, the Flannel Act was passed to combat the fall in wool sales. It was decreed that every corpse should be buried dressed entirely in wool. Living people were required to wear all-wool apparel from All Saints Day (November 1) until April.

Flax Bleaching Lay the skeins of flax out in the grass or hang somewhere in the full sun. The yellow particles in the flax are destroyed by the oxygen given off by the grass and in the air. The flax should be kept moist during this process.

Flax – Dressing The stages of breaking, scutching and hackling during flax preparation are known as flax dressing.

Flax Dyeing Flax can be dyed with synthetic dyes – follow maker's instructions; it can also be dyed by using natural dyes.

Flax Fibre *Bundles* of: see *Ultimates*

Flax, Green Also called *natural flax* is scutched flax, produced from deseeded straw without retting, etc.

Flax Jelly When spinning flax, moisture is required; this can be provided either as a bowl of warm water or as flax jelly, made by boiling some flax seeds in water, using approximately 1tsp flax seeds to one cup of water. Flax is spun S-twisted to follow the natural twist of the fibre when wet; continually moisten the fingers with either water or the jelly.

Flax Line The long, soft and silky fibres remaining after removing the tow. Colouring varies according to the area in which it was grown and the method of retting. Flax line is mainly beige in colour although, for example, Russian and Canadian flax tend to have a grey tone.

Flax *Linum antares* is more suitable for the production of linseed oil than for spinning.

Flax – Linum usitatissimum Botanically the flax family is called *Linaceae*. The name flax derives from the German *Flachs*. In France it is known as *lin*, in Italy *lino* and, in years gone by, in Ireland and Scotland as *lint*. It has the distinction of being the only natural fibre indigenous to Western Europe. The fibres are used for spinning linen yarn, and the seeds for linseed oil production. Flax was thought to have been discovered in prehistoric times. In Egypt the first known linen industry was set up in 4000 BC. Archaeologists have found both flax and flax yarn in primitive homes. In the Stone and Bronze ages, flax growing was part of the husbandry of the Swiss lake-dwellers who cultivated another variety. Evidence of flax in different stages of working was unearthed in the course of excavations of the oldest known of these lake-dwellings, which date from about 8000 BC. Flax is possibly the oldest known vegetable fibre used for textile purposes. Traditionally, flax was sown on Good Friday. Autumn flax produces a taller plant than spring flax; the latter is grown mainly for linseed oil. Irish flax is finer than Belgian flax.

Sources: flax is grown in many part of the world, mainly in Belgium, Bulgaria, Czechoslovakia, France, Holland, Hungary, Poland and Russia.

FLAX COMPOSITION: flax is approximately 70 per cent cellulose plus pectins and other substances. A rather complicated process yields the fibres from the stem of the plant. The fibres have an irregular surface and a natural twist which makes them easy to spin. The fibres, called *bundles*, are comprised of many small fibres called the *ultimates*, which are long, thin, single cells lying side by side and overlapping along their lengths. These are embedded in pectic substances that lie between the cortex and the woody core, in what appears to be a single fibre. They are tapered at both ends. If a single strand is pulled out of a strick of flax and appears to have tiny, whiskery pieces branching out, these are *ultimates*. The spinner is enabled to smooth and contain the ultimates because of the pectinous gum and by moistening the fingers during spinning. During hackling or combing some of the ultimates are torn away from the main stem; these are eventually spun as *flax tow*.

FLAX – GROWTH: flax is an annual, the seeds are sown in the spring closely together (around 2,000 per sq m) to produce tall, slender growth. The length and thickness uniformity is assisted by uniformity of sowing. Branching is only required at the top of the plant where the flowers, which are blue or white in colour, produce the seed capsules. (If the plants are grown for seed only, they are spaced well apart to enable them to branch out more.) Flax grows to a height of between 91.5cm and 121.9cm (3 to 4ft). It requires soil of good quality, with

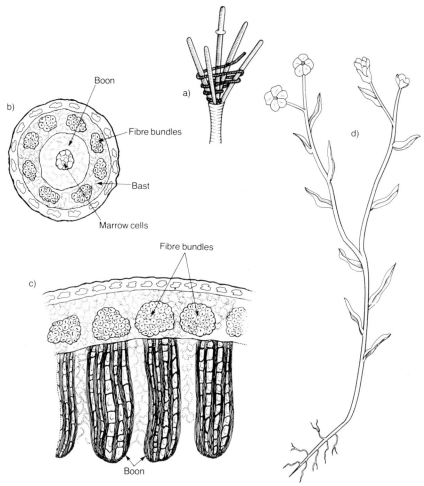

Fig 16 *FLAX*: a) fork distaff – 'tow', coarse flax fibres remaining after hackling, are formed into a roving and this is wound around the prongs of the distaff. b) cross-section of the stem of flax; c) magnified section of stem of flax; d) flax – *linum usitatissimum*

sand in the composition, and an ample water supply. It takes about three months to reach maturity.

HARVESTING BY HAND: flax is ready to be harvested when about two thirds of the stem, from the root upwards, turns yellow in early summer. If delayed longer until the seeds are fully mature, the yield of fibre will be greater, but the bundles will have become coarser and their quality affected. The flax is pulled by hand (see also mechanisation of flax), including the root, to obtain the maximum fibre length. Long flax is called *flax line*. After harvesting, flax is stooked, or laid out to dry; it is then necessary to remove the seed capsules.

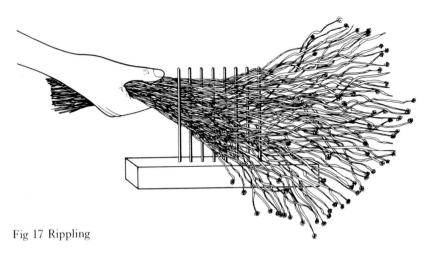

Fig 17 Rippling

RIPPLING (deseeding) – also called *bolling*. This is done by drawing the flax through a coarse comb called a rippler (or *rippler comb*) – a coarse comb with metal teeth that consists of a line of pointed nails standing out from a board clamped to a bench. Deseeding also can be done in the field. From earliest times it was a process done by hand, today it is done by machine. After rippling, the flax is further dried by standing in stooks.

RETTING (a rotting process): the fibres running the whole length of the plant are obtained by rotting away the outer covering and inner pith. This process is known as *retting*. The flax bundles, called *beets* or *sheaves*, are submerged in water. Fermentation, which is a natural process, gradually sets in, and this separates the fibres from each other; the bacteria dissolve the softer cells of the bark and rot the gum holding the fibres to the inner core.

Fermentation is affected by the temperature of the water, warm water hastens the process. If permitted to go on too long this could damage the fibre cells so timing is most important. There are various forms of retting and the colour of the flax, which is mainly a beige colour, is affected by the retting form used. Whatever the type of retting – ie pond retting; dew retting; river retting; or tank retting – the end requirement is the same, to separate the fibres from each other and the outer stem and inner wooden core. It usually takes about two weeks to complete.

TYPES OF RETTING:-
Dew retting is a rather slow process that can take a month to complete. It is preferable to have damp weather. The flax is laid out on the grass and thereby exposed to the elements and bacteria, and is

turned occasionally; usually takes from 14 to 28 days. The resulting fibre is a dark grey tone and coarser than water-retted flax. It reacts differently to the bleaching process, so therefore it is not advisable to mix it with other fibres.

Pond retting is sometimes called *stagnant water retting*: this is a fairly quick process, as the presence of the organic matter aids fermentation, which decomposes the adhesive substances that bind the fibres about the inner woody core of the plant stem. The flax is soaked in the water in the same way as already stated.

Tank retting: the stalk bundles are placed in tanks, root downwards, then weighted to hold down.

River retting or *running water retting*: a method practised in Belgium. Whilst this takes longer, it produces a good quality fibre, pale beige in colour, the result of the cleansing action of constantly slow-running water.

Whatever the retting process used, it has reached completion when the fibres are easily obtained following exposure. After retting, and to completely remove the adhesive content, the flax is laid out in the open air, and then dried. This is called *grassing*.

BREAKING, also called *beetling*, follows retting. This can only be satisfactorily carried out if the flax has been well dried and is brittle. In Sweden the flax is dried in sauna cabins. The dried flax, which now

Fig 18 Breaking the retted flax

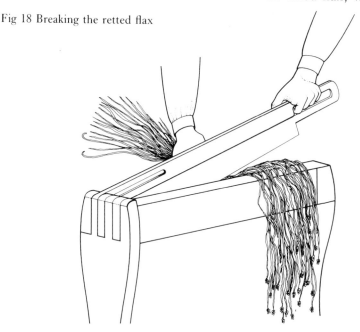

resembles straw, is beaten to loosen the fibres from the inner core of the stem. From early times until the 14th century, mallets were used; then stands were developed that had a hinged blade breaker mounted on the top, called a *break* or *brake*. The flax is laid on top of the stand, which has shallow grooves in it and, while being pounded with the wooden blade, it is moved backwards and forwards. The fibres bend during this process and the woody core breaks up and gradually falls away.

SCUTCHING is also called *swingling*. A bundle of flax stems is held in the left hand, shaken out loosely, and placed through a slot in the top of an upright wooden board constructed on a wooden stand called a *scutching board* or stock. The boon and bark are then beaten out of the flax, by using a wooden *scutching blade* (also called *scutching knife, scutching sword* and *flax swingle*) held in the right hand and with a downward stroke. As the beating continues, only the fibres remain. First one side is treated then, when sufficiently scutched, it is reversed and the opposite side treated likewise. Following this, the end held is reversed so that it also can be treated. Scutching assists in straightening the fibres. Any fibres that have become broken and dropped away (called *tow*), can be used for a rough spun yarn.

Scutching
blade held
in right hand

Fig 19 Scutching

HACKLING, also called *hetcheling* or *heckling* and known as *flax dressing*, is the combing of the fibres to separate and arrange them in a parallel position. This is achieved by drawing the fibres through a series of combs called *hackes, hackles, hatchel, heckles,* or *hetchels*. These consist of rows of pointed teeth (called *tines*) of varying sizes, mounted on a board called a *hackle board*. The first *hackle*, which is the coarsest setting of teeth, is called the *ruffler* (also referred to as

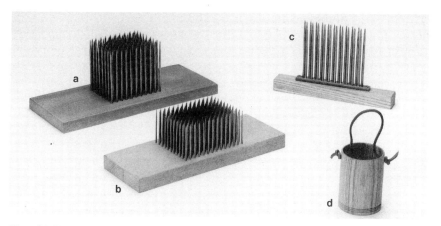

Plate 26 *FLAX TOOLS*: a) ruffer, 168 pins; b) dresser, 284 pins; c) rippler, 21 pins; d) water pot or flax cup

ruffer and *rougher*). The hackles graduate from coarse to fine; the process starts with the coarsest teeth and works towards the finest. As the fibres are worked back and forth the short coarse *tow* is removed from the long *line*, and the bundles become divided and finer according to the quality of the flax. Finally the *line* is twisted into hanks called *stricks, heads*, or *queues*, ready for spinning. Earlier hackle boards often had a hole each end to enable them to be secured whilst in use. Others could be steadied by a foot placed in an opening at one end of the board and the hackling done by drawing the flax across the teeth towards the body. To grow and process flax is a most interesting and satisfying project for the handspinner enthusiast; if this is not possible, well prepared flax can be obtained and is inexpensive to buy.

MECHANISATION OF FLAX PRODUCTION began when hand scutching was replaced by the introduction of the Flemish mill in about 1870. The modern method of turbine scutching was first introduced by C. Vansteenkiste of Ypres in 1922. Today, all the flax processes of pulling, rippling, scutching and hackling are mechanised. The flax is harvested from early July to mid-August, it is dried in the fields by spreading to form swaithes or alternatively tied in 3–4 kilo bundles which are stooked. If too green the fibres are weak. Over-ripe, dark green/brown, the stems are already lignified and the fibres strong but brittle so a great amount of tow. When yellow the flax is at its most suitable. Retting is also done in large warm water storage tanks by bacterial fermentation. When the flax has been thoroughly dried it is taken to the Scutch Mill where the stem, already loosened from the fibre, is finally removed by passing through a pair of round toothed cylinders; it is then rubbed and beaten by turbine blades which removes the tow and waste woody matter (shiv or shive). The fibre layer produced by the scutcher is then separated into "hands". Once this stage has been completed the raw material is shipped to the country where it is to be processed, eg Northern Ireland for Irish linen. It is then hackled by being passed through a series of pins that are graduated in fineness, it comes out well combed, clean and sleek, resembling golden hair. The tresses of fibre which lie evenly together are laid lengthwise, with the end pieces overlapping on slowly moving leather belts. These conduct the fibres over more sets of pins and then in between rollers, gradually drawing the separate lengths into a continuous ribbon of fibre which becomes finer and finer almost to the size of thread. It is then given a twist on the roving frame, which gives it support during the spinning process. Flax is the strongest natural fibre.

See *Bullen; Chenevote; Codilla; Diss; Distaff; Fine Counts; Irish Linen; Lea; Linen; Linseed Oil; Lint; Shive; White or Yellow Flax*

Flax – Seeds Used for making flax jelly, also the basis of *linseed oil*. See *Flax Jelly; Linseed Oil*

Flax Spinning – Crosscombed If using a free standing dressed distaff, this should be placed to the left of the wheel, nearly opposite the orifice and in line with the spinner. The water container, if not incorporated in the wheel design, should be within easy access of the spinner's left hand when required, so as to moisten the fingers to assist adherence of the flax fibres.

Attach an S-spun cotton or linen leader yarn to the bobbin, sufficiently long to reach the flax supply, and bring it out through the orifice. Moisten thumb and first finger of the left hand with the water – they should not be too wet – and pull down a few flax fibres from the base of the fibre supply on the distaff, *fig 20*. Some spinners find it more comfortable to use the thumb placed on the first and second fingers of the left hand; others prefer to use the thumb and index finger and the third finger as a support.

Twist to join the fibres to the leader, and treadle anticlockwise slowly, at first, keeping the tension on the band fairly loose, at the same time holding the left hand approximately 7.6cm to 10.3cm (3 to 4in) from where the fibres are being drawn down from the distaff. The anticlockwise direction to produce an S-twisted yarn is due to this being the natural fibrillar direction of the twist in the fibre. The thread should pass between the thumb and first finger of the left hand and pass over the second, third and fourth fingers.

Some spinners prefer to only use the left hand for pulling down fibres, twisting with a rolling action, smoothing and winding on, only employing the right hand to take over when the left hand requires

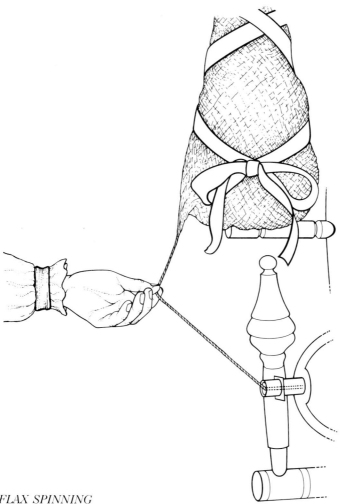

Fig 20 *FLAX SPINNING*

remoistening. However, the right hand can be most useful in assisting
control of the thread; alternatively the fibres may be both drafted and
controlled by the left hand moving downwards towards the orifice
never closer than 20.4cm (8in) and the moistened right hand is then
used to smooth the thread upwards towards the fibre supply on the
distaff. The flax should be drawn down very evenly, with a constant
supply if the end result is to be an even yarn. The actual spinning
action is a rolling one with the hand turning very slightly *towards* the
orifice on the downward movement, and rolling *away* from the orifice
when moving back towards the fibre supply; the thumb rolls over the
index finger. The thumb and index fingers are used to control the
twist and to permit its insertion into the forming thread on the journey

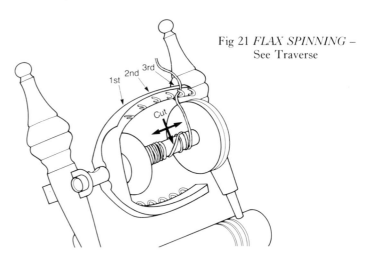

Fig 21 *FLAX SPINNING* –
See Traverse

back to the fibre supply, while simultaneously smoothing with moist fingers any fibre ends.

From time to time it will become necessary to turn the distaff; the fibre supply should be drawn down evenly and the appearance of the dressed flax retained. When the ribbon is reached, then undo and re-tie further up.

Once a controlled, even pace of spinning is established, both the tension and spinning can be increased. Throughout the spinning, moisten the fingers when necessary otherwise the thread will not be smooth. A common problem is that the thread becomes very thin and may break. This can be caused by overtwisting or maybe the treadling in relation to the spinning has increased; the drive band may be too tight, or the hand is working too slowly. To prevent this problem occurring, a rolling back-and-forth action can be used between the fingers, which should gather more fibres into the thread. Alternatively, move the left hand upwards to the distaff, and twist towards the wheel to enable more fibres to catch on; whilst doing this, care should be taken to avoid the twist running up into the fibre supply. Another problem is when the end is lost on the bobbin; if gaps are left between the placing of the yarn on the hooks of the flyer, it will be easier to trace an end that breaks. Alternatively, the diagonal formed can be cut, thus enabling spinning to restart (*fig 21*).

SPINNING WITH NON CROSSCOMBED FLAX, FIBRES STRAIGHT DOWN: the distaff is placed to the left of the spinner, and the water bowl within easy reach. The same spinning techniques are used as already described; however, care should be taken with this hanging down arrangement of fibre supply, otherwise too many fibres may be drawn down and collected at one time. Both hands can be used, the left hand holding a bunch of fibres, and the right hand drafting the required amount.

SPINNING USING FLAX TOW: the *ultimates* that are torn loose from the main strands during the preparation of flax are collected and spun as *flax tow*. It is obtainable as roving and can be woven around the prongs of a type of distaff called *tow forks* (see *fig 16a*). Spin similarly as a worsted spin, smoothing backwards with moistened fingers. Flax may be spun dried however, if a rough spiky yarn is required. Any remaining short lengths of tow may be carded and spun from a rolag.

SPINNING FLAX ON THE GREAT WHEEL: the same techniques are used as on a treadle wheel. Long fibres as flax line for example, may be tied around the spinner's waist.

SPINDLE SPINNING FLAX: place the dressed distaff to the left of the spinner and make sure the water supply is within each reach. Tie a leader yarn to the spindle as for spindle spinning. Moisten the fingers on both the left and right hands and join the fibre supply to the leader yarn. Rotate the spindle with the right hand in an anticlockwise direction and use a stroking action to produce a smooth, even yarn. Particular care should be taken over the twist control.

In earlier times, the natives in the Sudan, when spindle spinning flax, held the thread near the mouth and, as the thread grew, passed it between their lips to moisten and smooth. The spindle with the whorl downwards was twisted with the right hand, using the thumb, first and second fingers, the spindle then dropped and spun. It was controlled with the fingers closed around it without actually touching it and gave a short spin. Saliva was the main means of moistening the flax in earlier times; resin was often chewed to increase the flow of saliva.
See *Bucking Tubs; Water Pots*

Flax Top Commercially prepared flax.

Flax Tow Also called *hurd*, is the outer parts of the inner stem, coarser short lengths comprised of *ultimates*, which remain in the hackle during flax preparation process. Can be carded and spun.

Flax Wheels The yarn is usually spun anticlockwise; some flax wheels have the whorl attached to the spindle by a tapered fit.

Flax – Wild *Linum angustifolium* is a common weed in the Mediterranean area.

Flax Yarn Bundle The standard length by which wet-spun flax yarns are bought and sold; traditionally a 'bundle' contained 60,000yd of yarn (54,864m).

Fleece The protective coat of a sheep or goat, comprising hair and wool. The hair repels the water, and the wool acts as insulation. Wool absorbs water. With breeding the hair (*kemp*) has been considerably reduced. The animal is usually sheared once a year yielding wool shorn from live sheep as opposed to skin-wool, ie that from the skins of dead animals. See *Dead Wool*

Fleece – Preparation Methods

Type	Method	Type of Spin
1 *Drum carding*	Batts, then into rovings	Worsted type; short drafting action
2 *Flick carding*	Spinning direct from the fleece, wool flicked	Semi-worsted; short drafting action
3a *Hand carding*	Make rolags (roll from top to bottom of carder)	Woollen spin; long draw, or for semi-woollen, using short drafting action
3b *Hand carding*	Make rolags (roll from side of carder across to opposite side making fibres parallel)	Worsted type
4a *Combing* (*dog comb*)	Make into rovings – completely aligned	Worsted type; Short drafting action
4b *Combing*	Tops prepared by the true combing process, ie wool-combs, pad, etc	True worsted; use a short drafting action and insert a high twist
5 *Teasing*	Spinning direct from the fleece, wool teased	Semi-worsted; short drafting action.

CHOOSING A FLEECE: variables occur, not only between breeds of sheep, reared in different areas, but also within the actual flocks themselves and individual sheep. It can take some while to really learn how to choose a fleece; there are so many considerations to take into account. As a general rule, a knowledge of breeds is useful for making the final choice of fleece for a particular project. Wool is the fibre most used by handspinners; it is easy to use, has a wide choice, and the end products are almost limitless. The British Wool Marketing Board lists many different registered breeds, and in addition to these, many crossbreds are available. Wool is obtained from all over the world from many well known British breeds in addition to merino stock. In Britain alone, more than twenty million sheep belong to more than sixty different breeds. Rare breeds, which are being protected, are also available (see end of book for Rare Breeds Survival Trust).

Downland breeds have soft fibres suitable for clothing and knitwear; Mountain breeds have harsher fleece, suitable for rugs and hard wearing materials; Longwool and Lustre breeds are useful for worsted spinning. Most fleece contain both soft and harsh fibres.

Usually, however unskilled at choosing a fleece a new handspinner may be, sight and touch can be relied on, even if knowledge of the source of the fleece, eg crossbred, is unknown. The fibre length, fineness, crimp, lustre and density of staple and the colour can be seen; add to this touch, ie the handle of the wool, and the final choice should be satisfactory.

CONDITIONS THAT CAN AFFECT A FLEECE:

a) *weather*: fleece can be affected by wind, rain, snow and sun

b) *environment*: fleece from hill sheep, for example, may be affected by weather, bracken etc; whatever the environment, it will affect fleece in one way or another and have both good and bad influences. For example, in-housing, the modern technique of housing sheep over winter on straw/sawdust, results in much foreign matter in the fleece.

c) *feeding*: trough-fed sheep rub their chests and necks against the edges, and grains and other matter then become embedded in the fleece. Inadequate feeding may produce weak areas in the staple length.

d) *illness*: may produce a check in the fleece growth. Where this happens in the fleece relates to the time the check occurred, whether near to a previous shearing (when the weakness will show up near the tip), or, if only one or two months' growth of fleece, then check, the unevenness will be near the root.

e) *dipping stains*: these may have greatly marked the fleece. Dipping should kill mites, lice, etc, which can be carded out of the wool; however, the excretion often causes staining.

f) *marking paint*: if too liberally applied, may mark and spoil the fleece. Tar and paint are no longer necessary, as lanolin-based fluids are now available, which can easily be scoured out.

g) *discolorations*: when these occur in the fleece as a result of microbial action, they will not scour out. Warm wet conditions cause the micro-organisms to attack the wool, causing tenderness. In Britain the most common microbial fault is *mycotic dermatitis* or lumpy wool. This causes encrustation and the fibres stick together.

It can therefore be seen how variations between fleece occur.

POINTS TO CONSIDER WHEN CHOOSING A FLEECE:

a) *tenderness*: there should be no weak places along the staple, which can be caused by lack of food or illness. Often, at the end of winter, when the sheep may have had less food, there is a weakness in the

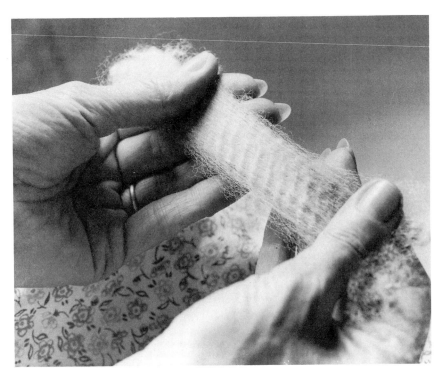

Plate 27 Testing a lock

growth (the break), then, as spring approaches, the strength of the growth increases. Therefore, when the sheep is shorn, the weak area may well come where the shears cut so the problem is removed. If shearing is delayed for any reason, the weakness will remain and show up. Tenderness can be caused by a variety of conditions, eg cessation of growth; reduction in food or in the quality of nutrition; recent lambing. The fibre may have been affected by fungus. Certain bacteria secrete enzymes which attack the intercellular cement of the fibre. Test for weakness by holding a lock of the fleece at both ends (top and base of staple) between the hands and giving it a sharp tug; it will break across the weakest area. Alternatively, flip or twang the taut staple with a finger of the right hand.

b) *dirt and vegetable matter*: a clean fleece is desirable. Avoid a dirty fleece, which will not only add to the cost (because of additional weight), but can make extra work at the scouring stage. Avoid a straw-and-vegetable-encrusted fleece, cleaning this can waste considerable time. Extreme dust may occur in a fleece where sheep have been grazed in wide, open windswept areas, the wool wax causes dust to stick to the fleece.

c) *cotty fleece*: will be matted and, if too badly affected, will be of little use.

d) *kemp*: will not dye well.

e) *second clip ends*: a problem that arises when the shearing has been delayed causing the new growth also to be clipped. (The first clip is recognised by the tips of the staples being more pointed and fine. Subsequent shearings have a more rounded fleece.) Also occurs when the shearer has cut twice (second cuts).

f) *crimp*: a close crimp should produce a fluffy yarn and, due to the many air pockets, it will be very warm. A well spaced crimp, often a Longwool, will produce a smoother compact yarn as there is less trapped air. It will have a more lustrous appearance.

g) *colour*: consider the overall colouring and whether the quantities will be sufficient for the project to be executed, bearing in mind the proposed preparation method and the type of spin.

See *Break; Burr; Fleece Suitability; Hog Fleece; Tender; Tippy Wool; Webby*

Fleece – Clip A farmer may sell his full yield of fleeces, classed as *washed* or *greasy*, to the British Wool Marketing Board. This refers to the fact that he has run his flock through a clean dip to remove excess dirt approximately three days before shearing. Not to be confused with the terms *scouring* and *in the grease*.
See *Arra; Frowsy; Gummy*

Fleece – Dry A fleece that has been stored for some while may become 'dry'. This can be rectified, in many cases, by laying it out in the sun to warm, or by spinning in a warm room, with the fleece laid near a fire or radiator, which will cause the oil to rise. If, however, the natural grease has been lost it may be necessary to dress it.
See *Emulsion – Dressing*

Fleece – Dry Cleaning How successful this means of cleaning is, relies on the original condition of the fleece. It is a particularly suitable method for those spinners who prefer to spin 'in the grease', as it removes dust and organic matter, which makes the carding process easier.

METHOD: unroll the fleece, skirt where necessary. Turn the fleece shorn side uppermost onto a wire mesh tray preferably in the open air. Gently shake the fleece, area to area, without disturbing it too much. Due to the scales on the fibre, the dirt will be shed to the fibre tips and then fall off through the mesh. See *Fleece – Sorting*

Fleece – Pick A top quality fleece in any class.

Fleece – Quantity to Purchase A freshly shorn fleece is easier to spin than one that has been stored. The grease, when just shorn, is soft and facilitates ease of spinning. When purchasing for a particular project, allowance must be made for yolk and grease, which can account for more than half the fleece weight. When scoured, this will cause a drastic reduction in quantity. The grease will harden in stored fleece, so will require warming in the sun or in a warm room for a while before spinning.

Fleece – Scouring Removes dirt and grease from a fleece by washing. In olden times, three parts water to one of urine were used as the scouring agent. A house-to-house collection of urine was made in many European towns until the last century. To replace urine, various plant roots could be used, eg *soapwort* (*Saponaria officinalis*), which was used in ancient Italy and Greece. Yucca roots were used by Mexican peasants. Plant ash was the most common scouring agent (see *Barilla*). In earlier times tar and butter were smeared onto the fleece and then had to be removed. Chemical dips and marking fluids have to be removed from fleece today. The industrial process removes staining by chemical means. There are a variety of reasons for washing a fleece. A spinner may prefer to work with a clean fleece rather than a greasy raw one. The fleece may require scouring before dyeing. A particular fleece may be excessively dirty, or may smell of insecticides. Once spun, the dirt is difficult to remove. Whatever the reason, the following should be observed.

Do's

Always add the soap to the water and mix well before adding the fleece. Once a fleece is lowered into a soap solution it can 'kill' the solution, making it go flat. Allow for this by adding sufficient quantities of soap to the original solution.

◇

When using soap flakes, dissolve them in hot water, then allow to cool to hand hot.

◇

Stergene is excellent to use, and mixes easily.

◇

Handle the fleece as little as possible.

◇

Don'ts

Do not agitate the fleece. The gelatin scales soften and protrude in warm water; agitation will cause them to smash together and matting will occur.

◇

Whilst it is preferable to avoid using detergents whenever possible, at times when requiring all dirt and grease to be removed (before dyeing, for example, or for an extremely dirty fleece) a detergent may be the answer. Mild soap and warm water will remove the dirt only, not the grease. Too much detergent will dry the wool. An alternative to detergent is to use washing soda, approxi-

Do's

Avoid extremes of temperature, otherwise felting will occur. If the fibres, in their softened state, are suddenly immersed in cold water the scales will be congealed together permanently.

◇

Place a fine fleece in a mesh bag during scouring.

◇

Fleece can be placed in a cotton bag and spun dried.

◇

Preferable to wash small, rather than large, quantities of fleece.

◇

Do soak a rather soiled fleece in warm water before preparing and use a soapy solution. It can be soaked overnight.

◇

Avoid small pieces of wool going down the plug hole; this can quickly cause a blocked pipe.

◇

Oil scoured fleece before spinning since most of the grease will have been removed during scouring, especially if hot water was used.

◇

Always rinse the fleece thoroughly. Soap contains an *alkali*, which will affect the dyeing if not completely rinsed away.

mately ½tsp to 4.5*l* (1 gal) of soapy water.

◇

Never place a fleece in a tumble drier – this would cause felting.

◇

Never run water directly onto the fleece.

◇

Try not to disturb the fibres too much, as they will require sorting.

◇

Never squeeze or wring a fleece.

◇

When the wool is wet, do not allow it to support its own weight, as this will cause overstretching. Place in a colander or suitable container.

◇

Lustre wools should not be washed at a temperature higher than 35°C (95°F) as this would cause damage to the lustre.

Yarn Scouring Always wash clean spun wool, ie wool not spun 'in the grease'. It is a mistaken concept that clean wool requires no washing. It is necessary to set the twist and preshrink the wool and to remove any oil which may have been added. However, in some cases, provided the fleece was well scoured originally, it requires a clean warm water rinse only. Always ensure that the skein is carefully tied first (see *fig 22*). After rinsing, the skeins require hanging with the addition of weights, to even out the twist (*fig 23a*). The weight to be determined by the amount of twist in the yarn. If overtwisted,

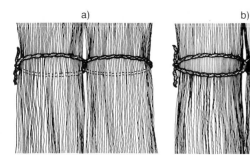

Fig 22 Wool: the correct method of tying a skein after winding onto a skeiner and prior to removing to scour. The skein is tied in several places with yarn, in a figure-of-eight. a) shows the figure-of-eight and how it should be placed around the skein; b) shows a solid view of the figure-of-eight; c) completed skein

Fig 23 Yarn – scouring

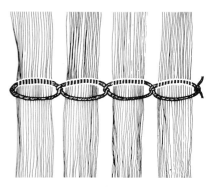

Half hitch

Fig 24 Linen skeins require more ties than wool. Linen tangles very easily, so the ties must be firm to help control this. The half hitch is suitable to hold ties in place

increase the weight. A plastic bottle filled with water can be adjusted according to the amount of weight required. Do not leave the weights on too long; remove it when the skein is slightly damp. If left too long, the yarn will lose its natural elasticity.

Singles yarn requires a rod to be placed through the skein at top and bottom and the weights added to the bottom (*fig 23b*). Singles will otherwise kink badly.

METHOD OF SCOURING

- 1 Shake the fleece gently to open the locks. Place shorn side uppermost in a container, eg colander for smaller quantities, or, for larger quantities, in a wooden box, with a mesh base, made to fit the sink (turned upside down this has the double purpose of a drying rack).
- 2 Fill a sink with tepid water and lower the container and fleece into it. The rather impacted fibres may possibly impede the water from coming up through them to the top, so gently press the fibres. The soaking time depends on the amount of dirt in the fleece; it can be for a short time or overnight. When the water is dirty, lift the container out and drain away the water.
- 3 Make a warm soapy solution and place the container and fleece in it. Gently move the fleece around. When the water is dirty, remove container and drain. If necessary, prepare a second soap solution and repeat.
- 4 Fill the sink with clean water to the same temperature as the solution from which the fleece has been removed. A point to note: some people mistakenly think that the rinsing water should be at the same temperature as the original soap solution. If used at this temperature, felting might occur, because the water and the fibres will have cooled during the soaking time. Therefore, place the container of fleece in clean water at the same temperature as the cooled solution.
- 5 Continue rinsing and draining away until the fleece is thoroughly rinsed, always taking into account the water temperature at all times.
- 6 Place the container and fleece where they can dry, away from direct heat; alternatively, spin dry. If laid out to dry naturally, from time to time gently loosen the fibre mass to permit circulation of air. When dry, it is ready to card, or whatever is required. If dyeing immediately, it can be left damp.

Spun yarn is treated in the same way as fleece. First the skeins must be tied carefully (see *fig 22*). Then, at the drying stage, the skeins are weighted (see *fig 23*). Handle as little as possible throughout the scouring process. Linen requires spaced tying (see *fig 24*).

ADDITIVES

Fabric softener may be added; alternatively a cream hair conditioner
Lemon juice added to warm water will impart lustre to the fibres
White vinegar added to the rinse will counteract alkalinity of the soda
and, if added to warm water when rinsing, will remove any scum that
has formed. See *Barilla; Carbonising*

Fleece – Second Cuts These appear in a fleece as short fibres
approximately 1.3cm (½in) long, caused by the shearer not cutting
close enough to the animal's skin the first time and therefore having to
go over a second time.

Fleece – Sorting A fleece can be sorted indoors or outdoors. Space is
necessary as a fleece can attain large proportions once it is no longer
condensed on the sheep. Indoors, cover the floor with paper or
sheeting. Outdoors, a wire mesh-covered frame laid on bricks to raise
it from the ground is ideal, as it permits the dirt, etc, to fall through.

After shearing, the fleece is dropped to the ground, cut side downwards. The roller then folds it into three, lengthways. It is then rolled
up firmly from the tail to the neck, and usually the neckband is
twisted, then bound around the fleece and tucked in (see *plate 28*).

Plate 28 A rolled up
fleece secured by the
neck

SORTING METHOD
- 1 Untuck the neckband and undo carefully, letting it untwist.
  Unfold the folded fleece bundle, tips uppermost, taking care to
  retain its shape. This stage is very much dependent on how
  carefully the fleece was folded by the roller.
- 2 Some fleece are skirted before selling; if this has not been done,
  remove about 7.6cm (3in) around the edges, ie legs, britch, belly

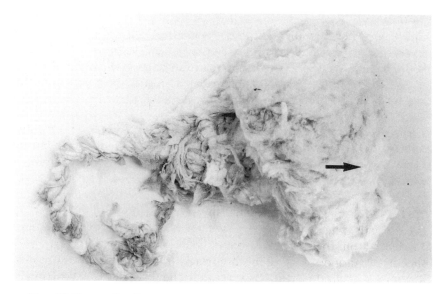

Plate 29 To unroll a fleece; undo the neck and roll open, see arrow direction

area and head. Remove also any other short, dirty ends (*taglocks*).

- 3 Examine the fleece in various areas. Some may show up as better than others, or a fleece may well be comparable all over. Remove a lock, when necessary, to examine and test for any weakness; always replace the lock in the same position so as to disturb the fleece as little as possible.

- 4 Having become familiar with the fleece to be sorted, proceed to the next stage, the *sorting-off* (*removing*) of the poorer quality parts.

Most fleece can be sorted into at least three different qualities, many as much as five, and occasionally into eight or ten qualities. When the areas of the fleece are separated they should never be cut or torn apart. The hands should be used, palms downwards, following a natural parting of the locks then, by firm pressure on whatever surface is being used, the fleece is parted in opposite directions. Practice will show the spinner where to part the fleece, and by comparing staple samples this will indicate where one quality ends and another begins.

The project for which the fleece is intended should be kept firmly in mind. It may be necessary to mix various parts of the fleece to produce a consistent texture to the yarn. If the fleece is to be used for several different purposes, or if it is 'coloured', this again requires considera-tion, possibly with individual bagging-up of fibres. Careful sorting is essential to successful spinning. Poor, inadequate sorting could result in a poor end product with hours of wasted work.

Sort, using *fig 25* as a guide only, letting the fleece dictate the divisions to be made. Each division will be suitable for different spinning purposes, eg dyeing, knitting, weaving, etc. When examining and sorting the wool, the spinner is in effect selecting the fibre that has the desired characteristics for a specific yarn design. The spinner should take note also of the intrinsic qualities of fineness, crimp, lustre, texture, strength and dyeing capabilities. Bag and label as necessary; hessian sacks or strong brown paper sacks are suitable.

Sorting A Fleece – Wool Sorting Terms

- 1 *Head*. Known as *moiety*. Sometimes spelled *moity*. The finest, but if trough-fed, sheep are liable to have hay and seeds matted in the wool. Worsted Trade: *Top Knot*. Woollen Trade: *Poll Lock*
- 2 *Fore Legs* when irregular and poor are referred to as *brokes*. Worsted Trade: *Brokes* Woollen Trade: *Brokes*
- 3 *Shoulders, Extra* or *Super Diamond* are the best quality. Dense, strong and of good staple. Mostly flanks and shoulders. Worsted Trade: *Fine* Woollen Trade: *Picklock*
- 4 *Belly* is referred to as *Picklock*. A narrow strip on each edge of a shorn fleece. Short, tender, sometimes felted due to the sheep lying on it. Worsted Trade: *Seconds* Woollen Trade: *Seconds*
- 5 *Back* is referred to as *Diamond*. Second quality wool, less strong than shoulder; it is often short and yolk stained. May be more open and slightly longer. In poorer fleeces there may be no Extra Diamond. Worsted Trade: *Choice* Woollen Trade: *Choice*
- 6 *Rump* is termed *Prime*. Has the worst of the weather and tends to be thinner, drier and tender. Worsted Trade: *ABB* Woollen Trade: *ABB*

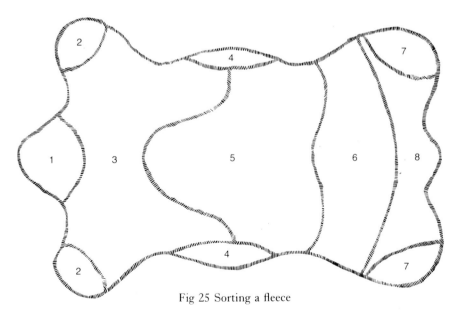

Fig 25 Sorting a fleece

- 7 *Hindlegs* also known as *Britch* or *Breech*. Has coarser fleece from the lower hind quarters, often with a high proportion of hair. Referred to as coarse. Is usually dirt encrusted and stained. Worsted Trade: *Cowtail* Woollen Trade: *Brown*
- 8 *Tail* and also *Belly*. Often very soiled and encrusted with manure; these areas are referred to as *Skirtings*.

EFFECTS OF BAD SORTING
a) the spun yarn could be very uneven due to different parts of the fleece giving varying results
b) wool which has been knitted could have tension problems
c) shrinkage could occur in different places in a garment, producing distortion
d) dyeing could be uneven, if a mixture of coarse and fine staples has been included.

With any craft (and spinning is no exception), careful and thorough preparation usually promotes a satisfactory end product. The constant rush of present day life tends to produce a desire in the individual to complete every task in as little time as possible, often to the detriment of a craft subject. The very nature of spinning, and the potential to be obtained from it, are a result of slowing down and completely relaxing.
See *Belly Wool; Cotted; Crutchings; Moit; Partitioning; Plain; Shafty; Skirting; Tags; Yield*

Fleece – Sources Go to a reputable stockist until you really know what to buy. It is necessary, for successful production, to rely on someone with good knowledge. Beware of friends who may offer you many different fibre types, more often than not, quite unsuitable, eg a fleece that has been stored for some years.

Fleece – Suitability Different fleece types are capable of producing a certain yarn type. Fine fleece will not necessarily produce a fine yarn, likewise neither will a strong wool always produce a thick yarn. Knowledge has to be built as to the desirability of one fleece over another to satisfy the spinner's particular requirements. If a test is made by taking a staple from a fleece, draft and twist it between the fingers and then permit it to double back on itself as it would when plied; compare this with other staples from the same fleece treated likewise using varying thicknesses and you will note that the way the yarn twisted itself into the plied position in the first sample, this is the one most closely related to the crimp pattern of the original staple, therefore, that will be the yarn which is easiest to spin from that particular fleece. The staple of a fleece should be able to be easily removed and the fibres should part easily in the hand.

Flick Carder Sometimes referred to as a *flicker comb*; it is a small tool used for carding, and has a longer handle than ordinary hand carders. Used singly, its purpose is to open and clean locks of wool. *Flicking method*: first protect the surface being worked on, ie the lap or table – a leather or a padded covering would be suitable. As this type of carder is not one of a pair, it will tear the undersurface being used. The action of the carder throughout is a gentle flicking one.

Hold the shorn ends of a bunch of fibres in the left hand (*fig 26a*), with the ends protruding over the knee. (If working on a table, the ends should lie free over the padding.) Using very light movements, almost a bounce, flick the tips of the fibres, which may have become joined due to weathering. Gradually the fibres will part and fan out. When the fibres have been opened out sufficiently and lie parallel to one another, reverse the fibres and treat the butt (*shorn*) ends similarly. Turn the fibres over and treat both the tip and butt ends of the underneath fibres in the same way. When the lock has been fully treated with the flick carder and is free from dirt and resembles a light fan (*fig 26b*) with the fibres aligned, yarn can be spun from it; it will be semi-worsted.

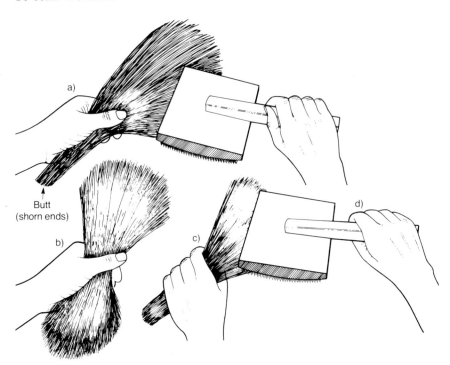

Fig 26 *FLICK CARDING*: a) shorn ends of the fibre held in the left hand b) fibres light and free from dirt c) alternative way of holding fibres preferred by some spinners d) a different way of holding the flicker; note position of thumb

Floor Swift A skein winder with two revolving, adjustable spools set in an upright stand placed on the floor.
See *Niddy Noddy*

Floss Also called *blaze* – a name given to the filaments of silk, extruded by the silkworm to anchor itself into position preparatory to spinning its cocoon.
See *Sericulture*

Flourette A spun silk, spun of long stapled, combed fibres.

Flyer Lead See *Bobbin Drag*

Flyer Wheel A spinning wheel that has a flyer type arrangement for spinning. In earlier times it was called the *flax wheel* as it was mainly used for flax spinning. The *wool wheel* was the spindle type wheel. The flyer wheels did not have treadles until the early sixteenth century. For details of the flyer complex, see *U-Flyer*.

Folding Twist The twist that is inserted into the yarns during plying or folding.
See *Plying; Twist Per Inch*

Folds A term usually related to the folded skin on the front of merino sheep, or to excessive skin on the body.
See *Development*

Footman See *Spinning – Learning to Spin.*

Fourchette Also called an *awl*. Used to pierce holes in the skin used to cover the cards (hand carders) in France in the eighteenth century.

Free A wool term to denote that it is free from any vegetable fault.

Fribby Wool containing a large amount of second cuts and sweat points.

Friction Band A cord or band which controls the revolutions of the spindle in relation to that of the bobbin.
See *Scotch Tensioner*

Friction Drag See *Bobbin Drag.*

Frieze A rough, fuzzy-faced sheep with a heavy woollen overcoating.

Frosty Face A defect occurring in merino sheep, whereby chalky white hairs cover the face.

Frowsy Dry, disordered fibre throughout the fleece, lacks springiness.

Fulling Is also called *milling* and *waulking*. From the French word *fouler* – to tread or trample, deriving from an Anglo-Saxon word meaning to moisten. The scouring, cleansing and thickening of different types of wool cloth. Similar to the felting process only not to such a degree. In earlier times, the fulling process was done by a *fuller*. Warn water was put into a tub containing a clay called *fuller's earth*. The cloth was placed in the tub and the fuller trampled it with his feet until the friction caused the fibres to matt together. This method continued in the British Isles until the twentieth century. Today this process is done by machinery. It is thought that the surnames Fuller and Walker may have derived from those earlier times when fulling was practised.

Fur Fibre Most fur fibres are better suited to blending with other fibres. They are useful in this way for producing very interesting yarns. The exception to this is the Angora rabbit, which has a very soft and silky coat. When examining the coat it is noticeable that a variation occurs in the fibres and it has a fine coarser content but, because even the coarse is indeed very fine, the two are often used together when spinning; they can also be used for blending. There are many fur fibres, all suitable for blending.

Fuzz Hairs A byproduct of the cotton crop. In some cotton varieties, for example Asiatic, Peruvian and United States, not all the extending cells of the cotton grow into long spinnable fibres and often only reach a few millimetres in length. These shorter hairs attain considerable girth, and by developing their secondary thickening to such an extent that the lumen is almost obliterated, these are called the *fuzz hairs*. These hairs, which can be white, green or brown, adhere firmly to the seed and, as they are so short, many remain after the ginning process. They then have to be removed by a special machine in a delinting process. The hairs are called *linters* and are sold for a variety of commercial uses. (Any residue remaining can be reginned and the products are termed 'first-cut linterns', 'second-cut linterns' etc, the lengths of the fibres in each successive cut becoming shorter.)

G

Galls Also called *oak galls; berry galls; gall nuts; gall apples; oak apples.* These are vegetable excrescences produced by insects (female gall wasps) attached to various trees (eg oak) and plants. They yield tannic and gallic acids, which act as mordants in natural dyeing.
See *Dyes and Dyeing*

Gandhi, Mahatma Gandhi wrote, 'For me nothing in the political world is more important than the spinning wheel'. He called spinning 'a sacrament' turning the mind 'Godward'. He used to spin most evenings; his clothes were handmade, and in spinning he found, according to his secretary Pyarcelal, 'rhythm, music, poetry, romance and even spiritual solace'. In Gandhi's quest to find work for his Indian peasants he founded a spinning movement to help supplement the poor farming yield. He used the spinning wheel as a symbol at the centre of the Congress Party flag, now the Indian Flag.
See *Charka*

Gare Long hairy fibres, not serrated, which will neither spin nor dye.

Garnetting The cutting up of previously spun yarns, which are reprocessed and respun in a mill as waste for lower-grade goods. The breaking-up of yarn waste is done on a machine called a *garnett*, a type of carding machine that contains rollers and cylinders covered with sawlike metallic teeth. The waste is considered to be garnetted once it takes on the appearance of a loose mass of fibres.

Gimp Yarn Also known as *gimp slub* is a 2 ply yarn in which one of the strands is held more loosely in the spinning than the other. The one strand is held as a tight core, whilst the other strand, or 'single', is paid out quickly and unevenly onto it, at irregular intervals.

Ginning A mechanical process that separates cotton fibres from the seeds.
See *Cotton; Fuzz Hairs*

Goat The goat, common *sp Capra hircus*, has been a part of the environment for decades, and is related to sheep. The fibre is mainly straight, coarse and stiff. It has a good lustre, is durable and, when spun, will not shrink or felt. The fibres from short-haired varieties can be added, or blended with other fibres where texturing is required.

137

Goat hair is available in a loose mass of short staple hair and also in combed strips of longer hair.

Before spinning, oil is usually added. Spin as camel hair. Wash after spinning and rinse well adding a little fabric softener.

Gold See under *Mineral Fibres*

Goutiere The triangular section piece of iron in the doubleur, used for bending teeth for carders. France, 1750.
See *Doubleur*

Grade (Wool) The standard by which wool is bought and sold.
See *Objective Measurement; Sale By Sample*

Grease Pots Small pots that were hung on spinning wheels in bygone days; possibly containing grease to lubricate the working parts on the wheel. Not to be confused with pots that contained water for flax spinning.

Great Wheel A quill-type spinning wheel that usually has a 121.9cm (4ft) drive wheel and an open pointed spindle, which is operated whilst standing and walking. The large wheel is turned by hand. Referred to by a variety of names: – *walking wheel; high wheel; big wheel*; and as *long wheel* in Ireland, *muckle wheel* in Scotland, *Welsh* or *great wheel* in Wales, *flanders wheel* in the Isle of Man, and as *Jersey cottage wheel, the short-fibre wheel*. In North America it is called the *wool* or *walking wheel*. It was occasionally used as a bobbin winder and referred to as bobbin wheel. 'Wool wheel' was the term used to distinguish a great wheel from a treadle or flax wheel. Some wheels had a drive wheel smaller than 121.9cm (4ft); earlier designs enabled the spinner to sit and spin – these wheels were thought to have been used for cotton spinning. The great wheel is thought to have reached Europe during the Middle Ages; the earlier examples were similar to today's wheels.

There are conflicting reports as to the origin of the great wheel. Some say it may have originated from the *charka* of similar composition, although the Indian wheels were close to the ground. Others say it may have its origin in China where it was used for unwinding silk from cocoons. The same principle of spinning from the spindle tip was used by Crompton in his Mule, and Hargreaves in his Jenny.

In 1802, an American, Amos Minor, patented his accelerating head, which greatly increased the efficiency of the great wheel. He added a further pulley to work with the one attached to the spindle shaft (the pulley whorl) and accelerated the speed of the spindle rotations. He started to manufacture it in 1810. See *Hoop-rimmed Spinning Wheels*

FIBRE PREPARATION AND TPI (*twists per inch*): the fibre preparation for spinning on a great wheel must be thorough. Unlike a treadle wheel, which leaves both hands free, with a great wheel the right hand turns the wheel whilst the left hand has to control the fibre supply. Careful consideration must be paid to the amount of draw in relation to the quantity of fibre released by the fingers of the left hand. The tpi are related to a) the number of turns of the drive wheel multiplied by b) the spindle rotation. The spinner, to produce a consistent yarn, must gauge the distance of a length of yarn and turn the wheel the exact number of times for this given length, thus inserting into each length the same number of twists. If this is not strictly adhered to, there will be many lengths of yarn with unrelated tpi. Some spinners tie a ribbon on one spoke of the wheel to indicate one complete turn. The rotation speed is also most important; do not start off turning the wheel too actively then slow down as tiredness occurs.

Drafting a yarn formation is achieved by moving back from the spindle and the point where the fibres are drafted; therefore, if 20 tpi are required, then after every 20 spindle turns the length of the yarn should be increased by 2.5cm (1in).

PLYING: As spinning on the great wheel is a Z-spin, the following should be observed when plying:

a) cross the drive band in front of the head to produce an S-twist, the wheel will then still be turned clockwise when plying. Whilst the drive belt could be left untouched and the wheel turned anticlockwise, this is too awkward to execute.

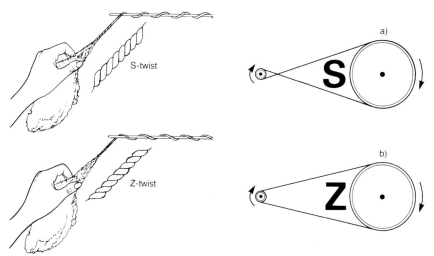

Fig 27 Plying on the great wheel a) closed band for S-twist; b) open band for Z-twist. Also shows correct 45° angle drawing of the fibre to the spindle

b) place the cops of yarn (or balls of yarn) onto a lazy kate on the left of the spinner. Attach the yarn ends either to a leader or tie them onto paper placed around the spindle shaft. Hold the singles between the fingers of the left hand at an angle of 45° from the spindle tip; the hold should be relaxed.

c) turn the wheel slightly in a clockwise direction and test the twist obtained. It must be relaxed and not overtwisted. If it twists back on itself, it is overtwisted; if the singles have not twisted together and joined, they are underplied. The plied yarn should be combined well and relaxed. When a suitable result has been obtained, continue to ply. When the length has been obtained, back off to clear the spindle tip, then wind on the plied yarn and continue. Keep a constant TPI.

SPINNING: *Woollen spin*

a) tension the belt

b) tie a Z-twisted leader cord around the spindle shaft; place the right hand on one of the spokes and turn the wheel clockwise, wind the cord on until a firm grip is obtained. When the yarn is to within about 25.4cm (10in) from the spindle tip, cease to rotate the wheel. (See *Note*.)

c) take a rolag with the left hand and attenuate it slightly. Place the leader cord on the fibre supply at an angle of 45° to the spindle tip. Turn the wheel with the right hand until twist has joined the fibre supply to the leader cord.

d) continue to turn the wheel, keeping the angle of the yarn to the spindle axis at 45°, and permitting slip-off from the tip, thus imparting twist. If yarn constantly overtwists, the wheel rotation is too rapid. If no twist is being imparted into the fibres, then possibly the angle of yarn in relation to the tip of the spindle is incorrect. The twist may tend to go to the thinnest places but will even out as the fibres become completely attenuated.

e) move backwards, attenuating the fibres with the left hand by permitting them to slip through the fingers (the tension of pulling off the spindle tip will assist the drafting) and by rotating the wheel clockwise to impart twist until further extension becomes impossible without losing contact with the wheel. (The arm should be fully extended without stretching, which would cause tiredness.)

f) stop the rotation of the wheel, back off (reverse) the wheel to remove the yarn from the tip of the spindle. Move the left hand in, parallel to the drive band. Turn the wheel in a clockwise direction and move forward as the yarn winds onto the spindle shaft. Careful attention should be paid to the build up of the cop (or cone) (see *fig 28a & b*). Work from the whorl end and allow sufficient yarn to travel the length of the spindle and off the tip with sufficient to

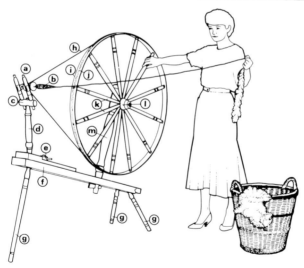

Plate 30 *GREAT WHEEL SPINNING*: final attenuation before winding the spun yarn onto the spindle; note the position of the right hand on the wheel and the arm, which is relaxed and not overstretched. The plate also shows the nomenclature of the great wheel: a) spindle head; b) spindle; c) mother-of-all; d) head post; e) tension device; f) bench, table or stock; g) legs) h) drive band; i) rim; j) groove; k) axle; l) hub; m) great wheel post

Plate 31 *GREAT WHEEL SPINNING*: winding-on; the spun yarn is parallel to the drive band and ready to be wound onto the spindle. The right hand position will now change from that shown (for backing-off) to the position shown in Plate 30. On the left hand side of the plate is a double treadle wheel particularly suitable for disabled people. This wheel also has Braille labelling

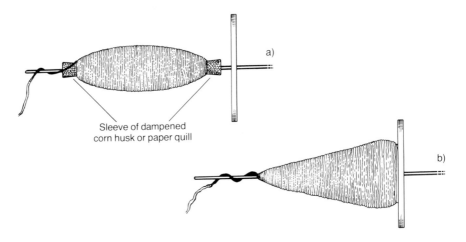

a)

Sleeve of dampened
corn husk or paper quill

b)

Fig 28 Build-up of yarn on great wheel spindle: a) cop; b) cone

start spinning with, approximately 25.4cm (10in) from the spindle tip.

g) recommence spinning by holding the yarn at 45° as before. As with a long draw, the spinner should hold the rolag in such a way as to permit a section to be attenuated per one length of yarn. (See *Twists Per Inch*)

h) when the cop has built up sufficiently, it should cover about half the spindle shaft and be tapered both ends; slip it off the spindle shaft and store until required.

Note: the traditional way of starting to spin was to wrap a corn husk around the spindle, leaving the tip exposed, and secured in place by tying at both ends with thin thread. A few fibres were caught in the husk crack and, as the spindle was rotated, the fibres became attached and a short length of yarn was twisted. The wheel was then backed off and the yarn wound on to secure; the spinner then commenced spinning.

To spin on a great wheel is to experience the craft of handspinning to its fullest extent, a journey into the past. In earlier times it was associated with wool; today it is capable of producing an equally satisfactory worsted spin. Use fine quality combed fibre. Divide the top into equal lengths and as the draft is executed, if the fibres are controlled as they enter the twist maintaining their alignment, a satisfactory product will result.

In England, students of spinning tend not to learn on a great wheel, preferring possibly the mobility of some treadle wheels. Those who become involved with spinning, and who wish to experience all aspects of the craft, often turn to the great wheel at a later stage. It is interesting to note that those who learned to spin on a treadle wheel using their right hand as the front hand and the left hand as the back hand (drafting) find the transfer to a great wheel a natural progression, whereas those who were trained with left hand to the front and right hand for drafting require time to become adjusted. Whether they are naturally right or left handed seems not to influence this at all. See *Bat Head; Builds; Cone; Cop; Minor's Head*

Green Flax In some cases flax fibres can be processed entirely by hand without retting.

Grège French word for raw silk as it comes from the filature. Usually white and exceptionally soft and lustrous. Raw silk is considered the best as it is taken direct from the cocoon. It is available as prepared rovings for handspinning.
See *Sericulture*

Grey (in the) Also referred to as *in the grease*. Fibre containing dirt and grease that has not been scoured.

Group Projects SPINNING: whether in schools, amongst disabled people, in an adult education craft class, as part of an elderly club group or for personal study, spinning is a suitable subject for group projects as the contents of this book prove. In a group where, for example, it is necessary to break the task down into separate units, with so many facets from history to techniques and design, this craft can offer a wide scope. Plate 32 shows a group project which was designed by elderly members of a craft group in a Senior Citizens' club. They met regularly, each set working on a different aspect, then at the end the various aspects were gathered together and exhibited at an Age Concern Annual Craft Show. The craft met the needs of both men and women within the group, and they had the satisfaction of knowing their work had given pleasure, not only to themselves, but to others.

In a school, choice could be made by each child to study and write a

Plate 32 *GROUP PROJECT*: built on a turntable, each section at base level shows an aspect related to spinning from the shepherd model shearing sheep in the foreground to the production of yarn. The top elevation, when turned, shows both the outside and inside of a cottage, with various spinning and fibre preparations being executed. The project, including painted backcloth, turntable and all contents ie models of spinning wheels, people, animals, knitted surround to the base, etc, was made by a group of poeple at an Over 60s Club

project on a particular related subject (for example, 'wool'), then they could exchange their knowledge with other members of the class, and finally combine the individual projects as part of an end-of-term group exhibition.

From the teaching aspect, it is vital to plan the project carefully; this can be done by the teacher alone, or by consulting the members of the group/class after acquainting them with the possibilities of the craft. Once the group has been motivated it is necessary to begin work on the project as soon as possible; if there is too much time between planning and the actual commencement, people lose interest. The planning and preparation should take into consideration the needs of the individual members of the group, particularly if it involves disabled people. The practicalities of the size of the project related to possible transporting to exhibitions is an important factor. In a group there may well be slow learners, who, whilst they could have much to contribute to the group, require a slower pace to make sure their enjoyment of the exercise is not marred by pressure. Work cards can be very useful here to help individuals working alone at their own pace. Use experienced group members to benefit the task in hand.

Careful co-ordination and monitoring of all the items must be done throughout; hours of work may be wasted if the co-ordination is below standard.

Pacing is very important if completion is required by a given time. One very important point to be considered is the scale of one person's work in relation to another; this particularly applies where models are involved.

When setting up, or laying out a project, care should be taken to present each exhibit/item in as uncluttered a way as possible. Colour co-ordination should be considered. Some work may not be to the general standard of others, which can present a problem; it should, however, be included, providing it is to as high a standard as the individual is capable of achieving.

Group projects provide interest for everyone, and often those people less capable can bask in the glory of the end project, which may motivate them for future craft work. Other groups viewing the exhibit may well be encouraged to try something similar, and so the pleasure is extended.

Guanaco Referred to by some authorities as *Auchinea lama* and by others as *Lama guanicoe*, it is found in the wild in Peru, Bolivia, parts of the Argentine and Chile and related to the vicuna of the high Andes of South America; sometimes domesticated. The fibre resembles cashmere. The softest fibres come from the young guanaco and are very fine, silky down of a creamy honey beige. The more mature animals have a deep caramel brown coat. Spin guanaco as cashmere.

Guide Hooks Also called *hecks*: the small hooks placed on the flyer arms to guide the yarn onto the bobbin; they are either situated on opposite sides of the flyer arms, or on the same side.

Guild System of Production The first guild (Anglo-Saxon *'gild'* or money) had been organised by weavers by the twelfth century. The medieval guild was built around a single craft in a town; membership was compulsory. There were three basic classes: masters, journeymen and apprentices. The masters organised the craft, including the charges and techniques and they set the rules. The masters were the employers of the apprentices, having served already their own seven years' apprenticeship. Once an apprentice had ended his indentures, he became a journeyman (*journee*). To become a master, a journeyman had to submit a piece of his own work to the guild for examination. This piece was known as 'the masterpiece' and on its merits rested the fate of the candidate.

The guild looked after the poor amongst its members and worked closely with the Church.

Gummy Grease, which has solidified down in the fleece, and is very difficult to scour out. Also a term used for an old sheep that has lost its incisor teeth.

Gum Waste Also called *thread waste*. This consists of silk that has been damaged and discarded after passing into the form of raw silk, more often during re-reeling. It contains no twist and is a valuable source of material for the silk spinner. See *Sericulture; Silk*

Gut The filament obtained when a mature silkworm is cut open to remove its silk glands. The filament is stretched to about a half-yard length. It is transparent in water and used for fishing lead lines and for surgical sutures.

An extract from an Abbey & Imbrie NY, *Fishing Tackle Catalogue*, dated 1923, describes how silkworms are fed for six weeks on mulberry leaves, then gathered in baskets and tipped into tubs of vinegar and water, where they die. They are left in the solution for several hours, which solidifies the 'liquid silk' so that it can be drawn out in the form of gut. These strands of gut are then dried in the sun. The surface film is either scraped off or dissolved away. The various sizes of gut are then carefully sorted. It is a misnomer to call the gut 'catgut'. Today, synthetic materials are used.

Hackes Also known as *hackle; heckles; hatchel; hetchel.*
See *Flax – Linum usitatissimum*

Hair Fibres Long, and often coarse, fibres which contain a medulla (hollow core). Appear in some breeds as an outer protective layer over down, eg camel. In the textile industry the term 'wool' is used for the covering on sheep, and 'hair' for other fibres of animal origin, eg alpaca, camel, cashmere, mohair, etc. However, problems can occur where the animal has two coats as already mentioned, in which case the shorter fibre may be referred to as 'wool'; it should always be clearly stated, eg cashmere wool etc.
See also *Dog*

Handle of Wool The feel of the wool, its texture, and whether it is harsh or soft.

Handspinning Is also known as *finger spinning*. The very beginning of spinning is unknown, although as an art it was well advanced in the early Stone Age. In the evolution of spinning three stages were involved:

a) to attenuate the fibres; b) twist them; c) wind them

The most primitive form of spinning used fibres and the hands to form the thread; in earliest times this was done by using the thumb and index finger. In this process the production rate is very slow, as attenuation, twisting and winding are all completely separate actions. To increase the rate of production the thread can be rolled on the thigh, using one hand, while the other hand draws out the thread. It is thought that in past times the fibres may also have been rolled on the ground. In ancient Egypt, women prepared flax rove for respinning, by rolling the fibre on the thigh.

Handspinning can be useful in determining the potential of a fibre. Take a sample from the fleece, tease, then twist; the result will show what it is capable of producing.

Handspun Yarn Often referred to as *fingering yarn*. The word fingering arose because noils, which appeared occasionally in the fibre, caused the spinner to roll (finger) the noil between the fingers to reduce it in size. Many knitting yarns used today, whether manmade or handspun, are referred to as *fingering yarns*.

147

Hank An amount of yarn that has been coiled, eg an ounce (or 28gm) of yarn. Of silk it measures 120yd (about 110m).

Hank Holders Also called *skein holders* and, in England, *wool winders*. See *Swifts*

Harsh A term describing wool lacking in softness.

Hemp A fibre from the *Cannabis sativa*, is an annual, which grows from 30.5cm to 2.438m (3 to 8ft) high. It originated somewhere north of Tibet and spread to China where it was being spun and woven into clothing as early as 2800 BC. It was introduced into Europe in the fifth century AD and reached America in 1645. In earlier times the peasants wore hemp and the wealthy silk. Hemp was the first fibre used for textiles in Japan.

Hemp is a native of temperate Asia and is grown in Europe. It is found in many temperate and tropical areas all over the world, but the best examples come from the Orient. Russia is the largest producer. It grows easily, providing that the soil is rich and moist and that the seeds are planted carefully. If they are too closely set, they will produce spindly stems; if too far apart, the stems will be coarse. There are both male and female plants, the female being the stronger. The male is picked first and the female left to enable the seeds to ripen. These seeds can produce an oil yield of as much as 30 per cent. The colour of hemp varies considerably according to the method of retting used. Tones range from light grey, beige, brown to almost black. Normal retting time is ten days for the male and three weeks for the female plants. The longer the retting, the softer the fibres, although this weakens the fibres. Hemp is often compared with flax and similarities do exist, although hemp has several disadvantages:

1 Hemp is processed as flax.
2 Bundle formation of the fibres in the stem is not so clean as with flax. The outer fibrils spiral in a right-hand direction.
3 Hemp is longer than flax.
4 Hemp does not consist of so pure a cellulose as flax.
5 If bleached, hemp loses strength.
6 Hemp lacks flexibility.
7 Hemp takes more time to mature than flax.
8 Hemp lacks the quality of flax.
9 Hemp is not so easy to spin as flax.

Hemp is available in sliver form.

SPINNING WITH HEMP ROVING: cut the fibres into approximately 30.5cm (12in) lengths. Draw out into a long rove. Dampen as flax.

(Some spinners use oil rather than water.) It can also be spun from a distaff.

Fine hemp, when woven, is similar to linen in appearance. The woven material made from hemp yarn is also called *hemp*. Hemp is used for making sacking, coarse canvas, rope, cord and for the warp yarn in carpet manufacture. Various narcotics are extracted from the stalk, flowers and leaves of hemp, eg *marijuana*.

HEMP TYPES:
Common hemp: grows in France, Germany, Russia, and other European countries to a height of 1.52m to 2.13m (5 to 7ft).

Bologna or *Piedmontese hemp*, also called *great hemp*: grows in Italy, Yugoslavia and Hungary 3.66m to 4.88m (12 to 16ft) high.

Cannapa piccola or *small hemp*: grows in Italy.

China hemp: grows in China to a height of 3.66m to 6.10m (12–20ft).

Sometimes pulled but is usually cut when the lower leaves turn yellow.
A point to note: the following fibres produced in various parts of the world are not hemps at all: *Indian hemp; Manila hemp; New Zealand hemp; Sisal hemp*.
See *Batching; Flax*

Hemp – Manila See *Abaca*.

Henequen – Yucatan sisal (*Agave fourcroydes*). The primary leaf fibres are agave (or aloe) fibres. It is golden-white in colour and the fibres are scraped from the inside of the leaves.

Highlander Is native to Scotland and thought to be a descendant of the *Kyloe*, or *black cattle*, which the Celts drove north and west during their departure before the arrival of the English. Very hardy, with handsome heads having widespread horns, and a very thick undercoat covered by hair. The colour varies from red, brindle, black or a mixture. Both the under- and the topcoat can be spun into yarn. May require controlling with an oil emulsion spray before spinning.

Hog Also called a *hogget* is a sheep that is unshorn, and is between 12 and 15 months old.

Hog Fleece Fleece from the first shearing of a yearling sheep; it is preferable to a ewe or a wether.

Hogget Wool First fleece of a sheep that was not shorn as a lamb.

Whit
ite · In
Whit

H / I

city · *Interlotting · Intermittent Spinning · Irish Line*
· *Interlotting · Intermittent Spinning · Irish Linen · Ix*
city · *Interlotting · Intermittent Spinning · Irish Line*

Hoop-Rimmed Spinning Wheel These great wheels were used in woollen mills during the seventeenth century. They were of similar construction to the earlier waggon wheels where the wheelwrights made wheels that had a hub, radial spokes and a rim often consisting of several broad *felloes* (outer circles). Some wheels, however, had a rim consisting of a basic broad thin strip of wood, which was joined together by splicing; these were the *hoop-rimmed* spinning wheels.
See *Great Wheel*

Horsehair Suitable to mix and spin with wool, in proportion of one part wool to two parts hair, which helps to produce a strong yarn. Horsehair is used for rugmaking in Scandinavia. Carpets made from it are very stiff and coarse in texture.

Huarizo A crossbreed from a female alpaca and a male llama.

Hungerfine An extremely thin wool, often the result of starvation.

Indigo White A term used in relation to the indigo vat when white particles appear as it reaches a certain stage in the process. Indigotin, the active dyestuff in indigo, can produce deep tones of blue. In earlier times Navajo Indians obtained indigo from Mexico. The process they used was a long one. First the indigo was dissolved in urine and the yarn immersed in same; the longer the period, the darker the blue tone obtained. The wool had to be rinsed many times. Only urine of a young child was used, it was the Navajos' belief that if urine from someone not still a virgin was used the resulting dye would streak the wool and the colour would not be 'fast'.

To obtain a good dye with indigo, chemical facts must be taken into consideration. It is insoluble in water and has to be reduced by fermentation (caused by micro-organisms) with ammonia furnishing the alkaline solution. The result of this reduction is referred to as *indigo white* and is soluble in water, which enters the wool and turns it blue when exposed to air. The colour is fast, the blue a result of oxidation and being insoluble in water. See *Dyes and Dyeing*

Insulating Capacity Wool has excellent insulating properties that protect the wearer from both extremes of heat and cold.

Interlotting The grouping, in a broker's store, of various odd bales from various owners, into larger even lines rather than small lots.

150

Intermittent Spinning An example of this is spinning on a great wheel, where the procedure consists of drawing out and spinning the fibre, then pausing to reverse the wheel to clear the spindle tip, then resuming the previous wheel direction to wind the yarn on. By using a treadle wheel, the yarn is automatically wound onto the bobbin as it is spun. The long draw, using a treadle wheel, is similar to the great wheel procedure.

Irish Linen It is comfortable to wear in warm weather. It gives up its moisture into the surrounding atmosphere more rapidly than any other textile. When purified and bleached, it has a lustrous surface. It is hygroscopic, that is, sensitive to moisture and absorbs up to one-fifth of its own oven-dry weight of water without being damp on the surface. When linen is washed, a minute micro-molecular layer is removed around each fibre; with each wash the surface comes up new.

There is evidence that linen fabrics were in use in England around 370 BC, probably introduced by the trading Phoenicians as early as 900 BC. Linen was made in Ireland early in the thirteenth century and probably even earlier than that.

In the reign of Queen Elizabeth I linen making started to really develop as an Irish industry. In 1633, Charles I appointed Thomas Wentworth, Earl of Strafford as his Lord Deputy in Ireland; among his other duties he was to oversee development of the linen industry. Strafford, in establishing a successful linen industry, also brought about the demise of the Irish woollen trade. In early Ireland both flax and wool were spun, but England did not encourage the woollen industry in her colonies, so by the late eighteenth century flax only was in use.

Louis Crommelin, a Huguenot refugee and a skilled weaver, visited the Irish farmers and advised them on all aspects of flax production. The farmers' wives were also included as they were responsible for bleaching the subsequent cloth. For this purpose they used buttermilk and a lye made by dissolving in water the ash of burnt seaweed. Crommelin laid the foundation on which the modern industry is based.

The flax crop today in Northern Ireland is small, and entirely for experimental purposes. Flax for the industry is imported from Europe, but Irish linen cannot be surpassed for its excellence, even though the raw materials are no longer grown in Ireland. See *Flax*

Ixtle A leaf fibre from the *tula ixtle* of Mexico. Used for mats, brushes and baskets.

151

ieces ·   *and Kakeme · Keba · Kemp · Kenaf · Keratin · Kerme*
es · Joi   *l Kakeme · Keba · Kemp · Kenaf · Keratin · Kermes ·*
ieces ·   *and Kakeme · Keba · Kemp · Kenaf · Keratin · Kerme*

J

Jaw Pieces Wool shorn from underneath the jaw of sheep; it usually contains vegetable matter and tends to be matted or felted.

Joins To produce a consistent yarn it is essential to have good joins. Some spinning methods required a good overlap, eg the long draw. Integration of fibre with the yarn coming from the spindle is essential; the fibre should not just wrap itself around the yarn. Weak joins will produce weakness in the yarn, and constant breaking may occur.

Jürgen, Johann A wood carver of Wattenbuttel in Brunswick who was thought to have invented the treadle spinning wheel in 1530, although it had been designed some years previously by Leonardo da Vinci; sketches showed this, although it seems as if it was an idea that was not put to practical use.
See *Leonardo da Vinci*

Jute *Sp Corchorus capsularis* generally yields white jute and *Corchorus olitorius*, dark jute, come mainly from India and Pakistan. The fibre is used for *burlap* and *twine*.

Jute was first introduced into Europe from India at the close of the eighteenth century. An annual, it belongs to the Lime tree group, and can grow to 4.57m (15ft) in height. It resembles hemp, but is a harder fibre. It is available in brown tones. The fibres are very long, but have very little elasticity. They occur in bundles in concentric layers around a woody core. The ultimates, of which the bundles are composed, are much shorter than flax and hemp; the exterior of the fibre is smooth. It will rot if exposed to moisture over long periods. Jute can be dyed but not bleached. If spinning with a spinning wheel, use the worsted method.

It is raised as European flax although cut, not pulled; then it is retted and scutched. Retting may take from ten to twenty days. The cortical layer is stripped from the stems in the form of coarse ribbons of fibre, which is then washed and hung in the open air to dry. The jute is sent to market in drums or rolls to be graded and is then made up into bales of about 181.6kg (400lb).

Jute is mainly used for making sacking, string bags, tarpaulins, bases for carpets, etc. When woven for industrial use, it is often given a special moisture resistant finish. Hessian is a jute fabric.

d Mohair · Knickerbocker Yarn · Knitting Yarn · Kno
ohair · Knickerbocker Yarn · Knitting Yarn · Knops
d Mohair · Knickerbocker Yarn · Knitting Yarn · Kno

· Jaw P
aw Piec
· Jaw P

Kake and Kakeme Terms used by the Japanese cocoon markets. *Kake* refers to the market price which is divided by the yield. The word *kake* replaces the word *yen*.

Kapok A unicellular seed hair obtained from the seed pods of the kapok tree or silk-cotton tree (*Ceiba pentandra*). The soft lustrous fibre is 2cm to 4.5cm (¾ to 1¾in) in length and coloured grey and tawny. The chief commercial producers are Indonesia, Thailand, Cambodia, Laos and Vietnam. However, the tree is found in tropical regions of both hemispheres. It is used as a soft filling for toys, pillows, mattresses and sound insulation, etc. It is easier to spin if blended with wool in the grease, as the grease holds the fibres in place. The fibre is sometimes called *ceba, ceiba, jaua cotton, silk cotton, silk floss*, etc.

Kashmir Fibre from the Tibetan goat, Capra hircus. Used in 'Cashmere' and 'Paisley' shawls. See *Cashmere*

Keba A raw silk form available from Japan. It is a loose silk filament that is first spun by the silkworm to enclose its area and construct the support for the cocoon. Collected after the worm has changed into pupa stage. The fibre is fluffy and easy to work with. Keba is unique as it is the only raw single filament form to be made into spun yarn. See *Blaze; Sericulture; Silk*

Kemp Often found in sheep raised in wet regions, also in mountain breeds eg Welsh and Scottish Blackface. Kemp sometimes the result of poorly bred sheep. They are short, coarse, wavy opaque fibres, usually from central primary follicles, which possess a wide central air canal (the *medulla*) at the expense of the cortical layer. Often chalky white in appearance, although reddish in some Welsh breeds. They have a pointed tip and tapering root and are shed periodically into the fleece. Kemp fibres have a poor dye absorption due to their opacity, and they are not hair fibres. Hair fibres are not as thick as kemps and the central medulla does not usually occupy such a great width.

Kenaf *Hibiscus cannabinus* is a bast fibre available in India and is similar to jute. The fibre length is 7.6cm to 10.3cm (3 to 4in).

Keratin Substance forming wool fibre, composed approximately of 50.5 per cent carbon, 6.8 per cent hydrogen, 16.8 per cent nitrogen, 20.5 per cent oxygen and 5.4 per cent sulphur. Classed as protein.

amb's Wool · Lanolin · Lantern · Lazy Kate · Lea · Leasing · Leonardo da Vinc
b's Wool · Lanolin · Lantern · Lazy Kate · Lea · Leasing · Leonardo da Vinci ·
amb's Wool · Lanolin · Lantern · Lazy Kate · Lea · Leasing · Leonardo da Vinc

Kermes A red coloured dye obtained from the bodies of insects found in the evergreen kermes oak (*Quercus coccinea*) and used in ancient times.

Kid Mohair The fibre shorn from a young Angora goat. The best of all Angora fleece.

Knickerbocker Yarn Also called *knop yarn* and *nepp yarn*. An attractive yarn made on the woollen system whereby contrasting spots are incorporated on the surface either during the spinning process or introduced during the latter stages of carding.

Knitting Derived from the Anglo-Saxon *cnyttan*, which meant the weaving of threads by hand. There are various forms of knitting. To generalise however, whatever form is used, a fabric is constructed by using a series of interlocking loops.

Knitting Yarn The main criterion when designing a yarn suitable for knitting, is that whatever design is incorporated in the yarn it should be even in presentation. Distortion will occur if the yarn has a tight twist as a single; in this case it is wiser to ply singles together. However, a softly twisted yarn will hold its shape without the need to ply. When spinning yarn for knitting, tie a coloured thread at the start where the fibre is joined to the leader cord. When commencing knitting, start with this marked end, there will be less likelihood of the yarn 'pilling' then. Many knitting patterns are now on the market for use with handspun yarns. If requiring to use a pattern not specifically designed for handspun yarn, care should be taken (where possible) to spin the yarn, to the yarn size stated in the pattern. If a sample of the commercial yarn is available, comparison can be made by winding around a ruler to see how the handspun and commercial yarns compare, for example over 2.5cm (1in). Squares of the handspun should be knitted to test the tension, and any adjustments made; all that may be required is a change in knitting needles.

Knitting Yarn; Yorkshire Count is the number of hanks containing 234m (256yd) required for 0.45kg (1lb). However, a hand knitter is more likely to be interested in the diameter rather than in the yardage per 1lb, therefore commercial knitting yarns are marketed by the number of ply, eg 2 ply, 3 ply, 4 ply.

Knops Small, felted fibre pieces integrated in the yarn.

:o Dye · Linen · Linseed Oil · Llama · Lock · Loft · Lc
Dye · Linen · Linseed Oil · Llama · Lock · Loft · Loop
:o Dye · Linen · Linseed Oil · Llama · Lock · Loft · Lc
tre Woc
Wools ·
tre Woc

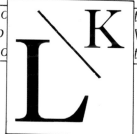

Knop Yarn A yarn, designed to contain bunches which predominate, comprised of one or more of its component threads either at regular or irregular intervals along its length. An interesting effect is produced if the knop yarn is bound with a thread in the reverse direction to the initial stage; this secures the knops and produces a spiral yarn in between. Also known as *boutonne*.

Knot A measurement related to yarn winders of past times. The circumference of the winder often measured two yards. Forty turns of the winder made a *knot* of 74.5m (80yd); if the winder was a click reel type it registered the amount, if without a clock or means of accounting for the amount, the spinner would tie a small knot in the yarn at this measurement. When seven *knots* had been wound there were 512m (560yd) of yarn or one skein. Today a skein does not always indicate an exact measurement. See *Skeiner*

Knubbs Also known as *frisson* or *strusa*. Knubbs provides the bulk of all the waste silk used by spinners. It is the outer layer of the cocoon that is removed before the single baves are isolated, and is very strong and gummy. Often workers were delegated to collect the knubbs for the reelers, pull them out straight and then hang them to dry in a parallel fashion before the gum hardened; the term *flowers and roots* applied to the inside and outside ends. See *Sericulture; Silk–Reeling*

Lamb A young sheep, with its mother, or up to five months old.

Lamb's Wool Fleece that has been shorn from the lamb at age seven months or less. The fleece is very soft to handle and, as it is so new, tends to fall open into separate staples, each with a small curly tip.

Lanolin Correct terminology, *anhydrous lanolin*. Secreted by special sebaceous glands in the skin of sheep so as to form a natural protective coating on the wool fibres. Chemically, it is a complex of esters of unique character. It is extracted from the natural wool, then refined and purified. Whilst it has the physical consistency of a soft grease, chemically it is a wax and completely different to the body fat of animals. The crude wax is removed from the wool by an aqueous washing process and then recovered from the wash water by high-speed centrifugal separators. The result is *centrifugal neutral wool grease* which yields the finished lanolin after intensive refining.

Lanolin is an unsurpassed softener for the human skin and for some animal types also. It has been recognised since Biblical times; 4,000 years ago the Egyptians used cosmetics with lanolin as the emollient. It was used by German and English chemists as far back as the early 1800s and is now listed in numerous pharmacopoeias, supplements and other compendia worldwide. Lanolin, with its unique combination of properties, can replace sebum (with which it has some chemical similarities). Sebum is present in normal healthy skin and, with other substances, controls the rate of water loss for the body through the epidermis and maintains a balanced water content within the skin. Loss of sebum results in excessive loss of water and dehydration of the skin, followed by dryness. Lanolin is a powerful water-in-oil emulsifier and thus can hold emulsified water in the skin. It is not completely impervious to water and thus does not stop up the pores but allows the natural rate of transpiration to take place. Other than the high grade lanolins used in skin products, it is an important constituent of pharmaceutical ointment bases; various grades exist for industrial or semi-industrial purposes, eg veterinary salves and creams, horticultural dressings, leather dressings, paint additives, marking fluids, textile and paper finishes, insulating compounds, putty, disinfectants, inks, polishes, rust preventatives, soaps, etc.

Lantern The top of a distaff having a lantern shaped frame. See *Distaff*

Laps The silk waste before combing into sliver or top.

Lazy Kate Also called a *bobbin rack* or *bobbin holder*. Used to store the full bobbins whilst plying the yarn. Many wheels are designed with built-in lazy kates. These are usually more suitable as a means of storing full bobbins rather than plying from them. See Plate 41

Lea Also called a *hank*. A standard measure principally for *flax*. An Act of Parliament (United Kingdom) established the length of a *lea* as 300yd (274.3m). In Scotland it is termed a *cut*. It is also known as a *rap*. The flax is wound on a reel, which has a circumference of 228.6cm (90in) to make each thread measure 2.275m (2½yd); 120 such threads form a lea of linen. A lea of cotton and a lea of worsted, however, contain only 80 threads.

Leader Also called *starter thread*. The name given to the yarn which is tied tightly to the bobbin on a spinning wheel then taken over the first flyer hook and brought out through the orifice with the aid of a hook. A strong Z-twisted spun woollen thread, or soft string, is suitable since the wheel will be turning clockwise. On a flyer wheel the leader should be approximately 3m (3yd) in length if operated by a new spinner, and at least 45.7cm (18in) for an established spinner.

Leaf Fibres See *Vegetable fibres*

Learning to Spin See *Spinning*

Leasing The insertion of a crossed traverse lease-cord into wraps of yarn on a reel, either to separate into specifically numbered groups or to prevent tangling during hank dyeing, etc. In the silk industry it is referred to as *lacing* and *halching*, the latter term is used when the lease-cord is coloured differently from the yarn.
Lease-cord synonyms are *lacing cord, lease-band* and *tie-band*.

Leonardo da Vinci There has always been a clash of opinion between historians as to who was the inventor of the bobbin and flyer wheel. Amongst Leonardo's papers were drawings with notes of this type of machine. However, paintings indicate that the bobbin flyer system evolved much earlier, possibly related to silk throwing.
See *Jürgen, Johann*

Leuco Dye A dye, somewhat reduced from the original, that may be regenerated by an oxidation process.

Level The even penetration of dye into material is referred to as level.

Lime *Tilia europaea*: a bast fibre used for cording mats and bags.

Line See under *Flax – Linum usitatissimum*

Linen Anglo-Saxon word meaning 'made from flax'. The word is used both for the spun yarn and the cloth made from it. Threads of the very finest quality have been found in the ancient tombs of Egypt; linen was described in the first century by the Roman historian, Pliny.
See *Fine Counts; Flax – Linum usitatissimum; Irish Linen; Linen Count; Tow Yarns*

Linen Count The number of leas containing 274.3m (300yd) required for 0.45kg (1lb).

Linseed Flax Varieties of flax cultivated for seed production.

Linseed Oil The seeds remaining after the rippling process during flax preparation yield up to 30 per cent linseed oil. The residue in the oil presses, combined with the seed husk, is used for cattle fodder.

Lint The term applied to flax when prepared for spinning. In olden times the waste material from flax was used for tinder. Lint is also the name given to a soft material used for dressing wounds.

Llama *Sp Lama Glama*: A member of the South American camel family. It thrives in the highlands where the pasture is thin. Raised in Peru and Argentina. A beast of burden that can carry equal to its own weight; in earlier times it was the only beast of burden until the Spaniards brought the horse. The wild form of the llama is called the guanaco.

Llama wool is easy to spin, it is long, fine, very dense and without grease or crimp. The fibre has more uniformity than alpaca; the scales are not so developed and it is not as silky or as strong. The staple length varies from 12.7cm to 28cm (5 to 11in). Llama are usually clipped every 12 to 18 months, with a yield of approximately 1.35kg to 2.70kg (3 to 6lb) per clip. Colouring varies; cream, grey, brown and black. There is often colour variation within a fleece. Spin as Alpaca.

Lock A tuft of wool taken from a fleece. The wool divides and forms into separate locks; usually the tips are joined due to weathering. A lock of wool may comprise of thousands of individual fibres. The locks are the staple (see Plate 19). See *Crimp; Staple*

Loft Also known as *hand* and sometimes referred to as *lofty*. This term is used to describe the way a lock of superior wool will open up in the hand with either gentle pulling or slight pressure. The individual fibres should separate easily and cleanly into an open arrangement of equal density throughout.

Long Draw See *Draw – Long*

Loop Yarn A fancy yarn, comprising a twisted core with an effect yarn wrapped around it, which produces a wavy outline to the surface.

Lot A parcel of wool that has been catalogued and offered as one line.

Lustre (degree of) The amount of the sheen or gloss on certain fibres, especially long wools, where the light is reflected more directly by the larger outside scales.

Lustre Wools Wools that have a long shiny staple, for example, the Leicester and Lincoln breeds of sheep.

ral Fibres · Minor's Head · Miscuit · Misti · Mohai ... ry Tree ·
ibres · Minor's Head · Miscuit · Misti · Mohair · Mc ... e · Mule
ral Fibres · Minor's Head · Miscuit · Misti · Mohai ... ry Tree ·

Maidens Sometimes called *sisters*.
See *Spinning – Learning to Spin*

Manmade Fibres This is the general term for all fibres that are produced from some form of raw material, whether cellulosic or chemical. The two main groups are regenerated fibres and synthetic fibres. They are made generally by forcing a chemically produced liquid through the fine holes of a jet, to form filaments. These are stretched and twisted into a filament yarn. Alternatively, many thousand filaments are gathered into a loose rope called a 'tow' and cut up into short lengths called 'staple fibres'. These are then carded or combed, just as cotton or wool, for spinning into yarns. Polypropylene fibre, a type of synthetic fibre, is more usually extruded as a strip rather than as filaments, and then split to form yarns.

REGENERATED FIBRES are a group of manmade fibres processed from naturally occurring cellulose materials, predominantly wood chips. The principal fibres in this group are *viscose* fibres. They were the first to be produced on a commercial scale at the beginning of this century, following the invention, patented in 1889 by Count Hilaire de Chardonnet, of a method of dissolving cellulose with chemicals into a viscous fluid. This fluid was forced through the fine holes of a jet to form filaments, which solidified into fine threads, much as silk is produced by the silkworm. These fibres were originally known as rayon, or artificial silk.

Viscose fibres in new and modified forms are still of major importance and until the 1960s were produced in larger quantities than all other manmade fibres put together. *Acetate* fibres were a later development, using cotton linters as the cellulose raw materials. Commercial production began around 1920. *Triacetate* fibres, chemically similar to acetate, were developed in the UK in the 1950s.

SYNTHETIC FIBRES are a group of manmade fibres processed from chemically synthesised polymers generally derived from petroleum. The first type to be produced commercially was *nylon* (now more commonly termed *polyamide*) – developed in the USA and launched in 1939. The next major type was *polyester* developed in the UK and produced on a large scale from 1955 onwards. Today, more polyester fibre is produced internationally than any other fibre. The third major synthetic fibre, *acrylic* was developed in Germany in the 1940s. *Polypropylene* fibres were introduced in the mid-fifties and have

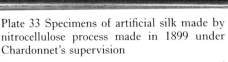

Plate 33 Specimens of artificial silk made by nitrocellulose process made in 1899 under Chardonnet's supervision

Plate 34 (*right*) Group of early apparatus used in making viscose, rayon including first spinning box, first flexible spindle and first viscose pump

grown substantially in importance in recent years. There are now hundreds of types of the various synthetic fibres produced worldwide and under different manufacturers' brand names.

Spinning methods using manmade fibres are similar to using natural fibres, eg the drafting zone is determined by the fibre length; the fibres can be spun as natural ones, however, care must be taken not to overtwist. Manmade fibres are especially useful for those people who are allergic to natural fibres, including those with certain chest conditions.

Marl Yarn Yarn comprising of mixed colours.

Matchings Similar qualities of fleece from several similar fleeces. Can be obtained from a specialist supplier and are obviously more expensive then.

Matt Become entangled.

Matted Also known as *cotted wool*. Wool that has become felted on the sheep's back, often caused by a bad season or disease.

Mawata Silk Also called *caps, silk flakes, bonnets, hankies*, etc. A Japanese word for expanded silk cocoons, frequently called wadding. The softened, degummed, pierced cocoons are pulled into a solid sheet form, then dried over a frame. They were never prepared in the mills for spinning; they make elegant inner linings for garments, jewellery cases, quilts, etc. Mawata takes several forms:

SILK FLOSS BATTING which come in sheets about 223.5cm × 152cm × 0.7cm (88in × 60in × ¼in) and weighing approximately 170g (6oz); used as linings for winter kimonos, etc.

SILK SQUARES contain the entire fibre from one cocoon. There is a dense place inside the cocoon where the silkworm did its last spinning. The fibre is very fine (*bassinett*) and breaks easily. The outside edge of the square, where it is very shiny, represents the reelable part.
   A pound of mawata should contain approximately 800 squares.

BOMBYX MORI (silkworm genus) MAWATA SILK CAPS: These are produced by using degummed cocoons and shaping them over a ceramic mould, then removing to dry by hanging up. They produce, if expanded evenly, a much more uniform fibre than found in a mawata square (hankie). Caps vary in weight from 28.4g to 85g (1oz to 3oz) and may consist of anything from 50 to 200 cocoons.

TUSSAH MAWATA SILK CAPS (also called *tusser, tussore* from the Sanskrit for 'shuttle') these are made from wild silk cocoons, of the oak-feeding *Antherea mylitta* from Northern China. The variety of tan tones are a result of the species of moths and the diet. This silk has great strength and is very durable.

METHOD To make mawata: cocoons, whole or pierced, are softened in an alkaline solution, but not fully degummed.
   Dissolve 1tsp washing soda in approx 2.27*l*–3.39*l* (2 to 3qts) of water for each 56g (2oz) of cocoons. Place a lid on the container to keep cocoons under the water. Heat very slowly to 90°C (195°F); the water should have a pH of 9. Simmer until cocoons become soft and collapse; this could take an hour or longer. Cool, then place the

cocoons in a pan of hand hot water large enough to work in. The cocoons must be kept submerged. Place hands in the water and, using the thumbs, open up a cocoon and remove the pupa. Using thumbs and finger tips, work from the centre and expand the cocoon into 20.4cm to 25.4cm (8in to 10in) square. Remove from the water lay either on paper or a towel, or stretch over a 20.4cm to 25.4cm (8in to 10in) frame, or, if making a *cap*, stretch over an inverted bowl. As the water cools, add more hot water, otherwise the silk will become difficult to expand. Treat each cocoon in the same way and stack them. They must become fully dry before using.

To use: take one square and, with thumb and index fingers in the corner, gently pull into a rectangle about 12.7cm × 60.9cm (5in × 24in). Now take your fingers and make an opening in the middle, gently pull apart into a rectangle going in the opposite direction. This circular roving, with noils evenly distributed, should now be continually drawn around with the hands approx 30.5cm (1ft) apart until of the required thickness. It can then be broken at the weakest place. This roving, without any spinning, can be used for knitting and weaving or can be spun. Use as little twist as possible for the project if softness is required. It requires no further degumming. Set twist of spun singles and plied yarns by spraying with warm water while the yarn is on the reel (or skeiner). Allow to dry before removing.

Bombyx mori caps: each layer of cap comprises several cocoons. To use, each layer must be separated as thinly as possible.

Method: one hand should be placed inside the cap and take hold of the top centre; using the other hand on the outside, start to pull a layer from top centre by pulling the hands apart; during this movement the cap should reverse itself as the newly pulled layer may not free itself from the cap. To achieve the parting, hold the cap edges with one hand and the new layer with other hand and using a sharp movement snap them apart. Continue to separate in the same way; the cap will keep reversing. Each separated layer is then treated as for *mawata squares*. The resulting roving should be carefully formed into swirls on paper to prevent tangling, and can then be spun.

An alternative method of spinning using silk caps is to open out the cap onto a table; the cap should be circular and comprise several layers. Separate the layers carefully into workable thickness. Place an umbrella type swift in a vertical position and cover with a smooth cloth. Lay the silk over this, arranging it evenly, with the cap hanging over the sides. Place on the left of the spinner at the wheel, and pull down a piece from the edge of the cap; twist slightly and join to the leader yarn. A long draw-out triangle will be formed. Using the right hand to lead the twist up to the triangle, begin to treadle; when the twist reaches the drawing-out triangle, pinch with the right hand to control the twist and pull the hand back towards the orifice which draws out more supply from the triangle. The spun yarn will wind onto the bobbin. The left hand is used to keep the draw-out smooth and regular, and to, when necessary, move around the cap. The right hand continues as described back and forth in a sweeping action.

TUSSAH CAPS, which are made from cocoons spun in semi-cultivated conditions, will contain dust and debris. These can be washed before using, or sometimes a gentle shaking is all that is required. They tend to be easier to take apart than *Bombyx mori caps* and have fewer layers than the white ones; useful for students learning the process. They are expanded as *Bombyx mori* caps into rovings.

Plate 35 a) and b) mawata; c) brick of silk; d) cocoon; e) cap of silk

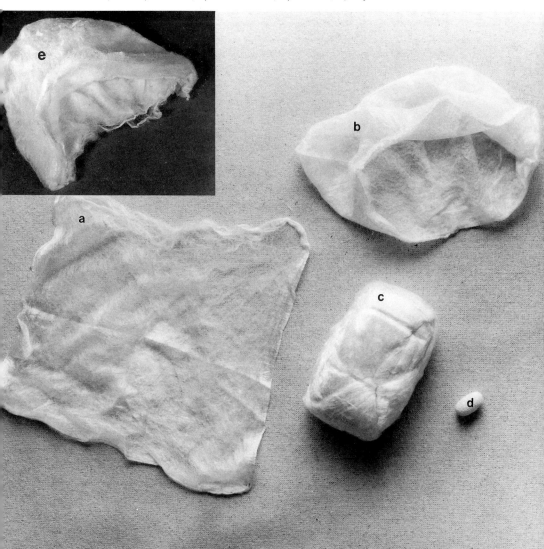

Meche A spun silk, soft, long stapled and white in colour.

Medullated Fibres Fibres that possess a medulla or core of air-filled cells. Hairy fibres have a coarse medulla and are difficult to dye.

Mercerisation – Cotton A process discovered by John Mercer in 1844 whereby combed cotton yarns are treated with a solution of caustic soda. This causes the fibres to swell and fill the air spaces. Mercerising improves the dyeing capability and also increases the lustre, but yarns treated in this way tend to lose the natural warmth and softness. Horace Low, in 1889, discovered that stretching the swollen materials, and then washing off, increased their lustre.

Merino Sheep Fine woolled sheep developed by the Spaniards around the twelfth century. Most of today's flocks have derived from this breed either directly or indirectly. Merino rams usually carry horns, the ewes do not. Strains of merino exist without horns. It has been famous for centuries for the fineness of the wool, and is the most important wool-producing breed of sheep in the world. The fleece is fine, it felts easily and is highly crimped. A full-blooded merino sheep would produce a fleece in the 70s and upwards. It is best reared in a dry climate; when the atmosphere is more moist, the wool becomes coarser. The greatest numbers are in Australia, South Africa and South America.

Plate 36 Merino Sheep

164

BRIEF HISTORY: in early Spain there were two types of sheep management; those which stayed in one area throughout the year and the migratory sheep, the *transhumantes*, which were the merino that were moved in large flocks, sometimes as many as 3,000, twice a year in very long journeys both north and south. These animals were owned mainly by the Crown, the monasteries and the nobility. They were grazed along the route, which was not popular with those whose grass they used. There were four main types of migratory sheep:

- 1 *The escurial type* were mainly royal flocks, which produced beautifully crimped fine wool.
- 2 *The Paular type*: these were associated with the Carthusian monastry at Paular. The fleece had very little surface felt and was soft and compact.
- 3 *The negrette type* were large animals with wool on their faces. The rams had very large horns. The wool was short and the animals had large folded skins.
- 4 *The infantado type* was similar to the negrette, however the rams' horns were closer set.

For a long time foreign sale of fine woolled sheep from Spain was forbidden then, in 1765, exportation was permitted to Saxony (East Germany). A further exportation occurred in 1774, again to Saxony. The sheep were of the *escurial* type. By 1802 there were 4,000 pure bred merinos in Saxony. In 1768 importations into Silesia from Spain occurred and in 1811 followed importations of *infantado* and *negrette* strains.

The Silesia merinos developed longer staple than the Saxony, although nearly as fine. The famous *Lichnowski* stud developed as a result of importations of negrette sheep by Maria Theresa, Empress of Austria. Between 1770 and 1801 Infantado sheep were imported to France and as a result Louis XVI's stud farm at Rambouillet was created. The Rambouillet type had big frames and very heavy fleeces, although not as fine as the Saxony types. These Rambouillet were a strong influence on merino development in North and South America and have extended all over the world. In 1791 a small flock of negrette was imported to England; it did not, however, prosper and was sold in 1804. Some animals were bought by Captain John MacArthur in 1797, who as a result became renowned for his influence on the early development of Australian wool. The merino was effactually introduced into the USA in 1802, followed by further very large importations. Merino breeding was, to a degree, concentrated in the state of Vermont; the type produced had large bodies, with a strong greasy fleece and large areas of wrinkled loose skin. The very wrinkled merino types are very difficult to shear and many double cuts occur. See *Botany Wool; Superfine Wool*

Metric Count A system applied to Continental yarns. It is the number of kilometre hanks per kilogram, ie the number of 496 yard hanks per pound.

Micron System This measures the diameter of the fibre in microns. 1 micron = 1/1000mm

Mildew See *Storing Fleece*

Mill Carding See under *Carding*

Milling See *Felting; Fulling*

Mineral Fibres SILVER: used since ancient times. King Herod of Judea had a tunic made entirely of silver.
GOLD: spun in England from the Iron Age. Used in a cloth found in the tomb of a Belgic chief. The Romans spun it also; a burial discovered in Rome in 1544 included a garment and pall holding 36lb of gold. See *Asbestos*

Mink *Mustela lutreola* (European mink) and, more important, the North American *M. vison* has two coats, the colouring dark brown to black. It is very soft.

Minor's Head Accelerating head for the great wheel, invented by Amos Minor around 1803, and comprising a small second wheel and drive belt; this increases the spindle speed.
See *Great Wheel*

Miscuit The French meaning 'half-done'. Silk which has been dyed in a half degummed condition.

Misti A crossbreed from a male alpaca and a female llama.

Moche Pronounced 'mosh', this term means a bale of raw silk as imported.

Mohair There are two claims as to the origin of the name *mohair*. The first states it was named after the old Turkish province of *Angora* now *Ankara*; the Angora goat was first domesticated there. The second states that the name comes from the Arabic *mukhayyar*; this is also used for the fabric made from wool and cotton, an imitation of real mohair.
The first European record of mohair was in 1554. In 1838 it was introduced into South Africa. The Angora goat was one of the first

Fig 29 *MINORS HEAD*:
a) accelerating wheel, short belt goes around pulley groove and down to the groove in the spindle d)
b) main drive belt to the wheel
c) uprights are longer than on a direct drive; they turn to adjust tension on the accelerating pulley
d) see a)
e) Spindle
f) leather bearings
g) screws in the uprights to adjust the second belt tension
h) flange
i) head post.

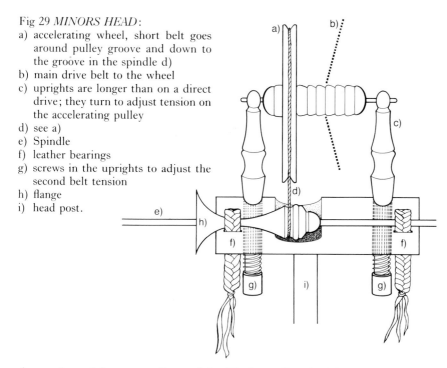

domesticated by man. Reared in Turkey, South Africa, Texas and California the animals have small heads, floppy ears, large bodies and short legs. The male has large twisted horns. Mohair is the yarn spun from the long, silky, lustrous strong hair of an Angora goat. Usually white in colour, it dyes well and resists dirt due to the smoothness of the fibre. It has hardly any felting qualities, although it does have a tendency to matt when wet. Mohair can be fine or coarse; it is graded according to the age of the animal. A kid will grow the finest hair and as the age progresses it becomes coarser and cheaper. A cross-section of the fibres shows an oval shape that can make processing difficult. The average length of the hair is 10.3cm to 25.4cm (4 to 10in), although it can grow to a length of 30.5cm (12in) according to whether it is shorn twice a year, as in the USA (which then tends to be on the short side); if grown especially for handspinning and shorn only once a year the length will be improved. Grows on average about 10.3cm to 15.3cm (4 to 6in) in six months. Raw mohair is not always available and commercially prepared mohair tends to have a large reduction in the natural waves. It is sometimes classified in the USA as *flat lock, fluffy fleece* and *tight lock*. This simply refers to the degree of wave in the locks; some locks have tight curls.

WASHING RAW MOHAIR: mohair appears in its raw state as either greyish or with a dull yellow colouring, but it becomes white once it

167

has been washed. If matted with dirt, soak overnight in warm water and washing soda. Wash with a detergent as for wool, adding a few drops of vinegar in the rinse to neutralize the soda and finish with a clear rinse. Sometimes small flakes of oil remain, these should card out. The mohair should be handled carefully to avoid breakage, otherwise it can produce short fibres in the finished garment. It is advisable to let the fibres rest during the various stages of processing.

SPINNING MOHAIR: allow to warm to room temperature before handling. Add slightly more twist than wool, although if it is too tightly spun it will be heavy. Can be spun just damp, after washing, as a means of control or, if it becomes dry, or is commercially prepared, spray with water from an atomiser. Can be spun as woollen or worsted, determined by the length available.

COMBED MOHAIR: after combing, spin, using the folded method over the right forefinger and draw-out. The drawing-out triangle will be long and the yarn produced semi-worsted. The short fibres that remain after the combing can be carded and spun as semi-woollen. Mohair kid is very soft and short-stapled, so make it into rolags and spin using a long draw. Mohair is sometimes spun in a loop form with the loops well spaced, if they are to be woven. The weaver can then produce a raised surface by brushing. Alternatively, a beautiful fine cloth can be woven from mohair yarn. Mohair is excellent for blending with most other fibres. With wool it produces a silky surface.

After spinning, skein off, dip in water to which has been added a few drops of lemon juice. Hang in skeins to dry, weighted. Can also be brushed to raise the surface whilst held on a swift, using a brush dipped in hot water.

Sometimes mohair is confused with the yarn from the Angora rabbit. Oriental mohair is called *camlet*, sometimes written as *camelot*; originally made from camels' hair, it is now made from a combination of hair, wool and/or silk.

Moit Vegetable matter, for example hay, twigs etc, in a fleece.

Molecular Crimp Each separate fibre type is comprised of chains of molecules; some fibres with shorter chains than others. Fibres having a larger molecular chain will be stronger than those with shorter chains. The molecular structure is firmly established, therefore when changes are imposed to affect this, it changes the fibre and therefore its feel. The molecular structure of wool is similar to a coiled spring, therefore this will enhance the springy texture.

Monofilament A length or strand of fibre that has been extruded, and is not composed of various lengths of fibre twisted together.

Montmorillonite A whitener used by Navajo Indians. It is a finely ground clay in which the white wool is rinsed; when the yarn is dry the powder falls out.

Moorit Also called *moor red* and is the soft warm red brown colour associated with a Shetland fleece.

Mother-of-All See *Spinning – Learning to spin; U-Flyer*

Moths The clothes moth is one of many insects which attack fibres. The larvae attack the sulphur-containing fibres. Wool is their preference, however, they do eat other fibres which they are unable to digest. Protection can be achieved by the use of moth balls and similar products. If a fleece has become contaminated it can be placed in a freezer, which will kill the offenders.

Mudag The Highland Scots kept their *rolagan* in an oval basket, the *mudag*, which had a hole in the centre of its side for the passage of wool when spinning. The hole may have had the same function as a *diz* in combing.

Mulberry Drawn Silk It is a cultivated silk with a shiny surface. Originating in China, it is the most important of the silks. It is reeled direct from the cocoons, in one continuous thread.
See *Silk*

Mulberry Tree Trees of the genus *Morus*, from which silkworm (*Bombyx mori*) feed. Whilst silkworms will eat lettuce leaves, this will often result in their not completing their life-span, or if they do, the silk will be very inferior to that produced by silkworms fed on mulberry leaves.

The mulberry tree produces leaf buds in May and continues to bear leaves into the autumn. The fruit of the mulberry is rather like a fleshy, slightly rough textured blackberry. There are various species – the *Morus rubra* has red berries, and the *Morus nigra* black berries. The Japanese grow *Morus alba*, a mulberry which has white berries. The original mulberry tree grew fairly tall, but today to facilitate harvesting, scientists have developed a tree that grows nearer to the ground. The quality of the growth is carefully monitored; good quality foliage produces as an end product, good quality silk. Tons of leaves have to be gathered and chopped up to provide food for many thousands of silkworms. In Japan, the main silk-producing country, the leaves are collected by the women and placed into baskets strapped to their backs.
See *Sericulture*

Mule In 1779, Samuel Crompton, using ideas of Hargreave's *jenny* and Arkwright's *water frame*, invented a spinning machine which he called a *mule* because it was a cross between these two. It still had the intermittent motion of the great wheel, however.

Mungo A manufactured wool made from wool waste, eg rags etc. It is obtained by the mechanical process of pulling the fabrics apart. The rags are classified according to how easily they can be torn apart; due to the milling, some are more heavily milled than others. The soft rags are pulled into *shoddy*, the hard rags into *mungo*; within these are differing groups, eg fine wools and coarse wools. Because of the poor condition of the materials used, only a short staple length results. The loose fibres are mixed with a small percentage of fresh wool and respun. The cloth made from this yarn is neither strong nor warm. See *Re-manufactured Materials*

Musa Plant See *Abaca* (also called *manila hemp*)

Mushy Wool that has been well weathered, resulting in excessive waste, and in it lacking in character.

Musk-Ox *Ovibos moschatus* are heavy animals with downward curving horns and found wild in Greenland and North America. They are being re-established in Alaska and domesticated in an attempt to bring back from almost extinction. They are not related to oxen but are almost an intermediate between sheep and oxen. Their thick coat consists of a very long stapled, dark brownish-black hair which reaches almost to the ground. Underneath this protective covering is an undercoat of down comprising fine, soft, light brown hairs with a fibre structure similar to cashmere, camel down and vicuna. As with the camel, this undercoat of down insulates the animal against the cold. Musk-oxen shed their down during the spring through the guard hairs. The Eskimo name for the soft fine down from domesticated musk-oxen is *qiviut*. To spin, remove the guard hairs, tease and spin as cashmere inserting a fair amount of twist. A very rare fibre.

and Flax · Niddy Noddy · Noggs · Noils · Noily Wo   *n · Nav*
d Flax · Niddy Noddy · Noggs · Noils · Noily Wool ·   *Navajo*
and Flax · Niddy Noddy · Noggs · Noils · Noily Wo   *n · Nav*

Nankeen See *Brown Cotton*

Navajo Plying A technique to enable making a 3-ply yarn from one single yarn.

TECHNIQUE: place one bobbin of singles yarn onto a lazy kate. Tie the end to the leader yarn from the orifice with a loop. Now proceed as if making a chain in crochet, or chaining a warp. Hold the first loop open with the thumb and third finger of the right hand; with the forefinger pull through a length of the singles yarn to form a second loop measuring approximately 15cm (6in); as the forefinger pulls the loop through, release the thumb and third finger on the first loop to hold open the second loop for the forefinger to pull through the third loop. Release the thumb and third finger for the forefinger to pull through the next loop, and continue in this way with the thumb and third finger holding each loop for the forefinger to bring through the next loop. Co-ordination is essential, as the left hand has to control the twist and feed the plied yarn onto the bobbin, whilst the right hand has to continue to form the chain. The wheel is turned clockwise or anti-

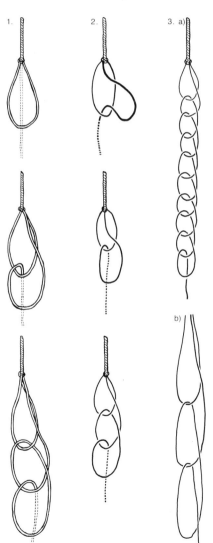

Fig 30 *NAVAJO PLYING*: Column 1, enlarged loops. Dotted lines indicate the strand to bring through each time; Column 2, stages of plying in singles; Columns 3, a) chain before twist is inserted. When forming, each chain should measure at least 15.3cm (6in). The chains in the diagram have been reduced in size to assist in the clarification of the method; 3b) a more accurate shaping of the chain before plying

171

clockwise according to the twist required. If difficulties are experienced in obtaining co-ordination and rhythm, a useful means of practising, before going onto the wheel, is to tie the end of a ball of string into a 15cm (6in) loop and attach it to a door handle or something similar. Practice the movements of the three fingers of the right hand in the sequence of forming the loops, making sure that the loops are of the same size. Once this has been mastered, it is easier to transfer to the wheel, as the right hand can then almost be forgotten and the concentration directed to the twist and feeding in.

Navajo Spinning Spinning and weaving are a part of the Navajo history and traditions. The Navajo word for 'teach' is 'show', which many teachers in the craft of handspinning would be wise to copy. The Navajo blankets are thought to have originated about 1780, the techniques possibly learned by the Navajos from their Pueblo neighbours as they travelled southwards. The true Navajo blanket is, by tradition, made from their spun yarns in colours of white, grey, black and red. In the past the blankets were much finer than today's examples. The Navajos drew the yarn across a piece of sandstone or corncob to remove any irregularities; a practice which dates back to prehistoric times, proved by the discoveries of grooved sandstone in the ruins. The earlier colourings of Navajo blankets/rugs were soft and natural; once commercial dyes became available to them, the colouring, in relation to the traditional colouring, was lost. Natural dyed blankets fetch a much higher price than *aniline-dyed* ones.

The Indians used *Dupont dyes* in the 1930s, but because acetic acid was required as a mordant and this was not safe in their *hopi* (house) with children and livestock there, they found difficulty in using the dyes. Old Navajo Dyes, manufactured by Wells & Richardson, were excellent to use as they matched the traditional colours of the old blankets.

Bound closely to the Navajo religion are sandpaintings. Here, the design for the tapestries is carefully outlined on the ground, covered in sand, and the design is filled in using dry paints and sand. The designs are very intricate; this is the main reason why Navajo weaving cannot even copy accurately the many colours incorporated in the sandpainting. Their religion teaches that if a sandpainting is made into a tapestry, deep significance abounds. Once the sandpainting has been used, it is destroyed.

Navajo blankets called *yei* (*yay*) *blankets*, which are based on sandpaintings, fetch a very high price. *Yeibichai* (pronounced *yaybichai*) blankets have designs that represent the Navajo gods.

The Navajo spin their yarns with a large heavy wooden spindle approximately 91.5cm (36in) long, with a whorl 10.3cm to 15.3cm (4 to 6in) in diameter, which is supported on the ground on the right of the spinner (if she is right-handed). The spinner sits on a stool or on the ground. The top of the shaft of the spindle should rest lightly against the right thigh and on the inside of the right thumb with all four fingers over it. The fibre supply is joined to the leader cord, which is not taken under the whorl but is wrapped clockwise around the shaft above the whorl. The spindle is twirled towards the body producing rhythm between thumb and first and second fingers and the palm of the hand rolling the stem against the side of the body. The fibre supply is held in the left hand, between thumb and first finger, with the palm turned uppermost. As the spindle is rotated up the body, the fibre is attenuated and, where necessary, jerked to produce desired yarn. The first spinning is usually a loose twist, approximately the thickness of a finger. It is then wound onto the lower part of the spindle, by holding the spindle away from the body in a vertical position and rotating it to wind on the yarn, leaving enough to come up the shaft to the tip to continue spinning. Practice is necessary to produce co-ordination of hand and spindle.

Students learning the art of Navajo spinning usually tend to hold the fibre supply too near to the spindle. The further away the attenuation is, the greater the uniformity of the yarn. Never pull sideways, always pull lengthways. It is a common fault, at first, that

Plate 37 View over spinner's shoulder, of thumb position while Navajo spindle spinning. The spindle is rolled back on the thigh by curling the fingers around the spindle in a rolling movement

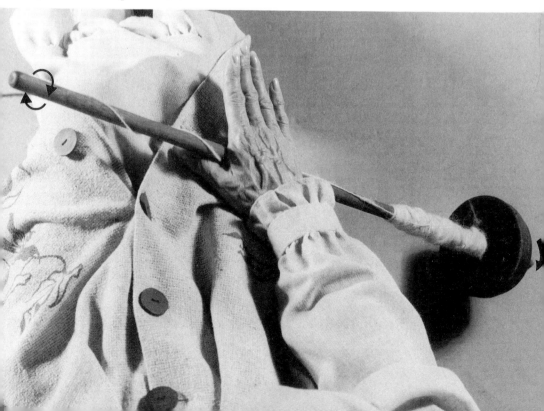

the fibres may become caught between two twists; if this occurs, cease to rotate the spindle, lay it against the thigh and using both hands disentangle the caught fibres. When the spindle is full, the spinning process may be repeated, to reduce the lightly twisted fibres to the required yarn size; it may be necessary to respin several times. When spinning weft, a loose twisting action of the thumb and forefinger is used at the same time that friction is pulling along the line of the staple from the spindle. With warp, the loose twist is held lightly between the thumb and forefinger with a twisting action; the left hand is nearer to the spindle than for weft and the spindle should be rotated at greater speed to impart a tighter twist. The cone of spun yarn above the whorl can be removed and wound into a skein.

The Navajo, when the spindle is full of spun yarn, wind it into a skein by placing it under the moccasin and up and over a bent knee. If a very tightly twisted warp yarn has been spun it is not skeined, but is wound into a large hard ball to contain the twist. This remains unwashed. The Navajo produce 2, 3 and 4 ply yarns which, whilst used as an edging for their blankets, are never used for their weaving.

PLYING METHOD – 2 ply: take two ends of spun yarn from separate supplies and tie both together to the leader yarn above the spindle whorl. Wrap the two strands around the shaft of the spindle and place over the left hand fingers. Roll the spindle on the thigh away from the body (in reverse to the original spin), feed the yarn from around the four fingers of the left hand. As it is plied, wind onto the shaft above the whorl.

Navajo Tea A plant whose stems, when used for dyeing, produce a pinkish tan colour. The Navajo Indians can use it rarely now, as it is in very short supply.

Needlepoint When spinning for a needlepoint project, it is essential to spin using the worsted method with a strong twist; the continual drawing through the canvas can quickly cause fraying.

Net Silk Old English term for *thrown silk*; this is the choicest yarn. The raw silk filaments, or strands, are processed into yarns by twisting and folding or both. The term is also used to describe fabrics produced from net silk.

Nettles Several varieties of nettle are grown for their fibres, these include those from the family *Urticaceae*. The stinging nettle (*Urtica dioica*), very common in the USA, is a fibre source obtained through the flax process; the resulting fibres tend to be rather weak and a poor yield. Nettle fibres tend to be grey or cream in colour. Ramie, obtained from the bast of *Boehmeria nivea*, a woody Asian plant, stingless and with broad leaves, is obtained by decortication as retting is not suitable. See *Ramie*

New Zealand Flax *Phormium tenax* is not a bast fibre. It is obtained from long, fan shaped leaves of a native lily. The fibres were already in use by the Maoris when the first settlers arrived. It grows both wild and cultivated. After three years the plant sends up a 4.6m (15ft) seed stalk. After six months the fronds reach maturity reaching 5cm to 7.6cm (2 to 3in) wide, 0.91m to 2.7m (3 to 9ft) long. The raw material in the leaves was obtained by being drawn over the edge of a shell and then washed in a stream. The prepared cream-coloured fibre was not unlike heavy quality flax. Similar processes were used on abaca, agave and yucca.

Niddy Noddy Also referred to as a *cross-reel* and, in Scotland, as *crois iarna*. A simple device for winding yarn. Usually 45.5cm (18in) long, making a skein 1yd long on one side; if both sides are used the measurement is doubled. A niddy noddy cannot be particularly accurate as the devices tend to vary according to both design and locality. One end of the arm on a niddy noddy allows the easy removal of the skein. It gains its name from the rocking movement back and forth, which is employed whilst winding the yarn.

Plate 38 Winding the spun yarn onto a niddy-noddy, the arrows indicate direction of winding

METHOD: hold the niddy noddy with the left hand, then proceed to wind the yarn (see arrowing), tilting the niddy noddy back and forth in a rocking movement to facilitate the winding. Finish the skein by tying the two loose ends together. Then tie the skein in four places, using natural wool or yarn, and allow room for movement. Form into a skein twist. If skeining from a single band scotch tension wheel, the bobbin of plied yarn is left on the flyer with the minimum of brake-band tension.
See *Skeiner*

Noggs The horizontal rows of wires per one inch, counted as the first row of twill in card clothing.

Noils The short fibres remaining on wool combs after preparation of *tops*. Can be used by the handspinner. Noils are the result of either 'second cut' shearing, or the poor diet of the sheep causing breakage, or of carding. They are also used in commercial woollen spinning and the felt trade. See *Combing*

Noily Wool Wool that has a large proportion of noils.

Nubs Also referred to as *neps, nips, nubbs,* etc. Often formed by learner spinners by accident and not design, these are small lumps or pieces of fibre alien to the fibre length being prepared. If they are used for actual yarn design, they can produce very interesting results. Nubs can be collected from carders during the carding process. Short pieces of fibre can be rolled into nubs by using the thumb and index finger. The most usual way of adding nubs is during the actual yarn formation when spinning, although they can be added during fibre preparation, usually at a final stage. Choice of method is determined by the regularity of nubs required in the yarn design. Uniformity can be produced to a degree whilst actually spinning the yarn. For a more abstract effect it is easier to introduce nubs at the fibre preparation stage. If adding them whilst spinning, it is necessary to ensure that fibres protruding from the nubs attach securely to the fibre in the yarn, otherwise they will fall out. When they occur in cotton, they are usually the result of immature, or dead, cotton hairs. When referring to flax, such lumps are naps.

Numerical Count System In the case of wool.
See *Yarn Counts*

rganzine · Orifice · Orkney Wheel · Overspin · Oxid
nzine · Orifice · Orkney Wheel · Overspin · Oxidisat
rganzine · Orifice · Orkney Wheel · Overspin · Oxid

Measi
asurei
Measi

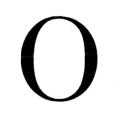

Objective Measurement A system introduced in recent years in Australia, New Zealand and South Africa for grading wools. See *Sale by Sample*

Occupational Therapy ASSESSMENT OF DISABLED PEOPLE AND SPINNING: spinning, whether with a hand spindle or on a wheel, is excellent for various disabling conditions. Before embarking on the craft, it is essential to obtain professional advice as to its suitability in relation to a client's particular personal disablement. It is wrong to generalise, as two people with the same condition may be affected quite differently; spinning may be suitable for one and not the other.

EQUIPMENT: spinning wheels can be costly for the individual who is possibly on a fixed income; however, when purchased for a day centre or craft class it can be shared, and also provides an opportunity for members of the group to try the craft to see if it is for them personally. Spinning wheels can usually be adapted, or converted, to meet personal needs once suitability as a craft has been determined. Double treadle wheels (see Plate 31) are comfortable to work with, especially where leg movement of the client may be weak. Electric wheels are available.

SUITABILITY AS A CRAFT: many people who have a disability are frustrated and tense; the craft of spinning, by virtue of its soothing rhythm, the use of natural materials, the creativity involved, the co-ordination of feet, hands and mind, quickly brings about complete relaxation. Often the client may have energy to expend without the physical means to do so, again, spinning can be most valuable. Being such a tactile craft, it is particularly suitable for blind or partially sighted people.

TEACHING: careful attention should be paid to planning the first lesson to ensure success otherwise clients can quickly lose interest. Make sure the wheel is secure and cannot slip on the floor. See that the lighting is good, and that the client/student is seated comfortably. Carefully consider each step and set a steady pace. When a client begins to tire, cease tuition immediately. If a group of mixed disability clients are to be involved, let each one work at their own pace until they are proficient at the task in hand. Do not leave out stroke cases; carding is possible if a right-handed hemiplegic is paired to a left-handed hemiplegic, each using the workable hand. Some clients, who

Plates 39–40 *HAND CARDING*: a right-handed hemiplegic paired with a left-handed hemiplegic, each using their workable hand (*right*) Teasing wool; a shared situation

may lack confidence, often work better if placed with a group (see Plate 40).

When teaching those who are blind or partially sighted, it is necessary to make them familiar with any equipment being used. At the early learning stages it is helpful to attach Braille labelling to the various parts, for example, on a wheel mark, mother-of-all, maidens, table, tension, etc; this will assist the client to remember the various names and thus aid the teaching. Generally, blind clients produce a far superior yarn to start with than sighted people; blindness brings a degree of isolation that can be turned to the benefit of the client, as distractions are easier to blot out if you can only hear them. Spinning lends itself to being taught in units, ie a step at a time; it is for the teacher to ensure that each stage is mastered before progressing to the next.

Whilst in an ordinary situation, not hampered by a disability, it is desirable to start with spinning on a spindle and then progress to a wheel, in the disabled area of work, this is not always possible. However, the value of studying a yarn through spindle spinning is not lost, because at a later date spindle spinning may be introduced in the form of the Navajo spindle, which is excellent in some wheelchair cases. Many crafts can be limited in what they can provide; once learned, that may be the extent to which they can be taken. They are also not always suitable for all age groups. Spinning, however, can be taken to whatever level, or extent, the individual wishes; there is almost unlimited potential. It is therefore particularly useful in a field where a person is going to be disabled for maybe a very long time and so is of continuing interest as a craft.

To date, spinning has not been considered deeply enough as a suitable subject for disabled people; with careful assessment and teaching it can assist more conditions than it would harm, and in doing so also improve the quality of life.

Oil For lubrication of a spinning wheel. See *Maintenance of a Spinning Wheel*

Spinning chair   Hebridean double-band spinning wheel   Lazy Kate

Plate 41 Parts of a spinning wheel to oil: a) treadle bar bearings – each end where the metal pins hold the bar to the front legs of the spinning wheel; b) wheel axle and groove – if the axle is not sealed because of the bearings, oil both axle and the groove it turns in; c) footman – oil at the top; d) front and back maidens – oil the bobbin bearings; e) shaft – remove bobbin and whorl, and oil the metal shaft of the flyer; f) tensioner and any wooden screws – oil occasionally to prevent locking

Oiling – Wool Early spinners used different types of substances including lard, butter, fish oil, and whale oil to oil their fleece. Olive oil, however, has long been regarded as the best for treating wool. A washed fleece should be oiled before carding to replace the natural oil removed during the scouring process. Two methods can be used.

a) add a few drops of olive oil to the teased washed fleece, then fold over the fibre mass to enclose the oil in the centre. Gently draw the fibres apart but do not handle too much as the final blending will take place naturally during the carding process.
b) if oiling a large amount of fleece, it is helpful to apply the oil using an atomiser which will produce a light even spray. Occasionally an unwashed fleece will require the addition of a little oil.

See *Emulsion – Dressing*

Open-Band Yarn One having an S-twist, ie looking up the yarn, the twist is seen to run from left to right, the opposite of *cross-band yarn*. See *S-Twist*; *Z-Twist*

Organzine Also known as *warp silk*, is a thrown silk from the best cocoons and used for warps. This has more twist than weft silk, called *tram*, which has very little twist. Organzine is made from two or more 'singles' – threads twisted in the opposite direction from the original twist. It is classed as one of the strongest and most elastic of the textile threads, taking into consideration its diameter.

Orifice See *Spinning – Learning to Spin*

Orkney Wheel In earlier times this style of wheel was referred to as *cottage wheels, German wheels* and *parlour wheels*. It is an upright flyer type wheel, very compact, with the spinning apparatus mounted above the wheel, which is constructed on the table or bench, above a treadle. A similar construction, although with two bobbin and flyer units to accommodate two spinners at a time, was designed later. These were called *gossip wheels* and *lovers' wheels*.

Overspin More than the optimum of twists in a given length of yarn; this causes snarling and often breaks.

Oxidisation Exposing the dyed material to the air in the indigo dyeing process.

ing · Plucked · Plying · Poll-Lock · Prepotency · Prob.
Plucked · Plying · Poll-Lock · Prepotency · Problem
ing · Plucked · Plying · Poll-Lock · Prepotency · Prob.

P

Pure Br
e Bred
Pure Br

Pack, Wool A traditional unit weight, 108.9kg (240lb) of wool.

Panteur The frame on which goat or calf skin was stretched to cover card (for carders) in France during the eighteenth century.

Pari A French term referring to the weight of raw silk before boiling-off. Par weighting is the weighting which returns degummed silk to its raw (pari) weight.

Partitioning The term used when fleece is divided into various qualities.

Pasteur, Louis Was responsible for the elimination of *pébrine* the most deadly of all silkworm diseases in 1865, which nearly wiped out the French silk industry. He proved *pébrine* was hereditary, a contagious blood infection; therefore by careful selection of disease-free moths for the supply of the next season's eggs, the problem was eradicated. The method advocated by Pasteur, known as *cellular*, is the foundation of present day practice. It consisted, after fertilization, of placing the moth into a small ring or cotton bag; there she lays her eggs and dies. The *graineur*, using a pestle and mortar, crushes a part of the body and examines the corpuscles under a microscope. If pébrine infection is present, it shows as minute oval bodies in the juices; the infected moth and eggs are immediately destroyed.
See *Sericulture*

Pick Fleece The best quality fleeces whatever the class.

Pied Wool See *Fellmongering* – section on *Sweating Method*

Piece, Flax A small handful that is the unit of the scutched flax.
See *Flax*

Pieced-Up An American term meaning spliced.

Piedmont Silks These silks from Italy are considered by many to be the best silks.

Pie Pieces Pieces of skin with wool still adhering to them, cut from skins during fellmongering. See *Fellmongering*

Pilling The main cause of pilling is when the loose ends of fibre work their way out of the twist in the yarn and these ends matt together when rubbed in any way; the resulting small balls are called *pills*. In a knitted garment, pilling may occur when it is new, but after a time, with wear, the pills drop off and pilling no longer occurs.

Some loosely twisted yarns may be susceptible to pilling although not all low twist fibres pill, for example, silk and linen. Cotton will pill with a low twist, but not with a high twist.

When handspinning knitting yarn mark, in some way, the end of the yarn nearest the starter cord (this can be done when skeining). Then, when commencing knitting, start from the marked end of the handspun. Less pilling will occur in this direction. If starting from the opposite end, you will be rubbing the yarn up the wrong way.

Pina A leaf fibre from the leaves of the pineapple plant (Ananas comosus), which produces a fine silky, lustrous fibre. Can be woven into an almost transparent material.

Pinna Shell *Pinna novilis*: in the early nineteenth century, divers obtained this 'fleece from the sea'. The shells measured approximately 45.7cm (18in) in length and contained tufts of cinnamon-gold coloured hairs comprising short fibres that could be spun. The shells were attached to the sea bed by bundles of fine brown threads called *byssus* (from the Greek). Recordings were made as early as the second century AD when a pinna industry existed. Items made from the combed fibres were very warm and soft.

Pirn This has two references: it can be a bare spool onto which yarn may be wound. If before starting to spin on a great wheel a brown paper pirn is formed to build the yarn onto it makes removal of the full cop from the spindle easier. A pirn is also a wooden or paper spool that has yarn wound onto it for weaving.

Plain Wool with straight fibres that are not in keeping with the particular breed.

Planking A term used in the wool combing process where the prepared slivers are laid side by side following the same direction, on the bench.
See *Combing*

Plasticity The amount wool will extend before breaking.

Plucked Also known as *fallen wool*, is pulled from sheep that have not been slaughtered, but have died from other causes, eg during

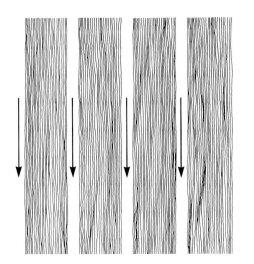  

Figs 31–2 *PLANKING*; (*right*) *PLIED YARN*: a) yarn originally spun Z-twit as a single plied 'S'-twist; b) yarn spun Z-twist as a single plied Z-twist also

lambing, etc. This does not spin or dye well and, due to its harsh handle, is never used for good quality cloth.

Ply Means a bend or fold from the French word *plier* to fold, a term used to describe the number of strands (singles) twisted together to make a required yarn, eg 2 ply comprised of two strands, 3 ply, three strands, etc.

Plying The twisting of two or more single yarns together in the opposite direction of the singles twist, ie if the original singles spun in a clockwise direction, they are then plied in an anticlockwise direction. Yarn which is plied is not twice the thickness of the original singles yarns; this is due to a certain amount of the original twist being removed during plying and thus the singles decrease in size accordingly.

Fancy yarns can be created by plying, using the singles in different ways.

A Z-twisted single plied with an S-twisted single, will give a different textured result from two Z-twists or two S-twists together because in the plying it adds twist to one and reduces twist in the other. Variations can also occur when tight singles are plied loosely or vice versa.

TPI (TWISTS PER INCH): when plying, try and obtain the same tpi as the original singles, taking into account the loss (possibly about half) caused by the reversal of the wheel direction. Usually the tighter the twist the greater the yarn strength.

183

When plying on a flyer wheel attention must be given to the twist, wind-on rates and treadling. The tension screw will require adjusting as the bobbin fills to increase the take-up, otherwise a slowing down of bobbin lead would increase the TPI.

PROBLEMS: if an overtwist occurred in various places in the original singles, this will cause twisting in the skein and a slant in the eventual knitting. The spinner should aim for evenness in both the singles and plied yarn, which will result in a well balanced skein of wool. If the singles being plied are not fed evenly into the wheel, and one is held more taut than another, this will cause the taut single to form an axis

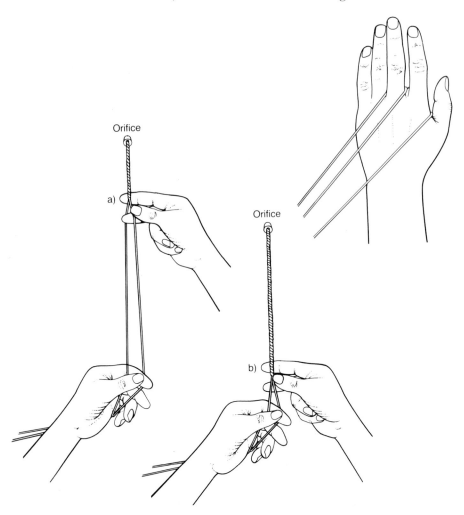

Figs 33–4 *PLYING*; (*top*) plying a three ply yarn: method for holding the singles coming from three bobbins on the lazy kate

for the second single to wrap around, with obvious results. A similar problem can arise if variations occur in the tension of the original singles, the axis can revert from one single to another.

PLYING METHOD: place two or more full bobbins onto a lazy kate (bobbin holder), the number determined by whether 2 ply, 3 ply etc, is required, the lazy kate being at the left side of the spinner. Secure the ends of the yarn to a leader yarn attached to the bobbin of the wheel, and brought out through the orifice (established spinners often adjust the tension so that it pulls the yarns directly onto the bobbin and not through the orifice. In this case the yarns are fed through the fingers of the right hand and the left hand is used to supply a constant feeding of yarn from the lazy kate). Hold the yarns being plied between the fingers of the left hand and in a direct line straight into the orifice (see *fig 33a*). The tension on the wheel should be sufficient to pull the yarn onto the bobbin. Begin to treadle in the reverse direction to the original singles spinning, and move the right hand up with the twist towards the body. At all times hold the yarns taut from the orifice to the body. When the twist reaches the left hand (*fig 33b*), pinch the plied yarns with the right hand and move it forward to permit rapid wind onto the bobbin. This will automatically pull and release more singles yarn from the lazy kate. Continue until the bobbins on the lazy kate are exhausted. From time to time check the twist and, when necessary, increase or reduce treadle action. As with ordinary spinning it will become necessary to change from one hook to another on the flyer. Account should be taken whilst plying of any differentials between the amounts of yarn on the bobbins placed on the lazy kate, the heavier bobbin will create more tension.

SKEINING: after plying, the plied yarns are wound onto a niddy noddy (skeiner) and are tied in several places and removed (see *fig 22*). It is then washed.

If plying from a cone produced by spindle spinning (eg, a great wheel), the cones will be stationary and the wind on from the tip of each cone.

PLYING ON A SINGLE BAND SCOTCH TENSION WHEEL: ply as for other wheels; however, it requires slightly more brakeband tension and faster treadling.

Poll-Lock A small lock of wool growing on the head of a sheep.

Prepotency The amount by which an individual animal can impress its characteristics onto a large proportion of progeny.

Problem	Cause and Remedy
Belt on wheel jumping	adjust alignment between drive wheel and pulleys. May also be caused if large join in the belt, eg a knot. Undo and make a neater join.
Belt on wheel slipping	a) increase tension b) the join in the drive band may be lumpy; sew the ends together c) cord may not be thick enough
Difficulty in joining the fibre supply; the ends part	a) a hairy leader yarn is easier to join onto b) open the ends of the leader and join fibre c) when spinning, do not spin to the end of the fibre supply; leave an untwisted end on which to join.
Fibres cease to draft; difficulty in drafting	a) the hands are most likely pulling at each end of the fibre length, move further apart b) the twist may have run up into the fibre supply and shortened the drawing-out triangle, which has then become less than the staple length. Cease to treadle and untwist the knotted fibres and return to the original triangle size. c) insufficient preparation of fibre d) fingers not working fast enough.
Fibres falling apart	insufficient twist has been inserted; either decrease the tension or hold back the yarn and treadle faster. On a scotch tension, decrease the tension.
Fibres matting together	fibres will become matted if held too tightly; relax and allow them to be drawn out freely.
Flyer not moving easily	the maidens may have been knocked out of alignment. Go to the end of the table on a Saxony type wheel (or the side of an upright wheel) and, holding a maiden in each hand, face the wheel, and line them up accurately.
Long draw: the yarn jumps from the hooks	the yarn was not held taut during the wind-on and, due to slackness, this caused jumping from the hooks. The yarn should be held taut until completely wound onto the bobbin.
Lumps forming in yarn	a) too many fibres in the triangle at one time; draft consistently with controlled amount of fibre b) twist entering the drafting area before the fibres are drawn out properly. Either draft more quickly or hold back twist slightly longer. c) lumps can be formed if the front hand moves to draft and twist the fibres. A fault often attributed to student spinners. The front hand should always be kept about 2.5cm to 3.3cm (1 to 1¼in) along the yarn

	behind the junction; if it pinches ahead of the twist into the drafting area this will form a slub.
Overtwisting	a) increase tension or b) draft more quickly or c) slow down treadling, or a combination of (b) and (c)
	d) increase tension on scotch tension; test for twist by relaxing the hold on the yarn so that it doubles back on itself; too many kinks show it is overtwisted.
Overtwisting and winding-on too slowly	increase tension.
Rolag becomes a bunch of fibres hard to draw	caused through gripping the rolag too tightly. The hand should be relaxed and holding the fibre supply lightly.

Single Band Wheel scotch tension system

Yarn twists and does not wind on	not sufficient tension. Tighten the brakeband tension knobs slightly. If the yarn pulls on too tightly, too much tension has been applied.
Overtwisting	a) slow down treadling
	b) yarn possibly has been held onto too long; once sufficient twist has been inserted, feed on immediately
	c) increase brakeband tension
	d) check yarn has not caught on a flyer hook.
Bobbin ceases to move	pull on the brakeband, this will often start it moving again. Increase tension as the bobbin fills.
Neither bobbin nor flyer rotates. Underspinning	tension may be too tight; reduce breakband tension, as the yarn is being pulled in too quickly. Increase treadling speed.
Single band wheel thick and thin yarn formation	this is caused by irregular drafting of fibres. Learn to be consistent and keep a constant, even number of fibres in the drafting zone.
Thinness in yarn, causing breaking	a) too few fibres in the drawing-out triangle
	b) the triangle may have become longer than the staple length
	c) the hand may be moving back too quickly. Continue to treadle and hold hand stationary, let more fibres draw out; continue spinning when the yarn is to the required thickness.
Treadling difficult	a) lessen the tension on the drive band or
	b) adjust the footman
	c) oil the wheel and the footman. Treadling should be adjusted to the rate and length of drafting and winding-on in relation to the yarn being spun.
Undertwist in yarn	a) hands are too close to the orifice and are feeding yarn in too quickly

b) tension too strong, taking the yarn in too quickly. Decrease tension on the driving band on the flyer wheel. Adjust the bobbin pulley on the scotch tension system.

Variation in twist   caused by irregular treadling. Keep an even feed-in of fibre and balanced, event readling.

Weak places in yarn   the front hand may be holding the twist back too long. Release twist to strengthen the yarn as it is drafted. Fleece may not be sorted well.

Wheel grabbing the yarn from the spinner's hand   the tension is too great, therefore inadequate twisting occurs. Reduce the tension slightly; if too loose, overtwist will result.

Wheel reversing in direction   the foot may not be placed on the footman correctly. The treadling should be at an even pace and thus keep the momentum. When starting the wheel, the crank should be a little to the right, which will make it easier to start treadling. Always try and cease to treadle with the crank in this position.

Sufficient fibre should be prepared for each spinning session to enable continuity of spinning. The rhythm is broken when stopping to prepare fibre.

Yarn winding on but no twist   both drive bands may be around bobbin whorl.

Yarn not winding on   a) yarn may be too thick for the size of the orifice

b) yarn may have a lump formed in it. Pull out, untwist the yarn and remove the lump, then recommence spinning.

c) yarn could be caught around a hook on the flyer.

d) yarn may have come off the hooks; this happens when the wheel is permitted to reverse

e) yarn may be tangled on the bobbin

f) insufficient tension

g) yarn may be incorrectly threaded; it should be over the bobbin, across the hooks, and through the top and eye of the orifice

h) a build-up of grease, dirt and dust may have occurred in the orifice, also possibly around the hooks. These places should be cleaned when necessary.

i) if the yarn is twisting but not winding onto the bobbin. Check as both bands may be around the spindle whorls.

The most likely common cause is (f). Increase tension. On a scotch tension system tighten the tension on the bobbin.

Protein Fibres Casein, groundnuts, maize and soya beans are all protein fibres and are always machine spun. Protein fibres feel warm because protein does not conduct the heat away from the body. Proteins are complex organic substances which are essential constituents of living cells. Wool is a protein.

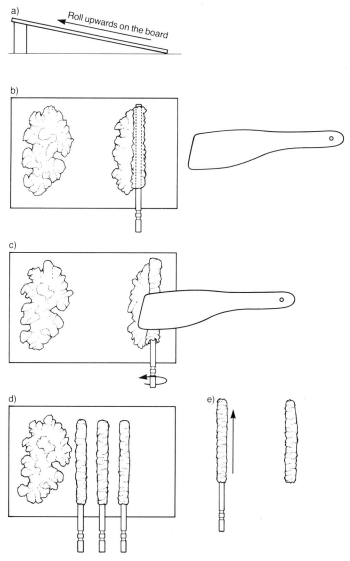

Fig 35 Making *PUNIS*: a) side view of slanting board; b) top view: pile of bowed (whipped) or carded cotton. Dowel rod lying on some of the cotton. Wooden spatula; c) rolling the cotton onto the dowel rod; d) cotton pressed around each piece of dowel; e) remove the cotton from the dowel by pushing off one end and use as a miniature rolag

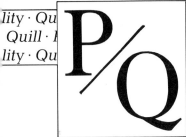

lity · Qu | Raw Wool · Reelers · Regain · Retting Pool · Rise · F
Quill · | v Wool · Reelers · Regain · Retting Pool · Rise · Rock
lity · Qu | Raw Wool · Reelers · Regain · Retting Pool · Rise · F

Pull A sample of fibres removed manually from a bulk of raw material to test for length, etc.

Pulled Wool See *Fellmongering*

Pulley The grooved whorl on the spindle of a spinning wheel.

Pulling – Flax See *Flax – Linum usitatissimum*

Pulling – Wool Removing wool from skins. The fibres are previously treated. The wool can be removed by hand or, if short in length, with a blunt knife held with both hands. If the puller is seated and removes the wool with his hands, it is referred to as 'knee pulling'. The wool is sorted by the puller as it is removed from the skin.

Punis The rolled pieces of cotton formed around a stick or piece of dowel for ease of cotton spinning.

METHOD: place a small pile of cotton that has been bowed previously, onto a board, table or smooth surface. Lay a smooth thin stick or piece of dowel rod onto the front edge of the cotton nearest to you; using a wooden spatula, place this on top of the dowel and cotton and proceed to roll gently to compress and wind the cotton onto the dowel rod. Repeat a second time to compress more tightly. Slip the compressed cotton fibres off the dowel rod and the *puni* is ready to spin. This method of preparation makes the cotton easy to handle and spin. Silk can be made into *punis* also.
See *Bowing*

Pure Bred A pure strain of animal from a recognised breed which has been kept pure for generations.

Quality When used in relation to wool, it refers mainly to the average fibre diameter.

Quill On a quill wheel, for example, a great wheel, the spinning is done at the tip of the quill, or spindle, which rotates and imparts twist. When spun, the yarn is guided by the spinner onto the spindle shaft.

R

Raddle Mark See *Branding*

Raffia A leaf fibre from the raffia palm, native to Madagascar. A coarse fibre used for making sacks, baskets, mats, etc.

To spin, soak well overnight, shake off excess water and hang as a straight strick of flax. Keep dampened during spinning. Feed in the fibres, a few at a time, until the required thickness is obtained. Skein the yarn.

Raise the Yolk See *Shearing*

Ramie Is sometimes spelt *ramee*, also called China grass (*sp Boehmeria nivea*) or *rhea* (*sp Boehmeria tenacissema*), or occasionally referred to as China linen. It is a perennial stem or bast fibre from a plant in the nettle family, *Urticaceae*, which grows in warm climates with a high rainfall. Used in China since ancient times for the domestic manufacture of what are called *grass cloths*. Ramie, which is obtained from China is called *China grass*. When India is the source, it is called *rhea*. It is harvested when the stalks turn yellow and usually produces three or four crops a year. The stems are from 91.5cm to 2.438m (3 to 8ft) high and each stem is approximately 1.3cm (½in) thick. The plants grow rapidly and have a high yield. The fibres in the stems are embedded in a gummy substance which permeates the cortical layer, making fibre extraction by the flax methods of retting and scutching very difficult. The lustrous fibre, therefore, is obtained after scraping, degumming and boiling off. (See *Decortication*).

Ramie is strong when wet, does not shrink, easily accepts dye, and resembles silk in its softness and fineness. It is suitable for blending with other fibres and, when used on its own, produces a soft lustrous yarn. It has little elasticity. It is available in roving form and as noil; the noil has a low lustre. Can be spun using the worsted spin, or as flax, jute and hemp. It is used for a variety of articles including fabrics which wrinkle less than linen, twines and high grade paper.

The Chinese prepare ramie for commerce by cutting it off close to the roots followed by peeling the fibre layers off by hand into long strips approx 1cm (¼in) wide. These are retted, scraped, then dried and sent to market. The fibres are therefore still embedded in the gum, which is removed mechanically, a decortication process. The resulting ultimates vary considerably in length, 2.5cm to 30.5cm (1 to 12in) and 25 to 75 microns in diameter.

Rams' Wool Usually stronger in quality and heavier in weight than ewes' wool.

Raw Silk The term given to the thread produced on a reeling machine. (The sericin has not been removed.) The threads from several cocoons, possibly up to eight in number, are fused together to produce a 20/22 denier.

Raw Wool Wool in its natural, dirty, unwashed state after shearing from the sheep.

Reclassing When wool is regraded to meet trade specifications.

Reel See *Bobbin*

Reelers Resembles a windmill, with prongs coming from a central axis; spun yarn is wound around the outside edges of the prongs to skein. This outside diameter determines the yardage. Yarn is usually wound directly onto the reeler from the bobbin of a spinning wheel by removing the drive band to permit easy rotation of the bobbin on the spindle. After winding onto the reeler, the skein is tied and removed ready for washing, dyeing, or whatever the requirement.

Reeling The winding of spun yarns into skeins. See *Niddy Noddy*

Reels Many styles exist, eg rotary reels; click reels; some turned by hand, others attached to spinning wheels. Their function is to provide a means of winding spun yarn. The circumference of the reels varies from area to area. See *Niddy Noddy; Reeler*

Reforzado See *Brown Cotton*

Regain The standard quantity of moisture added to completely dried out fibre in order to return it to its conditioned weight. In silk it is 11 per cent.

Re-Manufactured Materials

Are also referred to as *re-used wool* where appropriate. They are obtained by the disintegration of fabrics, mainly from old clothing and rags plus clippings from new, unused cloth. They may be all wool, or be comprised of previously re-manufactured materials, possibly with other fibre types. Whilst useful, it should be noted, that the rags require breaking up by tearing and teazing operations of a vigorous nature and, if being re-manufactured for a second time, the fibres will have already been subjected to considerable wear with accompanying deterioration. Some re-manufactured materials, by careful selection, can be incorporated in high class, good quality, woollen goods. Re-manufactured materials are usually classified into three groups according to the original cloth type from which they were obtained. Terms used to describe rags and shoddies:

Angolas – the wool and cotton are blended within the yarn

Berlins – fine woolled 'stockings' (meaning knitted rags)

cashmere – very fine-woolled (stockings)

Cheviots – wool rags of coarse quality

flannels – loosely finished rags, including blankets. These may contain some cotton or non-wool fibre.

linseys – strictly cotton warp, wool weft rags but also applied to other blended fabrics, eg 'linsey – stockings'

merinos – fine worsteds

serges – crossbred worsteds; strictly, these have a woollen weft

stockings – knitted rags

worsteds – woven fabrics made from worsted yarns, very lightly milled.

See *Extract; Mungo; Shoddy*

Re-Processed Wool Wool obtained from manufactured products, eg trade waste, clippings, etc; all new, not worn old rags. Whilst it can be labelled '100 per cent wool' or 'all wool', it will have lost its elasticity and be poorer.

Retting Also called *rotting*. See *Flax – Linum usitatissimum*

Retting-Pool Also called *routoir* or *retting-pond*. In the eighteenth century, anything people did not wish the Excise Officer to see was hidden in the retting-pool; the awful smell of the retting flax usually kept him at bay. The bundles of flax were weighted down in the water with planks on which stones were placed.

Ribbons See *Dressing a Distaff; Flax – Linum usitatissimum*

Rippler See *Flax – Linum usitatissimum*

Rippling See *Flax – Linum usitatissimum*

Rise, The A fleece starts growing again in the spring (*the rise*) and is usually clipped shortly afterwards. If the clipping is delayed for too long, then the new growth achieves a measurable length that presents itself on the underside of the fleece as short, fluffy ends to the fleece. These will make the wool more difficult to spin, and the result is a yarn of fluffy, but uneven, tufty nature. Take note of this when choosing a fleece. The wool (in *the rise*) is often rather yellow, due to an excess of wool grease.

Rock and Wheel A term referring to a cloth that had a tightly spun warp thread and a softer spun weft yarn.
See *Warp and Weft*

Rock Day On January 7, with the Christmas festivities over, spinsters began to spin again.

Rockings These were gatherings where women in earlier times met to spindle spin. The spindles usually had stone whorls called 'rocks' and it would seem safe to assume that this is the derivation of *rockings*.

Rock Salt The Navajo Indians boil the liquid produced for dyeing in *rock salt*, a mineral containing aluminium. The rock salt is heated in a frying pan or container in a process called *melting*; the melting point is very high. Rock salt can also be *burned* on hot coals, then transferred to the dyebath at the absolutely correct time; this requires much skill and practice. Sometimes salt and baking soda are substituted for rock salt. The dampened wool is immersed in the prepared dyebath, boiled until the desired colour is obtained, cooled and washed in soapweed suds (see *Yucca Root*), then rinsed and dried.

Rolagan The name used by Highland Scots for a rolag.
See *Mudag*

Rolags Fibres that have been hand carded and then rolled into a tubelike shape ready for spinning.

WOOLLEN METHOD (*fig 36*): the rolag is rolled from the bottom edge of the carder to the top edge. Arrows on the rolag in the diagram indicate the direction of the rolling. The fibres which are lying in the tube are arranged similarly to a coiled spring and will produce, if spun correctly, a soft, airy yarn because of the trapped air. To test for a

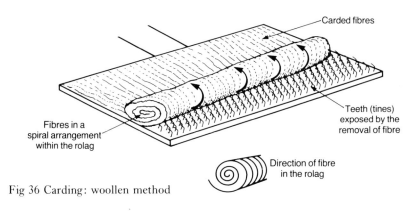

Carded fibres

Fibres in a
spiral arrangement
within the rolag

Teeth (tines)
exposed by the
removal of fibre

Direction of fibre
in the rolag

Fig 36 Carding: woollen method

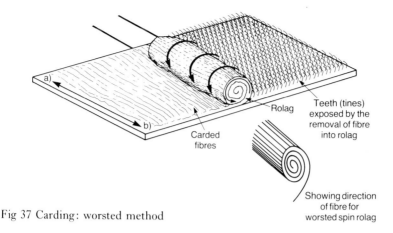

Teeth (tines)
exposed by the
removal of fibre
into rolag

Rolag

Carded
fibres

a)

b)

Showing direction
of fibre for
worsted spin rolag

Fig 37 Carding: worsted method

good rolag, hold it up to the light; it should appear of even texture throughout, open and have no dark patches of tangled fibres, dirt or noils.

WORSTED METHOD (*fig 37*): the fibres a–b are arranged as for the woollen method. When carded do not remove fibres from the length of the carder as for woollen but roll the fibres across the width of the carder. This leaves the fibres in a parallel arrangement. Arrows on rolag in *fig 37* indicate the direction of rolling. This arrangement will produce a smooth, sleek yarn.
See *Carding; Rolagan*

Rooing This process originated in earlier times. When sheep moulted they were plucked by the shepherds. Primitives still use the same process today. Certain breeds of sheep are suitable, usually those that have short fibres, for example, the *Soay*.

Root The end of the staple nearest to the sheep's body.

Rove To draw out and give the first twist to a thread ready for spinning; the process is referred to as *forming a rove*.

Roving A roving is made from *top* or *sliver*. The ropelike arrangement is drawn out to reduce its size and is slightly twisted to hold the fibres together; this continuous length is called a *roving*. The twist can be imparted by using a grasped handspindle or on a great wheel.
See *Combing; Epinetron*

Roving Builds See *Builds*

Roving Frame The machine on which roving is formed.

S

Saint Catherine The patron saint of spinners was a Christian martyr in Alexandria. In 307 AD she was condemned to be torn apart by the spokes of a wheel. November 25 is her saint's day. In earlier times in Europe, spinners were given a day off to celebrate St Catherine's Day.

Saint Distaff's Day Celebrated by spinners on January 7, the day after Twelfth Night. The spinners started work again after all the Christmas festivities had ceased.

Sale by Sample A type of selling used in Australia, New Zealand and South Africa. A sample, removed from a bale of wool, is analysed in a laboratory; a certificate is then issued giving the wool's characteristics. The samples and certificates may be examined by potential buyers before bidding begins, they can then decide which bales they wish to try and purchase. This is known as *sale by sample*.
See *Objective Measurement*

Salt, Sir Titus Was the first businessman to successfully spin alpaca hair in 1836; this produced an attractive extension to the woollen industry.

Saponification The conversion of fats and alkali to soap. See Plate 42, boiling soap in earlier times.

Schappe Silk Originally this was silk, which had been spun from fibre degummed by *schapping*; however, today the term is used as an alternative to *spun silk*.

Plate 42 Boiling soap

196

Schapping A Continental degumming process applied to silk waste which removes a proportion of the gum by a fermentation process but leaves up to 10 per cent of gum in the fibre.

Scotch Tensioner Also known as *Scotch tensioning system* is a small friction band, sometimes made of nylon, strong elastic or a small wire spring, attached to a peg, used on a single band treadle wheel as a means of tensioning control.
See *Single Band Wheel*

Scottish Wheel Women In the year 1578, women prisoners at Winchester were made to spin and knit at a 'corrective workshop'; they became known as the Scottish Wheel Women. In 1605 the Danes copied the idea.

Scouring See *Fleece – Scouring*

Scrooping At one time, when ladies required their handspun silk clothes to rustle, this was achieved by wetting the skeins with water and placing them in a bowl containing white vinegar. The skeins should be completely covered for approximately 10min, then removed and rinsed well in warm water. This is known as *scrooping*.

Scutching See *Flax-Linum usitatissimum*, section on *Scutching*.

Scutching Tow Is the waste that is broken from the strong fibre during the *scutching* process. It is used for spinning coarser yarns. If the flax is of poor quality, as much as 50 per cent can be wasted. The tow from the root end is coarser than the top flax, therefore during preparation the two are usually kept separate. When mechanically scutched by turbine, the front part of the machine may deal with the root and the second half with the top end. A separate machine deals with further scutching.

Seaming To stitch pieces of handspun knitting together, it is advisable to use a flat seam; it is less bulky and much neater if this method is used. Press the seams lightly on the wrong side if necessary.

Seats for Spinning In earlier times, stools were often used; however, a support for the spinner's back is desirable if long periods are to be spent spinning at a wheel. Height in relation to the orifice is very important. If the seat is too low, aching arms and back will develop quickly. The leg position should be such that the foot is not stretched out, but presses straight down on the treadle. If stretched out too far, the treadling will move the wheel further away from the spinner. The spinner should be seated at a comfortable height to the size of the spinning wheel being used and be positioned correctly. If you own more than one wheel, with varying heights and a chair is not available for each wheel, use a cushion to adjust the height. Spinning wheel manufacturers usually list in their catalogues chairs suitable for use with their wheel designs. See Plate 41.

Second Cuts Avoid at all times buying second cuts, which are very short pieces of wool that have been cut at both ends, often by an inefficient shearer who cuts the fleece and then has to go over the animal again as the first clip was not close enough. Second cuts during shearing can be eliminated by correct positioning of the sheep and the pattern of the shearing.

Seed Fibres See *Cotton*

Seedy A term used to describe wool which contains grass and certain other seeds.

Semi-Worsted The spinning of wool and hair fibres in such a way that they are not true worsted. Similarly semi-woollen is not a true woollen spin.

Sericin The natural silk gum extruded by the silkworm to hold its cocoon together.
See *Sericulture*

Sericulture The name given to the breeding of silkworms and the production of raw silk. The silkworm *Bombyx mori* is the species of silkworm most predominant in raw silk production. Today it is dependent on man, unlike the time when the insects lived wild and spun their silk in the branches of the mulberry tree. The mulberry (Latin *Morus* = *Mulberry*) is the essential raw material required. It can grow in many climates and has a bright green foliage. *Morus alba*, the white mulberry, is the best variety for sericulture. Whilst originally grown as a tree, farmers then proceeded to crop it by growing bushes that are cut down each year. Research has been extensive to produce a satisfactory end product. Vast quantities are required as silkworms always require fresh leaves.

Whilst *Bombyx mori can* be fed on different foods, eg lettuce, it then rarely finishes its life cycle or else the silk is inferior. The silkworm goes through a complete metamorphosis with four stages, egg, larva, pupa and adult. It takes only two months for the whole process from the time of egg laying, followed by hatching into a worm, becoming a moth and then dying.

EGGS: the silk moth lays approximately 600 to 800 eggs (40,000 eggs weigh approx. one ounce). Selective breeding increased the number of eggs laid by a female from the former 200 to 300 eggs. The eggs resemble tiny oval seeds and are called *graine*. When first laid, the eggs are yellow; if fertile they turn grey. Only eggs from healthy moths are used.

HATCHING: the eggs are scraped from the surface on which they were laid onto hatching trays. Within three to ten days the embryo inside the egg develops into a mature silkworm; the edges of the eggs darken as the worms form. Hatching starts early in the morning. The worm bites its way out of the shell at one end. First appears the head with a shiny tip and mouth, and gradually the silkworm emerges. The larva is tiny, with a black body with light spots. The body is covered with protective hairs that drop off as it grows. Some farmers lay cheese-cloth on top of the eggs; the worms crawl through this (it has a soft mesh) and the eggshells are caught and fall off. This not only helps the worms remove their shells, but separates the worms from the unhatched eggs and the eggshells.

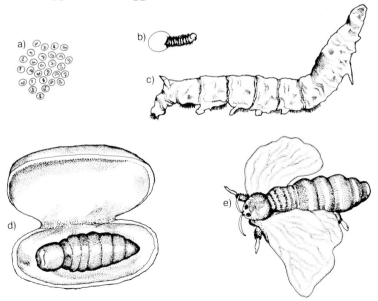

Fig 38 *SERICULTURE*: a) eggs; b) hatching silkworm; c) full-size silkworm ready to spin its cocoon; d) cocoon cut open to show chrysalis; e) moth

REARING: the silkworms are then spread on rearing trays and they start to feed on small chopped pieces of mulberry. The growth rate is considerable; the body comprises thirteen sections. Three pairs of legs behind the head are used to cling to leaves, twigs etc. There are also five stumpy and thick pairs of false legs (prolegs) to support the body and enable it to cling to surfaces. The silkworm has no heart or lungs; it breathes through small holes in the sides of its body. Blood which is yellow in colour is circulated by a pumplike organ at the back of its body. Silkworms have strong jaws and eat continually, working across each leaf in a line and then returning to start again. As the silkworm grows, the mulberry leaves no longer require to be chopped.

MOULTING: the silkworm continues to increase in size and outgrows its skin four times during the first four weeks. When this happens it ceases to feed and selects a quiet place where it attaches itself by a silken loop secured to the prolegs. It remains still, its head erect until transformation is complete (22hr). It then pushes its head upwards to break the skin and emerges with its new skin and recommences eating. During this process it must not be disturbed in any way. The time between moults varies, the first two take approximately 22hr, the third 27hr and the fourth longer. The times lengthen, due to the ever-increasing thickening of the skin. A particularly vital time is after the second moulting when the worm is very delicate and vulnerable. Then it is likely to develop contagious indigestion or other diseases, which could be spread to other silkworms.

INSTARS: the period of time between each moult is called an *instar*. Whilst the silkworm has four moults it has five instars. The first instar is from hatching to the end of the first moult; the last instar is from the end of the fourth moult until the next stage when the worm turns into a *pupa* inside its cocoon. During the instars the silkworm continues to eat, only ceasing on the rest days during the shedding of its skin. It consumes approximately fifty times its own weight, and its weight increases considerably.

At all times the environment must be controlled; silkworms do not like loud noises and require an even temperature 18° to 25°C (65° to 78°F) plus fresh air and no draughts. Cleanliness is of prime importance; any waste should be removed daily. To achieve this, nets of fresh mulberry are lowered onto the trays, the ever-hungry silkworms quickly crawl onto the leaves and can then be lifted onto fresh trays without actually being handled. More and more trays are employed as the silkworms increase in size.

SPINNING THE COCOON: the larva reaches maturity in about five weeks. It loses its green colouring and becomes transparent about the neck. It waves its head back and forth indicating it is ready to spin. It also ceases to eat because of the chemical changes that have taken place in its body; two glands (silk glands) have grown along the undersides of its body from head to tail and have become full of fluid. The narrow glands at the rear of the body contain a fluid called *fibroin*. At the middle and front of the silkworm's body, the glands are full and here a thick jellylike solution called *sericin* is produced. On its lower lip the silkworm has a small *spinneret* which has two holes on the inside and one on the outside. From the inside holes it extrudes twin filaments of sericin-coated fibroin. As these are forced out of the outside holes, the sericin cements them into a single strand of silk which hardens when exposed to air. With this now single thread called *bave*, comprising two *brins*, the silkworm makes the cocoon in which it rests during pupation.

Containers supplied by farmers for the silkworm at this stage vary. Some use individual cartons, others large trays divided into sections; smaller quantities of silkworm may be given twigs. The silkworm selects its site and spins between one anchorage and another to ensure that the cocoon will be firmly attached; this first spun silk is coarse. The silkworm rests briefly and then proceeds to envelop itself in silk, and the cocoon outline is formed. Inside the already-formed outline shape the larva moves its head back and forth in a figure-of-eight movement, forcing the liquid out of its glands in wet threads that adhere and cement to the outer threads. The figure-of-eight worked continuously enables the silkworm to form one long thread. At first it spins 22.9cm to 25.4cm (9 to 10in) a minute, then slows down to approximately 12.7cm (5in) a minute. It continues in this manner until all the secretions of fibroin, the silk forming substance, and sericin are exhausted; this usually takes from three to five days. The silkworm now moults for the fifth and last time, shedding its old skin within the cocoon by shrinking until it only measures 3.3cm (1¼in) in length. It now has a new skin containing a larger amount of *chitin* than in the old skin. The chitin is hard and forms a covering for many insects, eg beetles. This brings the *larval stage* to an end.

PUPA STAGE: usually takes about two weeks. During this time the silkworm is changing into the short, stubby body of a winged insect, with tiny scales growing over its body (these will give the adult silk-moth its dusty white appearance). Six long pointed legs are growing out of the pupa's body (*thorax*). A pair of feathery antennae are formed – long feelers with sense organs on each side of the moth's head. The large mouth is replaced by a small one as it will not eat – its life is so short. About ten to fourteen days later the pupa is ready to emerge as a silk moth; this it does early in the morning. It now has an alkaline liquid in its silk glands that dissolves a hole in one end of the cocoon large enough to permit the moth to escape. It emerges wet and wrinkled; it rests, and gradually the blood flows from the body into the veins of its wings and they expand. Fanning the wings back and forth hastens the drying process.

Due to the heavy weight of the body, the wings are not used for flying. The female moth tends to be more rotund than the male and is very inactive. When the female is ready to mate, she releases a perfume from the abdominal glands. The male has antennae comprised of 40,000 sensory nerve cells which pick up the scent from the female. He then executes a courting dance, his wings whirring continuously. They mate and in a few days he dies; his life span was 2 to 3 days.

The female lays her pale yellow and sticky eggs from a small organ in the tail (*ovipositor*). By twisting her tail to avoid laying one egg upon another she deposits them in neat rows. That task accomplished, she flutters, exhausted and dies. The eggs are then subjected to severe cold (not freezing, as this would kill them); hibernation is necessary before hatching by incubation. A mild solution of hydrochloric acid can affect the eggs in the same way as hibernation. When the mulberry starts to grow again in the spring, the eggs are brought out of hibernation for the next hatching, called the *crop*. Incubation can take about 30 days at a temperature of 20° to 30°C (68° to 86°F).

STIFLING: if raw silk is required most of the *pupae* are killed, whilst in the cocoons, to avoid the cocoons being damaged by the emergence of the silk moths; if the pupae were not killed, the cocoons could not be stored, as the moths would emerge in the natural way. If, however, production of eggs (*graine*) is the main object, then the moth is permitted to emerge and lay her eggs as already explained. Those cocoons selected to breed the next crop are sexed to see whether they contain male or female. This is done by placing them on a moving belt which is adjusted to let the heavier cocoons (usually female) drop into a container whilst the lighter ones (usually the males) continue on the belt. This method is not completely reliable. The Chinese used to stifle pupae not required for breeding by laying the cocoons out in the sun so that they cooked to death. Sometimes boiling water was used. Placing in ovens at 93°C (200°F) was another method; also hot air and steam. Today high frequency radio waves kill the pupae instantly. Whatever the method used the cocoons can be stored in airtight rooms until required.

BYPRODUCTS OF SERICULTURE
a) the litter from the silkworm beds ie droppings of rich undigested material. Used as winter feed for cattle.
b) pierced cocoons from places where the moths are permitted to emerge. Comprised almost entirely of silk other than the chrysalis shell and the caterpillar's last skin. In China and Japan, the

cocoons are boiled, then turned inside out and any animal matter removed; they provide wadding (*mawata*) for quilted winter wear. This is a good material for spinners as it has not been impaired by prior boiling or stifling.

c) from the reeling of 45kg (100lb) of raw silk can result some 50 to 68kg (110 to 150lb) of chrysalis residue. Used for several purposes, eg feeding fish, edible food for the peasants in the more primitive areas of silk-producing countries, for the manufacture of soap by the extraction of animal fat and the residue for agricultural fertilisers.

See *Bassines; Brins; Cortes, Hernando; Filament; Floss; Mulberry Tree; Pasteur, Louis; The Rising*

Seriplane A classification system drawn up by the International Silk Association related to the selling of raw silk. The main tests are for *evenness, soundness* and *cleanness*, for which purposes a seriplane is used. This winds the silk at preset spacing onto a blackboard where it is carefully examined under strong lights. Any fault found for cleanness is noted and this reduces the value of the silk. Photographs are used as a means of comparison for evenness and neatness. Denier accuracy is tested by winding 450m (492yd) lengths of silk into small skeins, which are then weighed. Any deviation from the average or mean denier is recorded and used in tests called *size deviations*. A variety of further tests are made for cohesion, tenacity and elongation.

Finally, by combining all the results, a correct grading is obtained. Electronic instruments are being developed to obtain an accurate quality grading.

Serrations The outer scales which project from the body of wool fibres. The quantity varies according to the breed; in a fine merino it is approximately 5,000 to the inch; in other breeds there may be only a few hundred to the inch. Wool is the only serrated textile fibre.

Setting the Twist A skein of singles, if left untreated, will twist into itself and tangle. To set the twist it is necessary to scour and dry the yarn under tension.

It is not necessary to set the twist on light to medium twist drawn silk; however, steaming is suitable for a higher twist in the yarn (provided, of course, that the yarn is not to be dyed).

METHOD: wind the yarn onto a skein winder. Heat some water in a kettle then, when it starts to boil, steam the yarn over the kettle spout; make sure that each end is steamed. Do not remove from winder, keep the yarn under tension. The steam will penetrate all the skeined layers. Allow to dry, then remove.

Shafty Term used to describe a wool staple which is long, compact and strong and coarser than *diamond*. Found towards the *britch* and the end of the fleece and a little behind the *poll-lock*. Not found in fine fleece.

Shakers An American religious sect, some of whose members designed and made many Saxony and high wheels during the late eighteenth and the nineteenth centuries.

Shearing In the past, gangs of men were hired to shear and they travelled from farm to farm. Due to their numbers they quickly sheared flocks of sheep using *shears*, or *dags* as they were often named. The sheep would be closely penned together so that the grease in the wool became warm and more supple for the shearer; this was called 'raising the yolk'. Then a sheep would be thrown onto its back and in this helpless state the fleece could be removed in one piece, a job requiring great skill to avoid injuring the animal. Large shearing scissors were developed in the eighteenth century and were approximately 25.4cm (10in) long; following these came the *spring-tined shears*, which greatly improved the speed of working as they had a steel spring between the blades of the scissors enabling them to spring back for the next cut. Mechanical shearing developed at the beginning of this century.

Today, the British Wool Marketing Board controls the quality of the wool they sell, which is a safeguard to the spinner. In earlier times the wool was baled, then sold to the merchants with no guarantee that the fleece on the inside of the bale would be as the outside of the bale. Many tricks were tried by putting good quality fleece on the outside and hay, matted fleece or even sacking on the inside of the bale. The merchants counteracted this trickery by using a *wool bale sampler*, similar to scissors with backward facing barbs, which they thrust into the centre of the bale, so that pieces of whatever material had been placed in it would catch onto the barbs. Around 1850, another testing device was developed called the *manchors balance* for weighing the fleece, this would indicate by the weight any 'doctored' bale.

Approximately one third of wool in Britain today is obtained from slaughtered sheep; it is inferior to that obtained from live animals and is mainly used in blanket, carpet and coarse material manufacture.

Shearing times vary from area to area; usually in Lowland and Southern areas shearing takes place in May/June, and in Northern areas in June/July.

In New Zealand and some other countries, some sheep are clipped twice; the short wool is used in carpets. This is called the second shear. See *Bales; Bloom; Fleece – Second Cuts; Hog Fleece; Lamb's Wool; Shears; Tegwool; Two-Shear; Wool Winding*

Shearing Terms
Mature fleece: fleece from a grown sheep, two years and older
Full fleece: fleece with twelve months' growth
First early shear: in spring with approx. six months' wool growth
Second shear: in autumn with approx. six months' wool growth
Pre-lamb shear: with twelve months' wool growth before lambing;
time varies according to area and husbandry.
See *Raise the Yolk*

Shearling A sheep usually between the ages of one and two years,
which has been only shorn once.

Shears The devices, often scissor type, which are used to remove the
fleece from sheep. See *Shearing*

Sheep *Sp Ovis aries*: there are still wild sheep, mainly in Asia and also
in Europe, North Africa and North America. They are mountain
dwellers, and have short coats which moult in the spring. Sheep with
very fat tails are found in many areas of Asia and Africa. During good
seasons they store fat in their tails and this helps them to survive
drought and cold winters. They are mainly kept for meat and milk.
The first domesticated sheep were descended from the European wild
sheep, the moufflon (*Ovis musimon*) and from the Asiatic moufflon
(*O. orientalis*), the urial (*O. vignei*) and the argali (*O. ammon*). The
wild urial ewes from South-West Asia have small horns and are
thought by some to be the main ancestor of domestic sheep. Britain's
Neolithic sheep came from the Continent; they were small and brown.
Bronze Age European sheep are thought to have been *urial-moufflon*
descendants. Sheep were domesticated in the Middle East about 9000
BC. In 1882 skeletal remains found in Swiss-lake dwellings, skulls with
and without horns, are thought to date to the Copper Age which
preceded the Bronze Age, and possibly of moufflon blood. It is
thought that until the beginning of the Bronze Age all sheep were of
the *turbary* type, well known from many Neolithic sites in Europe and
the Middle East. Turbary blood is considered to persist in the
Shetland and Soay breeds today. Descendants of native sheep exist
today, eg the *soay*, native sheep of the fourth century, live in the Isle
of Soay, south of the Isle of Skye. The Soay have a brown to fawn
coloured fleece weighing approximately .45 to .7kg (1 to 1½lb).
The *dunface*, a cross between imported white and native British
sheep, survived as a breed in the Highlands until 1850. It was small
with short erect horns, thin, and had a white face and legs. The wool
fibre was fine and measured about 7.6cm (3in) and the fleece weighed
approximately .45kg (1lb). The dunface were milked and lived with
the family as pets. About the fourteenth century the introduction of

white sheep called *Cheviots* brought change to Scottish sheep. The Cheviot gradually replaced the dunface in the Lowlands. The *North Ronaldsay*, the *Manx loghtan* and the *Hebridean* are also ancient types.

Britain's breeds have, over the centuries, greatly influenced the world's stock, surpassed only by the *merinos*. In England today exist about forty recognised breeds of sheep and many crossbreds. British wool commands the highest prices in the world for its type. There are about 90,000 wool producers in the UK, producing nearly 40 million kg of wool yearly, which is graded into national grades suitable for manufacturing requirements by the British Wool Marketing Board. Some farmers breed for meat rather than fibre, the latter a byproduct often used to assist in paying the vets' bills. With selective breeding, however, it has in some cases been possible to produce an acceptable fleece from an animal raised for its meat. Sheep breeds are chosen to reflect the need to use land and climatic conditions to the best advantage.

British wool breeds fall into three categories; possibly a development from the Middle Ages when sheep rearing and tillage had to work side by side. Today these categories are only a guide, as sheep may be reared in areas away from their original habitat, which can affect the characteristics of the wool.

Mountain and Hill, eg *Blackface, Herdwick* and *Welsh Mountain* have a staple that is medium to long 7.6cm to 17.8cm (3 to 7in). Usually contains kemps that can be white, red or black. Some Hill sheep have black faces and long hairy fleeces, others have white faces and shorter coarse fleeces sometimes referred to as *Green Hill* due to the fact they graze on grass on the hills.

Longwools and Lustres: these have long, lustrous, curly fleece with a staple length of 12.7cm to 45.7cm (5 to 18in). Some Kent breeds have soft semi-lustrous fleeces whilst others are sleek, eg *Lincoln* or *Devon Longwool*. The Longwool breeds often reflect their areas of origin, eg *Romney* from Romney Marsh in Kent, *Lincoln* from Lincolnshire, *Leicester* from Leicestershire, *Border Leicester* from the Scottish Border region. The *Romney* and crossbreeds derived from it, dominate the New Zealand flocks. In Australia the *Border Leicester* is often crossed with merinos to produce fat-lamb mothers, which in turn are bred to Shortwool sires to produce fat lambs.

Shortwools and Down: The short staple often below 10.3cm (4in). The wools are fine and crisp with good elasticity, eg the *Southdown*. The fine wool is not characteristic of British breeds; it originated from the merino breed in Spain. Other Down breeds were developed from the *Southdown* including *Dorset Down, Hampshire Down* and *Oxford*

Down. The Southdown, first bred in the South Downs of South East England, is an import fat-lamb sire in New Zealand.

CROSSBREEDING is carried out in all the major wool-producing countries to combine certain characteristics from different breeds and to form new types. The *Corriedale* is a classic early example. It was widely farmed in New Zealand, South America and in Australia and evolved by crossing the merino with English Longwool breeds, eg the Lincoln and Leicester, with Romney and Border Leicesters also, as sires to the initial half-breds. This breeding programme continued for decades and resulted in possibly the second most numerous sheep breed in the world. In England the Hill sheep remain pure-bred. The ewes have lambs in the hills and then are crossed with a ram from a long woolled breed. The ewes from this cross then provide grassland sheep and become mothers of fat lamb when mated to a Down ram. As long as a pure-bred ram is used, the crossbred wool will be between the types of both parental breeds.

MERINO: this requires a special mention, as it is the most important sheep breed in the world. Records show that it originated in Moorish Spain in the late Middle Ages and was the product of *Laodicean* and *Tarentine* sheep brought there by the Romans. It was prized by European breeders. Export from Spain of the animals was not allowed until 1765, when the merino went to Germany and then spread to become the world's finest sheep. Australia's first merinos arrived in the late 1790s via Dutch flocks, others went from France, Germany and North America. Merino fleeces can be found as fine as sixteen micrometres the renowned *superfine* or as broad as twenty-seven micrometres known as *strong*. The fibre is consistent in every way.

It can be difficult for a spinner to identify the exact breed of a fleece. However, it is possible by studying the character of the wool to assess its capabilities. Consideration should be given to the staple length, degree of crimp, soundness and all characteristics that may well dictate both the type of spin and method of preparation. At all times the design of the yarn should be foremost in all considerations and decisions. Over the centuries has evolved a fibre which is outstanding, with a variety of choice to supply man's needs.
See *Bottom Wool; Comeback; Ewe; Tup Ram; Tupping*

Female lamb – ewe
Male lamb – tup (in the North) *ram* (in the South).
Castrated lamb – weather or *weddar*
In England this denotes wool other than the first shearing. Can also indicate a male sheep which has been castrated as a lamb.
After weaning at 5 months old lambs become *ewes, tups*, or *wethers, hogs, hoggets* or *tegs*.

After shearing in spring or early summer
Females = theaves, thaves or *threaves* in the South; *gimmers* in the North. *Males = shearling* or *diamond tups* or *rams*, or in some districts *dinmonts*.

In autumn the females are mated and have their lambs five months later. When a few months later they are shorn again, they become *two-shear* or *two-toothed ewes*. Thereafter, each shearing denotes an additional year of a sheep's age, ie three-toothed or four-toothed ewe. After the age of four, age can no longer be proven because she grows no more teeth. When the teeth are worn out she is sold as *broken mouthed* and slaughtered. Hog wool is best. Wether Hogs give the biggest yield.

Shepherding Britain has always had a history of wool farming and industry. Trading in wool continued to grow through medieval times and in the eighteenth and nineteenth centuries. Due to his specialised knowledge, the shepherd was considered very highly in the community. In earlier times it was the custom to place a tuft of wool into the hand of a dead shepherd at his burial, which it was said would show his profession and at the same time explain to his Maker why he had been unable to attend worship regularly.

Shetland At one time the word 'Shetland' denoted that the garment material had been made entirely from wool off Shetland sheep; later the word referred to soft knitted woollen fabric, used mainly for sweaters.

Shive Sometimes referred to as *shove*. The broken boon after flax scutching, can be used as fuel. Shive is also a term used to describe small fragments of leaf and straw.

Shivey Wool Wool that has small particles of vegetable matter, other than burrs, in it.

Shoddy Shoddy is obtained from soft unmilled fabrics or fabrics that have been milled lightly. As re-manufactured material they disintegrate more easily and therefore the staple of the resulting fibre is better than mungo. Shoddy of the best quality is obtained from knitted materials, with fibre lengths between 1.3cm and 3–8cm (½in and 1½in). See *Extract; Mungo; Re-Manufactured Materials*

Short Draw See *Draw – Short*

Shrinkage The reduction in size of fabric, often due to washing. The word is used in the USA to describe weight loss that results after scouring greasy wool.

Silk Is a continuous fibre produced by the silkworm making its cocoon; it is the only natural fibre in filament form. It consists of two-thirds fibroin and is thus comparable to wool. When stripped of sericin, it appears transparent and rodlike, almost devoid of markings. Silk can absorb 30 per cent beyond its dry weight without feeling wet. It has a low weight for its volume and extraordinary strength and elasticity. It will stretch 10 to 20 per cent over its length without breaking. Silk can be distinguished from other fibres by the way it burns quickly, producing very little flame; it gives off an odour similar to burning feathers and leaves a bead of very little ash.

Si-Ling Chi is credited for discovering a worm spinning a cocoon is attributed to the wife of the Emperor of China in the year 2640 BC. For this reason she was called 'the Goddess of Silk', and temples were built in her name. In subsequent years each empress of China would dress in silk clothes and each spring would carry offerings to those temples. There are other versions of this story; another legend claims that a Chinese princess was having tea in her garden and a cocoon dropped in her cup from a tree and the hot liquid softened the fibre. On seeing this the princess pulled on the end of the thread and discovered a long continuous filament. The truth will never be known; it is a fact that the Chinese have cultivated spun and woven silk for approximately 5,000 years.

The origins of silk are unknown; a lost part of history. Silk in China is known to date back to 2500 BC. It is known that by 1500 BC spinning and weaving of silk was well advanced. In 125 BC the Silk Road was opened. As trade expanded, the secret of silk could be kept no longer and it became known in Japan and nearby countries and spread westwards through Persia and Turkey to middle Europe. By the fifteenth century it was established in Italy and France.

Because of the introduction of manmade fibres the silk market has been much affected. Silk can hold its own in the more exclusive markets where cost is not the main consideration, because no other fibre has yet been evolved to compare with all the desirable qualities of silk – it is unique.

SPINNING SILK: several different types of silk waste are available to the handspinner. Some are prepared, others are not. A tussah silk has flatter thicker filaments and the strands lay parallel. If a finer thread is required, use the thin filaments of the *Bombyx mori* silkworm. The methods of spinning vary according to the type being spun and the thread required. Spun silk yarns have less lustre due to the many ends, and therefore have more bulk and are softer. Reeled silks are the opposite. Silk fibres can be teased, carded or combed – whatever method is applicable. Rovings are possibly the easiest to cope with as they come prepared, having been degummed and cut into lengths.

Tops: these are well combed; a stage just before the roving or sliver form.

Mawata can be obtained. This has been prepared from matted cocoons and any remnants, by being stretched over a frame and the fibres arranged into a 25.4cm (10in) square sheet of soft silk. *Combed sliver* can be spun into a strong, smooth, lustrous yarn. It is available in a neat shape called a *brick* comprising a continuous supply that has been folded back and forth many times then formed into a brick shape with the end tucked in. *Knubbs, noils* and *wadding strips* are available, which have not been made into tops or rovings; whilst not so expensive, due to less processing, the quality is still there. These can be made into silk puni using a similar method as for cotton puni, whereby the silk is lightly carded into batts then rolled onto the dowel as for cotton.

To SPIN SILK: use light bobbin tension, dry hands (apply non-greasy cream if hands are at all rough) and a light touch. Insert just enough twist to provide the strength required. A comparable spin to worsted can be used, but a more delicate touch between thumb and forefinger of the hand holding the fibres is required. Use a shorter draw.

Mawata: take hold of the opposite corners and attenuate the sheet into a long, thin roving, then spin as wool. See under *mawata* for further details.

Brick: first undo the end and pull off a length, up to 15.3cm (6in). If a smooth strong yarn is required, or to produce a more bulky yarn, pull off shorter lengths. Spin using the folded method and do not overtwist. A forked distaff can also be used with the silk twisted between the prongs. With this method the silk is drawn down with the left hand although, unlike flax, it is spun dry. Treadling should be fairly rapid due to the short fibre length. Use only a few strands at a time. Tension should be adjusted to spin a strong thread.

Silk puni: these small puni rolags can be treated as the larger woollen rolags, ie join to the leader yarn, attenuate and allow a small amount of twist to enter as you continue to draw, until the length is spun to the required thickness; add more twist if needed for the necessary strength, then wind onto the bobbin; attach another puni and treat in the same way. Keep a supply of puni near to provide continuous action.

Degummed thrown waste – reeled silk: the best of the cocoon. Many variations are possible using this fibre form.

Rovings: remove from the bag and shake gently to allow to breathe. Break by gently pulling apart, then peel lengthways into pencil sizes, approximately 45.7cm (18in) long to start with, and allow the twist to gently run through as you make a long draw. Combed tussah will glide from one hand through the other if very little tension is set. Keep hands close together and well back from the orifice. The back hand holds the fibres and fans them out. Alternatively, roving can be folded over the forefinger and drafted out of the V-shaped fold.

Tops: spin as rovings, pulling off sufficient to use at one sitting. Avoid too much handling, as this results in a duller yarn.

Silk is very versatile and can be spun in many ways. It can be successfully blended with other fibres to produce yarns of great attraction and quality, especially if careful consideration is given to the content and properties of each fibre. It is excellent with other luxury fibres, eg alpaca and camel, and these blends produce really lustrous yarns.

After spinning, the silk should be skeined and soaked in lukewarm soap solution. Rinse well, place in a towel and dab lightly. Hang to dry and tension lightly. Silk should be handled carefully at all times to avoid tangling. To control at the skeining stage, strips cut from a soft plastic bag and used as ties are helpful. When soaking or rinsing skeins, if they are strung onto a ribbon or tape and suspended in the liquid, this helps to avoid tangling.

IRONING METHODS:
a) *tussah silk* items, iron when dry
b) *cultivated silk* items, iron whilst damp under a cloth, with moderate heat.

When the term 'spinning' is used in the silk industry, it refers to the manufacture of spun or schappe silk (composed of twisted staple) as distinct from raw silk (a combination of continuous filaments).
See *Artificial Silk; Byzantium; Gum Waste; Raw Silk; Sericulture; Silk Road*

Silk Moth These are of the order *Lepidoptera* from the Greek meaning 'scaly wings'. The lifespan of the silkworm/moth has been turned to a great advantage; the relationship between man, the silkworm and the plants called mulberry is unique.
EXAMPLES OF TYPES OF MOTH AND THEIR COCOONS: the colour and type of fibre is related to the food the silk caterpillars eat and the resulting cocoons.

Anaphe moth – Anaphe sp is prevalent in Africa. Feeds on fig leaves. Unlike other varieties producing wild silk, the caterpillars group together and spin a nest from which a number of moths emerge. The empty nests are collected as raw materials for the spinning industry.

Atlas moth – Attacus atlas Sylheticus is found throughout India. One of the largest of the silk moths and omnivorous (most caterpillars are vegetarians). The cocoons are open at one end.

Bombyx mori is the domesticated species of silkworm most predominant in raw silk production; they feed on mulberry leaves. The cocoons are beautiful because of selective breeding. Count – approx. 510 per lb from Japan and 860 per lb from India; the latter are smaller and less perfect. Some countries, for example, China have an equable climate plus a good supply of mulberry leaves enabling farmers to obtain from two to six crops of cocoons in one year; elsewhere, one crop is normal practice. If there is more than one crop, the worms are of the class referred to as *polyvoltines*; one crop only, and they are called *annuals* or *monovoltines*. Polyvoltine silk moths eggs will hatch out under normal conditions within a fortnight of laying; they require no hibernation. A typical cycle would be thirty days as a caterpillar, seven days as a cocoon and fifteen days between the emergence of the moth and the hatching of eggs. Seven cycles can therefore be completed in a year. The cocoons are not such good quality tending to be fluffy and smaller. The silk is less reliable – about half of that from monovoltines.

Eri silk moth – the *Cynthia moth, Samia cynthia* is also known as *Attacus ricini* or *Philosamia cynthia*. Wild silk is produced by the eri caterpillar of Bengal, Assam and Nepal, which feeds on a diet of leaves from the castor oil plant among others. It leaves an opening in the cocoon during construction for the emergence of the moth. *Cassilk* is the commercial name for some of these fibres.

Munea moth – Antherea assama produces wild silk of Assam, which is in the same class as *tussah* although the cocoon is not so hard and the filament finer and more brilliant.

Chinese tussah moth – Antherea pernyi is a native of China and Manchuria. Eats mainly oak leaves. It is semi-cultivated. Cocoons produced in Manchuria, where the weather is cold, are dark and heavy. The milder climate of Shantung gives a cocoon both lighter in colour and weight.

Indian tussah moth – Antherea mylitta is cultivated in the wild in Assam and other parts of India. Closely related to the tussah of Northern China. The cocoon is oval with a hard surface. It has a stalk composed of silk and gum, ending in a loop from which it is suspended from suitable trees until hatched. *Tussah* is brown in colour and varies from district to district according to the vegetation eaten by the silkworm. The filament is very strong and resistant to acid, alkali and sunlight.

Nistari moth A polyvoltine, native of Bengal. The cocoon are small, the sericin yellow.

Saturnids or *giant silkworm moths* best known of the wild silk moths – the eri moth is in this class. They have distinctive 'eye' markings on their wings.

Yama-mai silk – Antherea (samia) yama – mai is found in Japan. It produces a large green cocoon; the silk is white and strong.

Ailanthus is a silkworm of Europe, which is a cross of *A.cynthia* and *A.ricini*, was first bred by G. Meneville and is now widespread in the silk-growing regions.

Silk Noils Usually a byproduct of fibres rejected during reeling. They consist of the floss removed from the surface of the cocoon before it is boiled, also the basin waste removed after boiling, and from imperfect and hatched cocoons. The noils are carded and, when spun into a yarn, give a texture to the woven silk cloth. Silk noil is the name given to the yarn spun from this waste material; it is not a high quality but has a certain character. See *Spun Silk*

Silk Reeling The process in which cocoons, that have had their sericin softened by placing in warm water, are unwound in long continuous filament during the preparation of silk.

Cocoons: these may be white, cream or yellow, determined by the species of parent of the worm. Sizes vary, on average about 2.5cm to 5cm (1 to 2in) in length, with possibly a thousand metres (1100yd) of silk in each cocoon in one continuous filament (typical of *Bombyx mori*). The filament in a cocoon varies in thickness throughout its length; only a low percentage is reelable due to the weight of the sericin (about a quarter), and the pupa. It is not necessarily the large cocoons that are the best; the main criteria being that the walls are firm, compact and with a clean colour. Some defective cocoons can be reeled, eg those in which the worm has died, although staining may have occurred. When a worm is illnourished or unhealthy, it can spin a large, loosely constructed cocoon, which will require being reeled from cooler water; otherwise the filaments will soften too quickly and tangle. Cocoons are graded through a grill; whilst the general quality may be comparable whatever the size, those of like size will contain baves of like denier and this will facilitate the reeling of a regular count. Double cocoons, in which two silkworms have spun together, cannot be reeled, neither can cocoons from which the moth has escaped. These are used in the manufacture of spun silk.

To reel a cocoon, the outside end of the bave has to be found to unravel and wind into a hank. The cocoons are soaked in hot water, and the heat retained, to warm the sericin (gum) cementing the filament; this is referred to as the *floating method*. During this soften-ing process the water does not penetrate the cocoons, so they remain floating. Gradually the sericin begins to dissolve and the filaments will then adhere to a brush or rod when stirred. The outer layer of the cocoon is removed by jerking the brush, it is referred to as *knubbs* and is not as good as inner silk.

Methods of reeling have varied over the years. It can be done by simply soaking the cocoons as already described, then winding onto a piece of dowel, several filaments at a time. Whilst this is time consuming, it can be an interesting activity, especially for young children, to complete the study of the silkworm.

METHOD: place the cocoons in chemical free water and simmer for 15 to 30 min to soften the sericin. Using straw, a stick, or a piece of unsmoothed dowelling, catch the outer coarse filaments from each of the cocoons, continue pulling for a while and then lay aside; when there is a clear filament coming from each cocoon then is the time to commence reeling. Hold the fibres in your hand and begin winding onto either a reel, or a small *niddy noddy* or similar device; avoid stretching the silk as it is wound. The filaments merge between the fingers and are cemented together by the sericin to form a single thread. At all times the reeling should be executed over hot water. The denier must be even. As a cocoon becomes exhausted, pick up and join in a fresh cocoon. Watch the thread carefully, and if it becomes weak, tie a coloured thread to the end. The skein should be laced in several places to prevent tangling and removed from the skeiner, use whilst damp. See *Bassines; Floss; Sericulture*

Steam filature by steam boilers, was introduced in the nineteenth century in Europe to enable reelers to control the temperature; this was a great advance on the boiling by fire method, with its accompanying fluctuation in temperature.

AUTOMATIC REELING MACHINES were introduced first in Japan in 1949 to reduce labour costs. Over the years these have expanded and improved. An electronic gauge is set to the required size, the raw silk passes through this. A conveyor belt, with soaked cocoons with their ends in position, passes the reeling basin. When a drop in the denier size is registered by the gauge, it sets going a mechanism that picks up another cocoon. Thirteen to fifteen denier is the most common size of singles, which can require assembling together the filaments of five or more cocoons.

Whatever the method used, single filaments are no use in a commercial situation, so several baves are reeled together into a single strand. This can be achieved by a system of small pulleys arranged so that the thread is crossed with itself (*tavelette*) or with its neighbour (*chambon*). The crossing is termed *croisure* from the French. This provides cohesion and removes excess water. The thread is then wound onto a reel and formed into a skein. Cocoons vary in length and, as one drops off, it must be replaced otherwise the denier size will drop. Before automation reelers completed the join by placing the filament from a new cocoon over the little finger than lightly touched the thread already reeled and the sericin caused cohesion. A good reeler obtained a high standard of uniformity.

The product of silk reeling is known as *grege* or *singles*, and a skein, usually of 132cm (52in) circumference, is wound and when completed is crosslaced to maintain shape. Skeins are made up into bundles called *books* ready for marketing.

In Japan a co-operative may collect the cocoons from the farmers and then sell them to the silk filature factory. The cocoons are unwound onto reels called filatures and an official at the factory will decide on the fineness of the silk from each farmer's batch. The co-operative is then paid and in turn pays the farmer.

Mechanisation and science have been involved in trying to improve production. Whatever evolves in the future, the Mulberry and the silkworm still will be required to make it all possible.

Re-reel: if silk is reeled domestically, the product may be uneven and the skein rarely cross wound; it is then necessary to reel the silk a second time, this is known as re-reel.

See *Blaze; Book of Silk; Bourrette; Degumming; Doppione; Knubbs; Net Silk; Piedmont Silks; Seriplane; Spun Silk; Strusa; Tussah*

Silk Road Was opened about 126 BC and stretched across central Asia for 9,656km (6,000 miles) from *Changan*, the Chinese silk capital to *Rome*. It was the longest trade route of the Ancient World. As sea routes opened in the fifteenth and sixteenth centuries, the Silk Road began to decline in prosperity and cities along the road became deserted.

Silk Seed Also referred to as *graine*, is a name often given to silkworm eggs. See *Sericulture*

Silk Throwing The process which follows silk reeling, whereby several reeled silk monofilaments are twisted together into a single strand, thus making the thread much stronger. The strength of the twist inserted varies according to requirements, eg low twist for weft in weaving is referred to as *tram* and has more lustre. Warp yarns have a higher twist and are called *organzine* silk.

The first waste accumulates when skeins break or become tangled going through the cleaner blades; called *reelers'* or *winders' waste*, it appears as a single filament thread. During the throwing (twisting) process, a further waste can accumulate, referred to as *spinners'* or *doublers' waste*. *Doppione* waste occasionally occurs, due to irregularities of the reeled 'double' cocoons, whereby the skeins cannot be put through blades of the cleaner. Short, even lengths or threads cut from

Plate 43 Silk twister's wheel, cross and reeler

bobbins produce another source of waste which can either be *spinners'* or *reelers'*. See *Book of Silk; Net; Organzine; Sericulture; Tram Silk*

Silk Waste Also known as *unreeled silk*. The Japanese spin beautiful silk from silk waste, which they first turn into rovings on a silk roving maker. This has a flat, oblong wooden base with an upright stem at one end, at the top of which are 12.7cm to 15.3cm (5 to 6in) long split bamboo canes, turned rough side out and hammered vertically around the top to secure. When making a roving Japanese artisans wrap the silk waste, to hold, around the top of the bamboo. They sit on the ground with two shallow containers in front of them, one in line with the stem that will hold the roving, the other, containing dried beans, to the right. Moistening fingers on both hands with saliva, the workers pull and form the silk waste into thin rovings which they coil in the empty basket. Each complete coil is covered with a layer of beans. When the container is full of roving and beans, the roving is pulled out (through the bean layers) to be spun on a primitive type of charka. See *Bassines; Floss; Strusa*

Silkworm The larva of the *Bombyx mori* and of allied moths encloses its chrysalis in a cocoon of silk by ejecting a viscous substance called *fibroin* from two glands near its mouth. The two filaments extruded are cemented and coated together by a natural gum called *sericin* from a third gland. See *Sericin; Sericulture*

Silver See *Mineral Fibres*

Single Band Wheel With *scotch tensioning system*, sometimes referred to as *friction brake, scotch brake*, also *bobbin drag*: this type of U-flyer has a single drive band, from the wheel to the spindle whorl, which turns the spindle and flyer. The bobbin rotates without control because there is no drive, and so no draw-in or wind-on is possible. Therefore a friction brake is applied to the bobbin. This comprises a thin band with a stretch device made of strong elastic, or a small wire spring that is usually anchored to the mother-of-all on one side then is passed over the bobbin whorl to a peg, knob or screw attached to the opposite side. The peg can be screwed to tighten giving tension; this retards the bobbin and causes it to rotate slower than the flyer and wind-on of yarn occurs (the flyer rotating faster winds the yarn onto the bobbin). Several types of this adjustable brake system were all designed so that the bobbin will slip (run slower than the flyer) when required, thus causing yarn to wrap onto the bobbin. During spinning the tension is altered, when necessary, to adjust the twist and winding ratio. The bobbin can be changed very easily on the Ashford wheels by releasing the brake band and lifting off the full bobbin and replacing with an empty one; then the brake band is replaced. There is no need to remove the driving band.

With some flyer wheels, eg *double band*, wind-off is done in the opposite direction to wind-on, because the flyer rotates in the same direction as the wheel. Therefore, on a single band wheel, when the bobbin is full, the yarn is wound off in the same direction as when spinning, because the *flyer* winds the yarn on during spinning, whereas on a double band wheel, the *bobbin* winds on the yarn.

When necessary to replace the drive band on a single band wheel, place it once around the wheel and flyer whorl, overlap and join the ends by stitching together. See *Problems*

Singles Yarn A single spun yarn produced either from prepared or from raw fibres. If a singles yarn is spun clockwise it is normally plied anticlockwise or vice versa. See *S-Twist; Z-Twist*

Sinkage The loss of weight that occurs during the cleansing of wool, also any loss occurring during processing.

Sisal Sp *Agave fourcroydes, A. sisalana*, also called *sisal-grass* or *sisal hemp*. Thought to have been named after *Sisal*, a port in Yucatan.

This vegetable fibre is obtained from the leaves of the agave family. It is a relative of the *Amaryllis* family. It is a tall, tropical plant with long pointed leaves that contain a fibre used to make coarse fabric, sacks, ropes and twine. After harvesting, the pulp is cleaned from each side of the leaf; the remaining fibres up to 121.9cm (4ft) long are washed and dried in the sun. Whilst sisal can be dyed, it loses colour rapidly and even its natural creamy white colour quickly becomes yellow. It is sold in hanks.

Fig 39 Folding a Skein of Yarn: (1 and 2) twist the skein. Take loop at end a) through the loop at end b); 3, completed folded skein

Skein Having wound the yarn from the wheel onto a *niddy noddy* or similar skein winder, the skein produced by the winding is removed and washed. A skein is a coil of yarn (see *fig 39*).

Skein-Dyed Yarn dyed in skein form.

Skeiner Also called a *skein winder*. The revolving distaff was in use by the end of the Middle Ages for dispensing rovings; it developed into the present-day spinning accessories on which to wind spun yarn to form skeins. The simplest form is the *niddy noddy*; more sophisticated types to measure the wool were the *click-reel, clock-reel* and the *umbrella* type.

Skein Holders See *Swifts*

Skeining The winding of spun yarn onto a niddy noddy or similar implement, usually often plying.
See *Niddy Noddy*

Skin Wool See *Fellmongering*

Skirting The removal of the short ends and belly wool on the edges of the fleece.

Skirtings The parts of a sheep's fleece that usually require removing before classing, due to excessive dirt or staining. The water in which skirtings have been soaked makes an excellent liquid manure for the garden.

Slave Cotton See *Brown Cotton*

Slipe Lime-steeped wools, usually sold without being scoured.
See *Fellmongering*

Sliver Pronounced *slyver*, it is a continuous thick band of fibre with no twist and ready to either be twisted into roving or to be spun. A sliver was formed during the woolcombing process related to jigging. When the wool was jigged sufficiently it was pulled by the comber, with both hands, into a continuous rope called a sliver. The present day word sliver possibly derived from the earlier sleevers of woolcombing. See *Combing*

Sloughing-Off A term used in the silk trade when the cone of silk is slipping and loosely wound, and the silk slips off the cone.

Slub A place in a length of yarn where the fibre was not attenuated to the same dimension as the rest of the yarn. See *Fancy Yarns*

Slubbing The name given to the thick fibrous strands produced in the early stages of attenuation of the finished slivers preparatory to spinning the twisted fibre. Slubbing is produced from the sliver in a ropelike form about as thick as a pencil. See *Slubbings*

Slubbings Carding became mechanised around 1748 with Paul's invention of a carding cloth-covered roller-type machine. Arkwright developed a similar version in 1775. After carding, the slivers were passed through a drawing frame, also consisting of rollers, whose purpose was to draw out and impart a soft twist. This process was often repeated several times; the drawn out wool was then called a *slubbing*. The thinnest slubbings were called rovings.
See *Carding Schools*

Slub Cotton A yarn, produced by unevenly covering a cotton roving with a rayon thread.

Slubs The learner spinner often produces a yarn containing slubs, ie areas with less twist than others that produce soft thick lumps in the yarn. A more experienced spinner, when using slubs in a controlled way, can produce fancy yarns where the slub is an attractive feature. See *Fancy Yarns*

Slub Yarn Yarns designed partly in wool or cotton where the spinning is both tight and loose at regular intervals, eg *slub cotton*, *gimp yarn*.

Fig 40 *SLUB YARN*

Smearing See *Dipping – Sheep*

Snap A West of England term for a hank measuring 292.6m (320yd).

Snarl A fancy yarn with a kink or curl produced by permitting the twist to recede upon itself. Similar to *gimp yarns*.

Snarly Yarn A yarn having a tendency to twist upon itself unless held with sufficient tension.

Snitch The loop formed, before starting to spin, at the top of the spindle to hold the leader thread and spindle in a vertical position. When sufficient yarn is spun to nearly reach the ground, the *snitch* is undone and the yarn wound onto the spindle shaft. Another snitch is formed before restarting the spinning.

Sorting The preparation of wool for manufacture whereby fleeces are divided into matchings according to quality, number, length and colour.

Sound A term which denotes that wool has the tensile strength (soundness) to withstand the combing process satisfactorily.

Souple Silk Silk that is dyed in skein form with only a small amount of the sericin removed. This is much firmer, but less lustrous than fully degummed silk.

Soupling A process to produce softening in continuous filament silk yarns which are to be dyed in the gum. The yarns are treated in a warm soap solution and softened in an acid tartrate bath; this removes all but about 10 to 15 per cent of the gum in the fibre.

Spacer A ring, usually made of plastic, on some spinning wheels, eg Hebridean. It is placed on the whorl end of the spindle before the leather tab into which the spindle is inserted in the back maiden. The spacer saves excessive movement by the bobbin between the maidens.

Spider Silk Spiders' nests and webs are made of silk. They are raised for use as hairlines in telescopes and optical instruments. Some species of spiders spin the finest natural filament known. The large black and yellow common garden spider, *Araneus diadematus*, is one of the best types. It is not practicable to raise spiders on a large scale for silk.

Spindle A measure of yarn. In cotton a spindle of 18 hanks contains 13,826m (15,120yd). In linen, a spindle of 24 leas is 13,167m (14,400yd). See *Spyndle*

Spindle Ratio The ratio of a spindle whorl to the diameter of the wheel, which determines how many times the spindle must rotate to each complete turn of the wheel. See *Twists Per Inch*

Spindle Spinning In earliest times man twisted fibres between his fingers and then wound the length onto a stick. From this, without doubt, evolved the first spindles. Stone Age and Egyptian findings prove that spindles were used early in our history. Spindle spinning was already well established in *Neolithic* times and the only instrument in use for spinning until, at the earliest, the twelfth century AD. Thigh spinning was the first type of spinning and from this it was discovered that a stick with a weight at one end, when suspended, would revolve, and thus cause the fibres to be twisted, after which they could be wound onto the stick for storage. The suspended spindle was used in Ancient Egypt, Greece and Rome for centuries and they produced outstanding yarns. The world renowned *Dacca muslins* were produced on a supported spindle.

Spindles are used in most cultures in the world; the suspended type possibly more than any other, due to the mobility it permits, as the yarn can be spun whilst the spinner is walking.

There are many types of designs of hand spindles and they relate to the fibre and the method of spinning. The placing of the whorls varies considerably, as does their weight also. They are available in wood, ceramic or stone, which adds momentum to the spindle. The weight of the whorl should be taken into consideration to the yarn requirement; some whorls are placed at the top of the shafts, others at the bottom and occasionally in-between. They also provide a base on which to build the yarn. The size of the shafts varies accordingly, from the very thinnest, to as thick as in the Navajo design.

Plate 44 Drawing of spinning and weaving in Ancient Egypt

The spinning methods also vary, eg Tibetans sit on balconies to enable a longer length to be spun from their suspended spindles before they reach the ground. Salish Indians spin a thick roving over a beam.

It is beneficial to learn to spin on a spindle before working on a wheel. Unfortunately, all too often, students view the spindle as more suitable for children. It is a fact that students who learn to spin on a spindle adapt very quickly to spinning on a wheel. A spindle makes the study of the construction of yarn far easier than if it is studied while spinning on the wheel. Students should be aware that the quality of yarns spun over the centuries using spindles far surpasses what we produce today. Do not view the spindle with disdain. It is easy to make a yarn of sorts, but far more difficult to spin a really good yarn; any instrument that will make this possible is valuable.

CHOICE OF SPINDLE: do not be tempted by the most attractive design, or the most expensive. The main criteria are balance and weight. A slot or notch at the top of the shaft can, if placed correctly, provide a better balance than a half hitch method of leader yarn attachment. Hooks, similar to crochet hooks, are also satisfactory. A small metal hook can be inserted into the top of a spindle stem providing the diameter of the shaft is sufficient to take the screw without splitting.

SPINDLE TYPES AND SPINNING TECHNIQUES

Type and location	Description and use	Technique
1 *Bead Whorl spindle* Used in Africa, Asia, China and India, Ancient and Modern Mexico	produces a very fine even yarn with a high degree of twist from simultaneous drafting and twisting. Rotates at a higher rate than drop spindles. Shaft usually 16.6cm to 25.4cm (6½ to 10in), can be of metal or hardwood. Whorls usually bead but also of metal or clay. Spindle is supported in a cup or bowl.	see under *Supported Spindle Spinning*
2 *Grasped spindle* Used by Sudanese and in Ancient Egypt	a spindle grasped in both hands	a prepared rove is passed through a ring in the ceiling or on a door post, and is spun on a large spindle grasped in both hands. Passing through a ring produces the required tension and a longer spin. Attenuation and twisting is separate.

Plate 45 Ancient Egyptian spindle, 1375–1360 BC

SPINDLE TYPES AND SPINNING TECHNIQUES

Type and location	*Description and use*	*Technique*
3 *Hooked stick* Used by the Nomads of Sudan, also in Africa, Asia and Peru	by tradition, spinning is done on a stick that has a natural hook in the end, and is twisted with the right hand. A useful method of teaching children to spin, at little cost.	the stick is held in the right hand and is twisted between the fingers and thumbs. The previously teased fibre supply is held in the left hand. The stick is placed to the fibre and, as the right hand twists, it catches onto a few fibres; the left hand moves away, attenuating the fibres, whilst the right hand continues to twist the stick. When the left arm is fully stretched, wind the yarn onto the stick, leaving sufficient stick free at the base for holding, then spiral the yarn up to the hook and continue spinning. This is a fairly slow method and the yarn can be uneven, if care is not taken. The stick, if smooth, can be rolled against the thigh.
4 *High whorl spindle.* Egypt	the whorl is placed at the top of the shaft, usually with a hook in the top of the shaft, occasionally the spindle has two whorls. In a well designed spindle, the shaft is a good length to give space to store yarn and to allow hand rotation. The shaft is usually 30.5cm to 40.6cm (12 to 16in); the length varies with its origins and country.	a leader yarn is tied to the shaft below the whorl and brought up over the whorl, as for a drop spindle, and through the hook. Using the palm of the hand, the spindle shaft is swiftly rolled upwards on the right thigh to produce momentum. Then proceed as for a suspended spindle (drop). When the yarn is wound onto the shaft, make sure sufficient shaft remains clear for continued rotation by the palm of the hand. Disabled people often find the high whorl spindle

SPINDLE SPINNING

SPINDLE TYPES AND SPINNING TECHNIQUES

Type and location	Description and use	Technique
4 High whorl spindle. Egypt		easier to manipulate, providing it is well balanced; the momentum is easier to keep going than a drop spindle. An ordinary, well balanced spindle can be altered quite easily into a high whorl spindle.
5 Supported spindle: rotation against thigh	a small handspindle used in a similar way to the larger Navajo spindle	the spinner sits on the ground with the spindle supported against the thigh (choose which side of the body is best). The end of the spindle rests on the ground with the shank resting at an angle against the body. With the yarn at an angle of approx. 45° to the spindle shaft, the twist enters the yarn as the spindle is rotated, with the free hand attenuating the fibres. The spindle must be kept at the correct angle; if altered and it becomes parallel to the shaft it will unwind or if it is at right angles to the shaft, it will wind on. When an arm's length of yarn has been made, unwind from the shaft; hold it at right angles to the spindle and wind on.
Rotation of the spindle in the hand Practised by Sudanese Arabs	a difficult technique to learn; once learned it is a most attractive means of spinning. Used for wool spinning. The spindle is sometimes a stick, or a stick with a whorl at the top. The yarn produced is coarse and even. Used for weaving coverings called *shamlas*.	the spindle is held loosely in the right hand, in which it will be rotated. The rotation is achieved by the movement of the whole hand and the muscles of the palm; the fingers play very little part. The left hand controls the wool.

See *Distaff; Distaff – Hand; Navajo Spinning; Suspended Spindle Spinning*

Spinning – Learning to Spin It is necessary to become familiar with the parts of the spinning wheel (see Plate 46, *Hebridean wheel* shown.) Variations will occur according to the spinning wheel design.

1 *Wheel*: this has a rim comprised of several sections or *felloes*, a hub and spokes; its purpose is to drive the spindle and bobbin. The rim is curved to hold the drive band in place.
2 and 3 *Uprights* or *bearers*: these hold the wheel axle on which the wheel revolves. The uprights are slotted at the top of each one to support the wheel and are held in place by wooden pegs (5).
4 *Axle and crank* are usually permanently fixed to the hub. The axle can be either a metal shaft through the hub, or two short metal pins, one either side of the hub and inserted to hold in place.
5 *Wheel pegs*: these hold the wheel axle in place in slots at the top of the uprights, and prevent the wheel from jumping out.
6 *Head of footman*: this slots into the arm of the axle (the crank).
7 *Footman*, sometimes called *pitman, treadle rod, link-rod* or *con-rod*, is a length of wood linking the treadle to the crank as a connecting rod. The footman usually has an oblong or keyhole shape at the top, which fits over the knob at the end of the crank. Other designs are secured with a screw and nut, or washer and split pin arrangement. Cord is also used as a footman; this often has a leather tab piece at one end with a slit in it which enables it to fit firmly over the end of the crank.
8 *Treadle cord*: this connects the footman to the treadle. Can be adjusted when necessary.
9 *Treadle*: the means by which the wheel is revolved, by pressing the treadle up and down. It is attached at the front to the treadle bar (10) and at the back to the footman (7).
10 *Treadle bar*: the wooden bar on a spinning wheel to which the treadle is attached at the front; today, usually with nails, earlier designs had leather hinges. The bar is inserted between the front legs of the wheel by a metal pin at both ends (bearings), to facilitate movement when the treadle is in action; it pivots as the treadle moves up and down.
11 *Tension screw*: is a wooden screw with a handle, inserted into the table to adjust the tension on the driving band. It is connected to the extension of the mother-of-all (13).
12 *Table*, at times called *bench, platform, base* or *stock*: on which all the parts are constructed.
13 *Tension block under table*: this is attached to the tension block under the mother-of-all. The block is moved nearer the wheel by adjusting the tension screw (11) to lower the tension on the drive band, or to add tension by moving away from the wheel. It is attached to (18).

Plate 46 Parts of a Hebridean spinning wheel, see text

14 *Front Maiden:* 15 *Back Maiden:* sometimes called *sisters*, into which leather spindle support bearings are inserted. The front maiden has a square of leather with a hole in which the spindle with the orifice rests. The back maiden has a loop to hold the opposite end of the spindle in a horizontal position between the maidens. Both maidens are designed to twist in their sockets to facilitate removal of the spindle when the bobbin requires replacing. When the maiden is replaced, it is essential to ensure complete re-alignment.

16 *Leather bearings:* see under 15.

17 *Orifice:* the opening at the end of the spindle through which the yarn flows onto the hooks (*checks*) and then on to the bobbin. There is a collar on the spindle next to the orifice that prevents the spindle moving too much in the front leather bearing. Two 'eyes' (openings) are on each side of the spindle, behind the collar, through which the yarn winds onto the bobbin.

18 *Mother-of-all:* onto which the whole flyer assembly is cnstructed, ie the flyer, spindle, bobbin and the maidens. The circular block underneath the mother-of-all is part of the tensioning; it lies on top of a square opening in the top of the table, and is attached to the block (see 13) into which the tension screw is inserted.

19 *Bobbin:* this receives the spun yarn. It should run freely. Spinning wheels are usually supplied with spare bobbins.

20 *Flyer assembly:* see under 18.

21 *Bobbin whorl:* one loop of the drive band is passed around this.

22 *Spindle whorl:* the bobbin whorl (pulley) is smaller in diameter than the spindle whorl (pulley), so that the bobbin is turned faster than the flyer and thus winds the yarn onto the bobbin. The spindle whorl has a left hand thread.

23 *Flyer and guide hooks:* the flyer is a horseshoe-shaped piece of wood with small guide hooks, usually along each arm, to guide the spun yarn as it is wound onto the bobbin.

24 *Drive band:* the drive band connects the spindle to the large wheel, first passing around the large wheel then is looped once around the bobbin whorl and once around the spindle whorl.

25 *Spindle (or needle):* a metal shaft securely fixed to the centre of the U-shape of the flyer. It is usually made of brass, steel or cast iron. At one end is the orifice. On each side are holes, the 'eyes'. The spindle is placed between the front and back maidens in leather bearings in a horizontal position. The end placed in the back maiden is threaded, and onto this the spindle screw can be placed after the bobbin has been slipped onto the spindle. The screw often has a left handed direction, so that it will not loosen and unwind with the turning of the wheel.

a) first oil all the moveable parts on the wheel, ie remove the bobbin

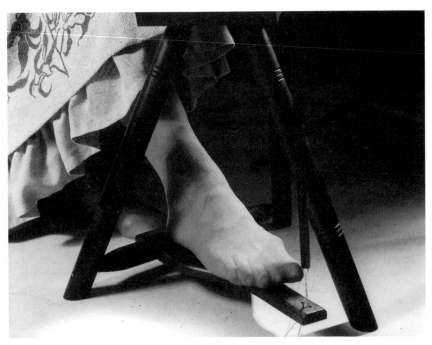

Plate 47 Correct placing of foot on treadle to obtain easy control and even pressure when required

Plate 48 Close-up of wheel showing crank in correct position to commence spinning

and, with a small amount of oil on your finger, rub over the metal spindle. Oil the crank on the footman. Oil the bar through the large wheel; if necessary, the wooden pegs on the uprights can be removed and the wheel raised for easy access.

b) release the tension so that it will not pull in the thread too quickly.

c) place a chair in front of the wheel with the orifice near to you and where easy foot movement is possible on the treadle. If the seat is placed too far back from the wheel, which would necessitate stretching the leg to reach the treadle, it will press the wheel constantly away from the spinner. Place the foot comfortably and evenly on the treadle.

d) turn the wheel so that the crank can be seen slightly to the right, ie if Z-twisting. Press down with the ball of the right foot on the treadle and at the same time, with the right hand placed on one of the wheel spokes (never on the wheel rim, which would eventually cause a build-up of grease and subsequent drive band slippage), flick the wheel to the right (clockwise). Practise until you can keep the wheel running in this direction. It should not be permitted to run anticlockwise. Practise stopping and starting; if the crank is always to the right when the wheel is stopped, it will make starting again easier. As you treadle, watch the footman and press down with your foot when it is at the top (slightly to the right). When the crank is at its highest position, the treadle will be also high and vice versa; at this position the wheel and treadle will be static and movement will be only possible if the wheel is started with the right hand. The first push on the treadle must be very firm to make the wheel complete a full turn; if rather tentative, the wheel will only turn part way and the problem of wheel reversal will occur. A clanking noise often indicates that the treadle is hitting the footman as it rises. Adjustment on the treadle cord may be required, or the noise may be due to the spinner lifting the foot from the treadle. It is essential at all times to keep the foot completely flat and in contact with the treadle to produce a smooth treadle action with no jerking foot movements. It is essential to practise alternating speeds; anyone can keep a wheel revolving once it has momentum, however, to be a successful spinner it is necessary to control the wheel, which can only be achieved by practice. Once treadling has been mastered, the next stage is spinning a yarn.

e) take a piece of either handspun or similar yarn, slightly hairy if possible, measuring about 3m (3yd), for the leader. It should have been spun in the same direction ie Z- or S-twisted, as the yarn to be spun. First tie around the bobbin shank (stem) and, using the thumb of the right hand, turn the bobbin towards the wheel so that the leader yarn wraps itself around the bobbin several times. Take the end of the leader yarn and place over the hooks, on one side of

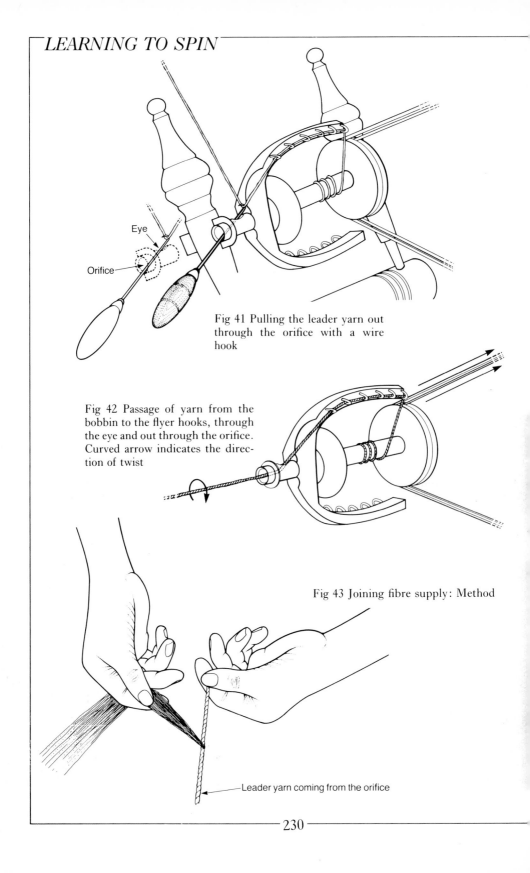

Eye

Orifice

Fig 41 Pulling the leader yarn out through the orifice with a wire hook

Fig 42 Passage of yarn from the bobbin to the flyer hooks, through the eye and out through the orifice. Curved arrow indicates the direction of twist

Fig 43 Joining fibre supply: Method

Leader yarn coming from the orifice

the flyer. Lay the yarn over the eye on the top of the spindle shaft. Insert the wire part of a threading hook into the orifice and out of the eye and catch hold of the yarn and pull it down through the eye and out of the orifice.

f) it is immaterial in the next stage whether the right or left hand is to the front. Some spinners prefer one way, others another; try both and see which is more comfortable and easy (see Plates 49 and 50). Take a previously prepared rolag and pulling the leader yarn well away from the orifice, hold the rolag in the left or right hand and pull a few fibres from the end. Hold the leader yarn in contact with the attenuated fibres and begin to treadle, whereby the fibres will quickly catch on to the leader and start to twist (*fig 43*).

METHOD 1: this stage can be difficult, as rapid treadling could result in the yarn parting from the fibre supply and disappearing; alternatively if the treadling is too slow, it may be difficult to keep the wheel

Plates 49–50 (*left*) fibre held in the left hand. The right hand will release the twist to enable it to enter the drafting zone. It is essential to hold the hands a little further apart than the actual staple length, otherwise drafting will be impossible (*right*) Fibre held in the right hand

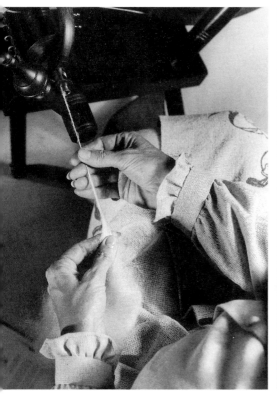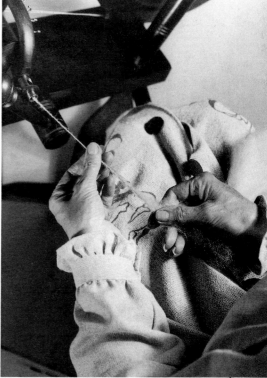

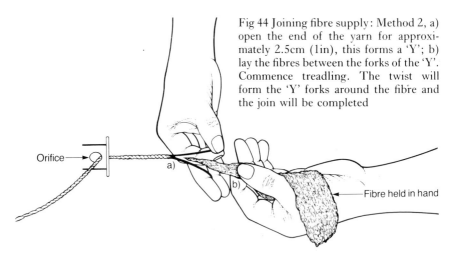

Fig 44 Joining fibre supply: Method 2, a) open the end of the yarn for approximately 2.5cm (1in), this forms a 'Y'; b) lay the fibres between the forks of the 'Y'. Commence treadling. The twist will form the 'Y' forks around the fibre and the join will be completed

Orifice

a)

b)

Fibre held in hand

revolving. It will quickly become apparent whether sufficient treadling practice has been done. Provided no problems have arisen, once the leader is joined to the fibre supply, hold the right hand about 15.3cm (6in) away from the orifice using the thumb and forefinger to control the twist. Draw back with the left hand and at the same time release and control the fibres to be spun. The twist must not be permitted to run up into the rolag, this would cause matting. Once sufficient twist has been inserted, allow the yarn to be wound onto the bobbin, then pinch again with the thumb and forefinger of the right hand to hold back the twist, draw out with the left hand to attenuate the fibres, release twist and allow to travel up the fibres and wind the yarn on. Continue in this way. See *Method 2 fig 44* for an alternative method of joining the fibre supply.

At first, the student tends to pull both ways with the hands which is called a *picking* movement, whereas a *drawing* movement is required. Students may become agitated and tense whilst concentrating on production of yarn without being aware that their treadling has become faster. Alternatively they may forget to treadle and the wheel is allowed to reverse, which then may cause the yarn to jump off the flyer hooks or become twisted around the spindle. When a problem occurs, immediately cease all activities, breathe deeply and relax. Find out the cause of the trouble, rectify it, then re-commence treadling, this time more slowly, which will give time to learn co-ordination of hands and treadling. Second and subsequent rolags are joined as the first.

Once a yarn can be produced, then consideration can be given to various spinning techniques. Practice is the only way to learn. Study what is being produced and how it is happening. Once confidence is gained, move the hands further apart and, when the twist is released to travel up the yarn, at the same time move the left hand backwards as far as is comfortable, then when sufficient twist has been inserted sweep the left hand towards the orifice to wind on the yarn. As the bobbin fills, alter the yarn around the flyer hooks so that an even fill of the bobbin occurs. The tension will require to be increased as the bobbin fills because of the additional weight and bulk.

Whilst it has been stressed how essential practice is, it is not advisable at first to sit for a long while at the wheel. The relaxation of spinning will not be apparent to students if they sit too long, become tense, and subsequently tired. Spend some time after a spinning session to discover the reasons for any problems or analyse why a successful yarn has been produced.

See *Bobbin; Footman; Long Draw; Mother-of-All; Orifice; Problems; Seats; Short Draw; Treadle Bar; Treadle Cord; U-Flyer*

Problems When Learning To Spin:

Problem	*Answer*
1 Treadling commences and immediately the leader yarn disappears out of the student's hands, jumps off the flyer hooks and wraps onto the bobbin	Release the tension more. Rethread the leader yarn pulling out a longer length well away from the orifice and try again.
2 Treadling commences and the leader yarn does not twist and the fibres are therefore not attached	a) possibly the original attaching of the leader yarn to the bobbin was not secure or too loose; the bobbin then rotates within the yarn. The leader must be securely tied and wrapped around the bobbin several times.
	b) the tension may be too slack.
3 The spinner's arms and shoulders ache	The chair may be too low necessitating reaching up to the orifice. Add a cushion to the chair to bring the spinner in line with the orifice height.
4 Spinner's treadling leg aches	The angle of the wheel in relation to the spinner may be wrong.
	a) adjust to obtain a comfortable position.
	b) the wheel parts may not be oiled sufficiently, so rectify this. Established spinners often oil their wheel several times during a spinning session.
5 The yarn keeps kinking and breaking	a) may be overtwisting so increase the tension.
	b) check there are no sharp edges on the orifice.

See also *Problems*

Spinifex Describes grass particles about 20mm (¾in) long which are smooth at one end and have three spines at the other. Can cause problems by adhering to the fleece.

Spinneret See *Manmade Fibres; Sericulture*

Spinning 'In the Grease' To some spinners this term means spinning with wool as it comes off the sheep's back, ie not scoured; the wool may be carded and prepared first. To other spinners it means wool spun directly from the fleece with no preparation.

Spinning Jenny Some authorities state the word 'jenny' means engine. The demise of handspinning began in 1765 when in England, James Hargreaves designed the spinning jenny. (See also *Cotton* – section on historical details). It had sixteen upright spindles that were turned by eight single driving bands. One hand was used to control the travelling carriage which fed the yarn onto the bobbin after the roving had been spun. The other hand turned a wheel, which turned

Plate 51 Hargreaves' spinning jenny

234

the spindles. He designed the spinning jenny to assist the output of his family who all earned their living by handspinning. He kept it hidden due to the strong feelings existing during that period by spinners and weavers over the threat of mechanisation; the machine was eventually discovered and destroyed. Hargreaves was threatened with death and forced to leave his home town. Within a comparatively short time, mechanisation had taken over. The word jenny also occurs in wool-combing. It is the preliminary pad which was used to hold the comb in a vertical position while the wool was being lashed on. See *Combing*

Spinning out of the Fold Also called the *folded lock method*: when spinning with a long-stapled combed fibre, fold a length of the fibre over the left forefinger, a length of about 25.4cm (10in) will be sufficient. Lay the leader (starter) cord in the centre of the fold and catch to join. The forefinger should at all times be in the centre of the fold and in line with the orifice and the fibres should be continually drawn out from the centre of the fold at the tip. The drawing-out triangle will be long.

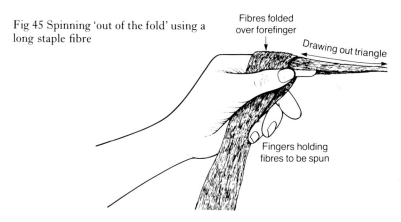

Fig 45 Spinning 'out of the fold' using a long staple fibre

Fibres folded over forefinger

Drawing out triangle

Fingers holding fibres to be spun

Spinning Quality The most important fibre characteristic in relation to a wool's spinning performance is fineness, for that will determine the degree of fineness of the yarn that can be produced from it. It is also desirable for it to be relatively free of elliptical cross-section, if a good spinning performance is to be obtained.

Spinning Schools Set across Europe between 1600 and 1750. These resembled factories producing the maximum output of standardised yarns. Children were employed for a minute wage from the age of six; sometimes as many as two hundred at a time sat on benches spinning. In the centre sat a grand mistress with a long stick to tap any child who was idle. In 1661, linen making as a Scottish industry was introduced, and again delegated to the poor. About 1727 the 'schools' were introduced into the Highlands.

Spinning Twist Also called *singles twist* is the twist that is inserted into the fibre during spinning.
See *Folding Twist*

Spinning, What It Is The twisting of short fibres together to form a strong continuous length of yarn or thread; the process has changed very little from earlier years until today. Possibly the first fibre to be spun was human hair.

Spinning Wheel A machine for spinning fibres of varying types into yarn. It consists of a wheel, driving band and spindle driven by hand (great wheel) or foot (treadle wheels). The spinning wheel imparts twist into the fibres, then winds the formed yarn onto the bobbin. The flyer was being used by 1480, the treadle early in the sixteenth century, although it was in more general use in the seventeenth century. However, mechanisation in the eighteenth century caused spinning to move from a domestic situation activity into an industrial one. Today's spinners are still in demand when a handweaver or knitter may require a specially designed yarn, often from more specialist fibres, eg camel, cashmere, etc.
See *Castle Wheel; Charka; Double Band Wheel (Saxony); Double Flax Wheel; Great Wheel; Hoop-Rimmed Spinning Wheel; Jürgen, Johann; Leonardo da Vinci; Occupational Therapy; Orkney Wheel; Shakers; Single Band Wheel (Scotch Tensioner)*

Spinning Wheels, Choosing
GENERAL CONSIDERATIONS: people are drawn to spinning in a variety of ways; it is essential to go to a reputable stockist who can give advice and recommend the wheel best suited to the individual's requirements. Wheels, as with any piece of furniture or equipment, can look very different in the display area in the shop; space should be taken into consideration; whether to chose a horizontal or upright wheel. An upright wheel takes up less floor space and is easier to transport. A horizontal wheel gives more room for a larger wheel; usually the orifice is at a more comfortable height and there is extra treadling space. It is wise, when choosing a wheel, to try out several types. Comfort is essential, as spinning often requires long periods of sitting at the wheel. The craft is very therapeutic; however, if the spinner's body and limbs ache due to incorrect positioning, eg if a chair is too low in relation to the wheel, requiring that the arms reach up to the orifice rather than are at a comfortable height in line with it, therapeutic values are quickly lost. Wheels, unless designed to be portable,

on the whole do not travel well, and quickly become damaged or broken because of excessive handling. If you intend to travel with a wheel to guild meetings, shows, etc, the facilities for transport should be considered. The Ashford traveller wheel is ideal for this purpose. *Cost*: wheels can be purchased assembled or in a packed flat form ready for assembly. The latter are usually less expensive, but if you purchase a wheel that requires assembly, buy from a reputable firm (see *Stockist* section at the end of the book). Spinning wheel plans are available; care should be taken, as many on the market are designed by people with very little knowledge of the craft of spinning, and they may have concentrated more on the visual, rather than the functional aspects of the wheel. In addition to the cost of the wheel are the various accessories, eg carders, etc. However, these need not all be purchased immediately; this equipment can be acquired gradually.

Part	Considerations
Bobbins	These should revolve easily on the spindle shaft and not be too small. An inside measurement of approximately 10.3cm (4in) is ideal. Spare bobbins are necessary.
Flyer	The flyer arms should not be shaped so that they cramp the bobbin. Measure the width of the open arms of the flyer, then measure the length of the bobbin; these measurements should correspond. All moving parts should be easy to use. The flyer should be well balanced; if it only has hooks (hecks) on one arm, the other arm should be sufficiently weighted to counteract this. The hooks, if on both arms, should be evenly spaced on the flyer to facilitate even build-up of yarn on the bobbin (see *fig 46, 1* and *2*).

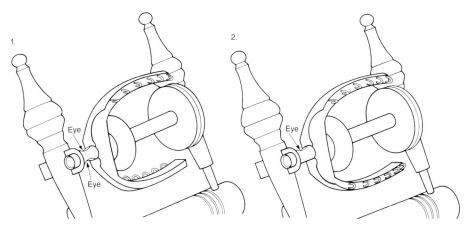

Fig 46 The flyer has hooks on each arm to balance. 1 Shows the hooks on opposite sides; in this design there should be two eyes (exit holes) in the spindle. 2 Shows hooks on the same side of the flyer arm, one for spinning and one for plying; there is only one exit hole

237

Maidens	Depending on the wheel design these may be adjustable. They should be in complete alignment to the wheel. If they have to be turned to remove the flyer assembly, check once they have returned to their original position that they firmly stay in place.
Orifice	A very important consideration, as one size orifice will not be capable of producing every yarn size. A small orifice will accept only fine yarn. A useful size of orifice for most spinners' requirements is up to 1.3cm (½in). There should be a clear passage for the yarn to be hooked out through the orifice.
Spindle whorl	These may screw or be a push fit. If a screw, it should fit in an anticlockwise direction to prevent unscrewing when the wheel is revolving clockwise. Secondhand wheels should be carefully examined in this area, as the whorl may have had its thread stripped by being screwed in the wrong direction.
Tensioners	On a double band wheel there is one tensioner; on a scotch tensioning system there are two, where the main one is set before spinning and the peg tensioning the brake is set during spinning. With either type of tensioning, check that they work satisfactorily and hold their position. Whilst they should not be too loose, alternatively, if too stiff they are difficult to use during spinning.
Treadle	There should be complete freedom of movement of the treadle; not too loose or too stiff. The table should not be in the way. The treadle should not be too narrow; the spinner's foot should be completely supported to permit good control. The treadle should not slope away from the spinner but should lie parallel to the ground or be just slightly raised.
Wheel	The wheel should not be noisy or vibrate. It should revolve smoothly and true, not warped in any way. With the band removed, and when treadling ceases, it should continue to revolve freely; below thirty revolutions may indicate some friction.
Woodwork	Good jointing with a smooth overall finish.

ANTIQUE WHEELS: a wheel to be used must be functional. Antique wheels can look very attractive in a shop or showroom but more often than not are made up of a variety of wheel parts, or may have been repaired with non-functional parts. Parts may be missing; warping can be a problem and also woodworm. Antique wheels can be very expensive so it is advisable, when purchasing, to employ the services of an expert.

Spinning Wheel Maintenance All mechanical parts should be lubricated whether spinning or not. Atmospheric conditions, eg central heating, sun, damp, etc, will greatly affect a wheel.

CHOICE OF LUBRICATION: choice of a suitable oil is a personal one; in fact one oil may well suit a particular wheel more than another.

TYPES:
3 in 1: a light oil that has a nozzle on the can for ease of application.
Sewing machine oil: a light oil that tends to attract dirt.
Neatsfoot oil: is available from saddlers and from hardware shops. Suitable for leatherwork.
Vaseline: tends to be sticky and messy to apply.

Some spinners favour axle grease. Once the oil has been selected, oil the following:
a) the bearings on each maiden.
b) axle bearings on the wheel.
c) metal bearings on the treadle bar.

During a spinning session, oil several times. When spinning fast, the orifice can become warm. Unfortunately, oil attracts dirt, which causes wear; therefore cleanliness is very important. Clean all working parts thoroughly from time to time.

FOOTMAN: check the cord that attaches the footman to the treadle. If it is too loose, it will bang the floor; if too tight, the foot will rest at an uncomfortable angle; it should be parallel to the ground or just slightly raised, never sloping backwards, as a badly adjusted treadle can be tiring in use.

DRIVE BAND: always check before spinning; if damaged or worn, replace.

SINGLE BAND WHEEL: place band once around the wheel and flyer pulley. Overlap the ends and join by splicing or sewing.

DOUBLE BAND WHEEL: loosen the tension screw to the point nearest the wheel. Remove the old band and replace with the new band, by passing it around the rim of the wheel, over the bobbin pulley, again around the wheel, then around the flyer pulley forming a crossover in the band. If the flyer pulley has two grooves, use the band around the groove with the smallest diameter; the larger diameter groove will give less twist to the yarn.

WHEEL GROOVES: these will need to be cleaned out from time to time as the driving band will collect dirt and impart it to the wheel, especially during the bobbin change. If cleaning with a knife, care should be taken not to damage the wood.

POLISHING THE WOODWORK: beeswax polish or a good furniture polish is ideal for the woodwork.

OILING THE WOODWORK: wheels treated with linseed oil will require repeated applications if they become dry. Care should be taken to avoid oiling the wheel grooves.

GENERAL: watch the wheel overall for any signs of wear and, if it becomes necessary to employ the services of a professional for any repair job, select someone used to working with spinning wheels. The parts of a spinning wheel are inter-related and therefore a badly executed repair job could have an adverse affect on the rest of the wheel. See *Drive Band; Spinning – Learning to Spin; U-Flyer*

Spinning Without a Spindle From the earliest times, spinning has evolved from the simple method of twisting fibres between the hands, or alternatively on the thighs. In Greece 600 to 400 years BC, the production of roving was well advanced by rolling on the thigh. The spinner used a foot rest and, as a protection for the leg, used a pottery *epinetron* or *onos*, which had a marked surface to prevent the fibres slipping.

The Aborigines in Australia spin on their thighs, using grasses.

Spinster The original means – 'a woman who spins', possibly as the spinning was usually performed by women. Later it became the term given to an unmarried woman unlikely to marry, hence the English noun 'spinster'. Today, the general term used for those who spin is 'spinner'.

Spiral or Corkscrew Yarn A fancy, 2 ply yarn with the two single strands held at even tension in the plying, one component smoothly spiralling around the other. There are various constructions, eg
a) two single ends of equal length containing S and Z twists respectively.
b) the plied yarn can be produced by delivering one or more of its components at a greater rate, the shorter length forming the base with the greater length spiralling around it.
c) the plied yarn consisting of two ends of equal length one coarser than the other, the finer forming the base and the coarser end spiralling around it.

Splice Attaching a new supply of fibre to spun yarn.

Springiness Wool of a springy texture can be tested to determine to what degree it will return to its natural state after being compressed.

Sprit-Flax The small pieces of woody epidermal tissue that adhere to the fibre strands.

Spun Silk When a cocoon becomes too fine for reeling, it is broken out and another cocoon joined in. The remnants of these cocoons, and the floss removed at the beginning of reeling, are used in the manufacture of *schappe* or *spun silk*, whereby they are torn up by machines into short lengths. Schappe or spun silk is composed of twisted staple and is not fully degummed. When purchasing spun silk, it is referred to as *combed* if all noil is removed, and *carded* when the noil is present. The procedures for spun silk are long, starting with the softening, followed by pulling-out; degumming; cocoon beating (the removal of pupa waste); opening and fulling (untangling and cutting); dressing (sorting lengths and noils); and finally drawing and spreading into *sheet* or lap form, sliver and the final thickness for spinning.

Silk has the image of a fine lustrous lightweight thread; however, heavy spun silk yarns can be produced, but they are costly due to the quantity of silk required.

Nubby spun silk is the process, during the spinning of the carded fibre, which produces an interesting texture in the woven material.
See *Silk Waste*

Spun Yarn A yarn consisting of fibres, either of regular or irregular length, bound together by twisting.

Spyndle Used in Scotland to describe the heavier linen yarns. Their quality is indicated by their weight per spyndle of 48 cuts or leas.

Squirrel Cage A vertical stand with two adjustable cylindrical cages which freely move; the skein of yarn is placed around these. Termed a *swift*.
See *Swift*

Staple A lock or tuft of fibres of similar properties, eg fibres growing from the sheep's skin naturally form themselves into small tapering locks or tufts called *staples*. Wool is described as being short, medium or long staple. The length of a staple is measured from base to tip without stretching. When it is stretched the fibre length can be determined. The staple length is rather hypothetical; if the staple is pointed, as for example in a Longwool, it really only states the length of the longest fibres since within the lock may be many shorter fibres, whereas a short wool with a square-shaped staple tends to be more uniform in length overall. The length of a staple does not denote its fineness, as variation in diameter occurs along the staple length. A suitable staple length for someone learning to spin is about 10.3cm to 12.7cm (4 to 5in).
See *Lock*

Staple Length The length of the staple from the base to the tip, measured when unstretched.

Staplers See *Broggers*

Staples See *Fairs*

Star Lots Parcels of wool containing less than the stated number of bales specified for sale in the main sale room.

Static Electricity This can be a problem when working with hair-type fibres or fine fibres at the preparation stage. Easily resolved by spraying the fibre with an oil and water emulsion (one part olive oil to one part water). See *Emulsion – Dressing*

Steam Silk Silk that is filature, not hand, reeled.

Steely Wool produced on pastures deficient in certain trace elements; it tends to lack character and has a steely sheen.

Stock See *Table*

Storing – Fleece Cotton pillowcases and hessian sacks are suitable storage containers for fleece. Plastic bags cause sweating. It is essential to thoroughly dry a fleece before storing otherwise it will quickly smell of mildew, which is caused by micro-organisms in the air. Mildew has considerable staining qualities. Humid places tend to encourage mildew which can damage cellulose, protein and also synthetic fibres. Moths are the main enemy; the fleece can be sprinkled with *paradichlorobenzene crystals*. It is advisable not to pack the fleece too tightly in the container; layers of paper can be used to divide the different qualities. It should be examined occasionally. The neck of the container should be secured by a tape, or similar, with a label noting the breed (or fleece type), date of sorting and any other relevant information.

Stoving A method used for bleaching wool, silk, hair or other keratinous materials in a moist condition. The material, after scouring, is placed in a closed chamber where it is exposed to burning sulphur dioxide. Wet stoving is the treatment of material with a solution of a sulphite or bisulphite.
   Wool yarns and also woven fabric can be bleached in this way, however, the white is not permanent.

Strand An individual component, eg a single, two-fold or multi-fold yarn, of a folded or cabled construction.

Straw, Tow This is flax straw in a damaged, broken condition, the result of threshing a flax crop too poor to be processed normally.

Strength Wool can be termed as *sound* or *tender*, relating to the ability of the fibres to withstand breakage during processing.

Stricks Also called *queues* and *strikes* (referring to jute) is the name given to small bundles of flax, straws, scutched flax or hackled flax.

Strike When the dye penetrates the fibre.

Striker A wooden cross into which dried teasels, *Dipsacus sylvestris fullonum*, were set. It is thought to have been used as a means of carding in earlier times. Other references tend to be of the opinion that the striker was used only for raising the nap on cloth during the finishing process.

Stripping The removal of dye from fibre.

Strong Wool The Australian term for crossbred sheep, sometimes also used for the British lustre wools. Any extra long staple wool from any wool clip may be referred to as 'strong wool'.

Strusa Also called *frisson*. Silk waste that has the appearance of coloured straw; it has to be degummed before spinning.
See *Degumming*

S-Twist Yarn spun in an anticlockwise direction, producing yarn with a twist opposite to Z-twisted. Early Egyptians spun with a S-twist.

Fig 47 Single 'S' spun yarn

Style A term used by professionals relating to the best attributes of the wool, ie good colour, elasticity, length and softness.

Suint The name given to the sweat secreted by sheep from the *sudoriferous* or sweat *gland*. Long wool breeds produce more suint than fine wool breeds. The grease in the fleece is insoluble in water. The suint, composed of soluble potassium salts, and soluble in cold water, acts as a cleanser to remove much of the grease from the wool.

Superfine Wool Wool mainly from Australian *Saxon merinos*, the most expensive and finest wool. Used for luxury knitwear and men's tailored suits made to the highest specifications.

Supported Spindle At first this may appear to be a more difficult means of spindle spinning; the student, if conversant with suspended spindle spinning, will miss the downward pull of the fibres produced by the weight of the whorl. To a degree, supported spindles have the added advantage in that they do not so easily break the thread and do not reverse direction, as they simply slow down and cease to rotate in the container. Bead spindles are suitable for spinning short fibres, eg cotton. A bead spindle is simple to make; it requires a thin shaft, approximately 17.8cm to 25.4cm (7 to 10in) ending in a sharp point to reduce friction. The shaft is then pushed through the centre of a suitable bead; sometimes it is necessary to glue it in place to secure. It is essential to keep the weight to a minimum. A spindle weighing up to 28g (1oz) is suitable.

TECHNIQUE:

a) place a suitable container, eg a cup turned upside down, either on the floor if the spinner intends to sit, or on a table. Spinning is done from the tip of the spindle, in some ways similar to spinning from the great wheel, except that the bead spindle is held in an upright position.

b) attach a leader yarn to the shaft. Alternatively, if preferred, catch a few fibres to the top of the shaft by moistening the tip (if the spindle has a hook then attach the fibres to this). The draw will be short; because of the shortness of the cotton fibres, a large amount of twist is necessary. With the spindle and container to the right of the body, draw out to the left, using the left hand turning the spindle clockwise with the right hand. Continue in this manner using a short draw of about 5cm (2in) of fibre, add the twist and attenuate the fibres from the tip of the spindle. When sufficient length of yarn has been spun, about 76.2cm (2½ft), remove from the tip of the spindle and wind onto the shaft in a clockwise direction, just above the bead whorl, spiralling up the shaft and leave sufficient to attach to the hook (or to work from the spindle tip, if the spindle has no hook).

c) twist the spindle with the right thumb and first finger as for suspended spindle spinning, then once it has gained momentum encircle the stem with them and draw out the cotton at an angle of approximately 45 degrees to the left using the left hand. The twist will enter the fibres from the spindle tip. Twist the spindle when necessary, and as the twist enters the unspun fibres, move the left hand at the same speed as the twist travels towards it. When sufficient length of spun yarn is obtained (usually arm's length), it is necessary to discontinue drafting, but maybe more twist will be required, in which case let the spindle continue to rotate until required twist is obtained. Wind the spun yarn onto the spindle shaft by lowering the left hand parallel to the spindle; still keeping the yarn taut, hold the spindle in an upright position and turn with the right hand in a clockwise direction; gradually move the left hand towards it, always keeping the yarn taut, until it is wound onto the shaft.

Problems	*Reason and Solution*
1 The yarn falls apart	This is related to the speed at which the left hand moves; it should not be too fast.
2 Thick lumps formed in the yarn	The left hand is drawing out too slowly, therefore the twist is entering the fibre mass and producing lumps.
3 Difficulty in controlling the fibre supply	Whilst a teased mass of fibres can be held in the hand, a student may tend to clutch this whilst learning to spin, because of tension and trying to learn several actions at one time. However, for both the learner and established spinner who require continuity of spinning, prepared *tops* are very suitable; these produce a smooth, even yarn. This fibre supply has to be stored somehow. A very lightweight hand distaff could be used, but is not so convenient as a cord-type bracelet distaff, which fits loosely around the left wrist, with the prepared tops wrapped around the base above the tassel. The bracelet should be of a rough texture to assist adhesion of the fibre; this is also suitable for cotton spinning, as shown in fig 48 (*left*).

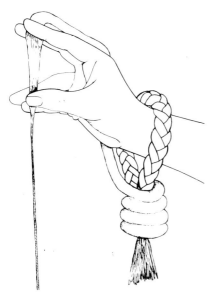

4 Spun yarn kinks whilst winding onto the spindle stem	This is caused by the spinner omitting to hold the yarn taut between both hands.

245

Suspended Spindle Spinning Also called *drop spindle*: with suspended spinning, the spindle hangs freely; the spinner draws the fibre supply and the weight of the spindle drafts by stretching it, ie the yarn is pulled at both ends. This is called *double drafting* and assists in producing a fine yarn. Two ways to twist: either twist the shaft with the thumb and first finger of the right hand then let the spindle hang freely to impart twist, or roll the spindle with the right palm against the right thigh then allow to spin freely as before.

Points to take into consideration:
1 Do not let the twist run up into the fibre supply as this will make continuation of drafting impossible.
2 When necessary to stop the spindle, secure it, otherwise it will untwist in the opposite direction.
3 When twisting the spindle, it should turn quickly in a balanced way, with no wobble.
4 When a rolag is lying over the left hand, take care that both ends do not become joined to the yarn being spun. This can be avoided by keeping the rolag to a workable length.
5 Heavier yarns require extra weight on the whorls when suspended spinning; plasticine can be added to the base, alternatively choose a spindle with a heavier whorl which would require no weight addition. To produce a really heavy yarn use a Navajo spindle which is supported.
6 Very fine or short staple yarns require the spindle to be supported.
7 The use of a bracelet distaff or stick distaff to store the fibre supply is a valuable addition when spindle spinning.
8 If the yarn continually breaks, this usually indicates inadequate twist or overtwist.
9 An inability to draft may indicate:-
   a) the twist has been allowed to run into the fibre supply
   b) the hands may be too close together and therefore pulling at both ends of the staple length.
10 If, when winding the spun yarn onto the spindle shaft for storing, the yarn becomes very tangled, this is because the spinner is omitting to keep the yarn taut between the right hand holding the spindle and the left hand.

TECHNIQUE
a) tie a 60.9cm (2yd) length of either handspun or yarn with a coarse texture Z-spun (if wishing to spin a Z-twisted yarn) to the shaft (stem) of the spindle about 0.7cm (¼in) above the whorl. Take the end down over the whorl round the point of the shaft, back over the whorl edge and to the top of the shaft. Secure either with a half-

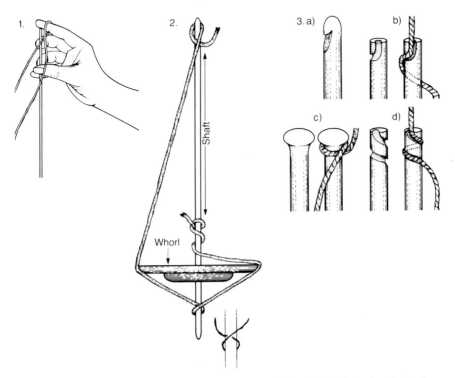

Fig 49 1 Placing the leader yarn to secure at the top of the spindle; 2 placing the leader yarn on the spindle top and base; 3 types of spindle tops: a) hook; b) slot; c) knob; d) groove

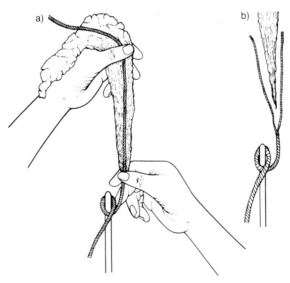

Fig 50 *SPINDLE SPINNING*: joining the fibre supply

hitch or place into the notch or slit depending on the design of the spindle (see *fig 49*).

b) fluff out the end of the yarn. Hold the prepared fibre in the left hand, let it lie over the back of the left hand. Place the leader yarn from the spindle onto the fibres, slightly attenuating them first. Hold both the fibres and the leader yarn with the left hand (see *fig 50a*).

c) using the right hand, twist the shaft of the spindle clockwise (it can be spun anticlockwise using an S-twisted leader yarn so long as spinning is continued in that same way, otherwise the twist will undo and the whole thing drop to the floor). Let the twist travel upwards and this will join the yarn and the fibre supply. Alternatively, use method b) (*fig 50*). The yarn is opened and the fibre laid inside the V formed. Hold together with the left hand and twist the spindle with the right hand to join.

d) move the right hand up to below the fibres, the actual distance between the hands is determined by the length of the staple. Slightly ease the left hand hold on the fibres and this will permit more fibres to be drawn down (drafted); the actual amount will determine the yarn size but it must be strong enough to support the weight of the spindle. When drafting, the right hand must hold back the twist and pull at the base of the drawing-out triangle. The right hand moves down to twist the spindle when necessary, then moves up with the twist, then drafts again.

e) when the spun yarn reaches the ground, slip the leader yarn from under the whorl and push off the half-hitch, or whatever method is used for securing at the top. The spindle is held in the right hand and the yarn is kept taut between the left hand and right hand, otherwise the yarn will quickly tangle. Wind the yarn onto the left hand in a figure-of-eight between thumb and little finger (across the palm). Keep the yarn taut between the left hand and the right hand, then wind the yarn onto the shaft starting nearest the whorl. Work backwards and forwards, spiralling up and down the shaft, to store the yarn into a cone shape, the widest part nearest the whorl. This will help to increase the momentum when spinning. Wind all but 30.5cm (12in) onto the shaft.

Fig 51 (*above*) *SPINDLE SPINNING*: drafting; the distance between the hands when drafting is determined by the staple length

Fig 52 (*below*) *SPINDLE SPINNING*: 1 Spindle spinning medium to long staple. Hand position; 2 some spinners prefer to twist the spindle on the stem; 3 alternative hand position for twisting the spindle; 4 spinning with a long staple fibre. When joining, place the leader yarn in the fold; 5 spinning a short staple fibre; draw out between first and third fingers; 6 remove cone from the spindle by sliding from the base

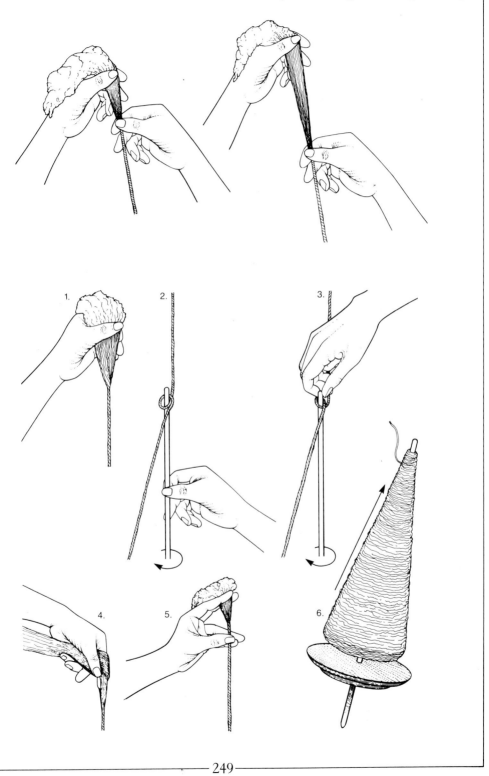

1.

2.

3.

4.

5.

6.

SUSPENDED SPINDLE SPINNING

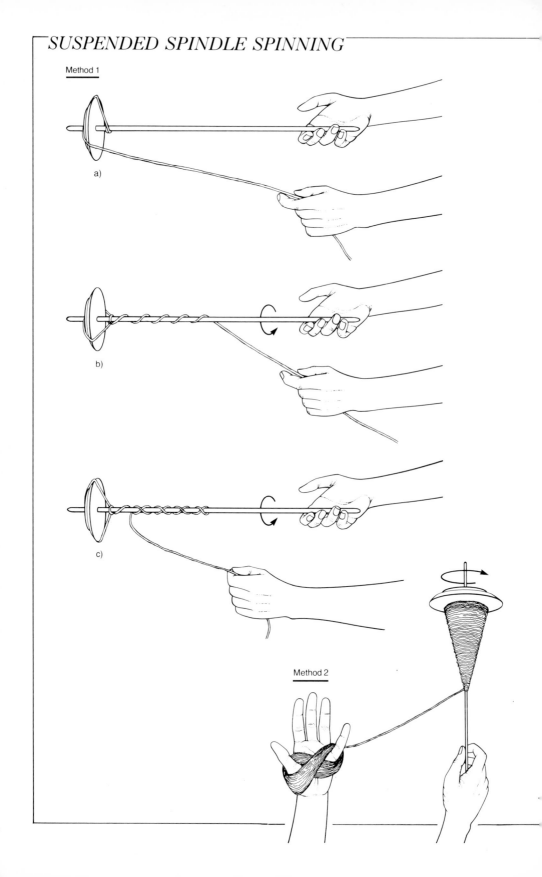

Method 1

a)

b)

c)

Method 2

f) replace the end of the yarn around the whorl and shaft as before and recommence spinning. If wishing at any time to stop the spindle, place against the inside of the left knee or foot; this will prevent it unwinding. When the spindle feels heavy, it is necessary to remove the yarn by slipping it off the shaft. A metal spike set into a piece of wood is a useful means of storing the cone of yarn. If the yarn is so tightly wound that it will not come off the spindle shaft in a cone, then it will be necessary to suspend the spindle horizontally by two pieces of string, and unwind the yarn into a ball or onto a niddy noddy or similar. As with wheel spinning, spinners vary in their style of work with hand spindles. Some may twist the spindle at the tip of the shaft (*fig 52, 3*) others prefer to twist holding the shaft further down (*fig 52, 2*), and others may draft by pulling the left hand away from the right hand. When winding the yarn onto the shaft, many spinners prefer to hold the yarn taut and wind on (see *fig 52*, Method 1); others wind onto the left hand first and then onto the spindle (see *fig 54*, Method 2.)

Suspended Spindle Plying

METHOD 1: take two (or more) balls (or cones) of the previously spun yarn. Place on the left hand side; join to the leader on the spindle, lay the yarn over the back of the left hand bringing at the same time through the thumb and index finger and spin in the opposite direction to the previously spun yarn, using the right hand. The tension must be even; the weight of the whorl should be sufficient to pull the yarn through the fingers, if not, the yarn can be pulled and controlled by the right hand. Plying removes a percentage of the twist in the original yarns, which should be taken into account in the original twist of the singles. Wash as spun yarn.

METHOD 2: a particularly useful method for physically disabled or blind people. Two or more full identical spindles are required, ie size, design and weight according to how many yarns are to be plied, plus an empty spindle. Attach and suspend the yarns in the same way as for Method 1. Place the full spindles over the spinner's shoulders and let them rest on the floor behind the spinner. Spin the spindle in an anti-clockwise direction, if plying Z-twisted yarns (or reverse if S-twisting) and impart the required amount of twist, drafting the singles with both hands and using the thumbs and fingers, until the spindle reaches the floor. Wind the plied yarn onto the spindle shaft and continue until all the singles have been plied.

Figs 53–4 *SUSPENDED SPINDLE SPINNING*: (*above*) winding the spun yarn; Method 1; (*below*) winding the spun yarn; Method 2

· Tease
easel · T
· Tease

S / **T**

ry Colours · Texture · Thread · Thrown Silk · Tines ·
Colours · Texture · Thread · Thrown Silk · Tines · Tip
ry Colours · Texture · Thread · Thrown Silk · Tines ·

Swifts Implements for holding hanks of yarn whilst being wound into balls. There are several types. The expanding umbrella-type swift can be obtained made in wood or plastic covered wires. It can be used vertically or horizontally clamped to a table and is often used in conjunction with a ball winder (see Plate 1). The *drum swift* sometimes referred to as a *wool rice* consists of two drums in a vertical position; the hank is wound around both. A slot in the construction permits adjustment when required. The drums revolve as the hank is wound. See *Squirrel Cage*

Synthetic Dyes Synthetic organic compounds were originally called *aniline* dyes because they derived from coal tar. The first artificial dyestuff was discovered in 1856 by William H. Perkin at the Royal College of Chemistry in London. It was a purple colour and he called it 'mauve'. By 1859 various other colours were discovered by chemists all synthesised from *aniline*. The discovery of such dyes originated in England, quickly followed by Germany which led the world in the technology of dyes for approximately the next fifty years. The early aniline dyes were fugitive (faded fast), later developments of azo compounds (also a derivative of coal tar) made fast colours which were very satisfactory. See *Aniline Dyes*

Synthetic Fibres See *Manmade Fibres*

Table Also called *platform, base* or *stock*. See *Spinning – Learning to Spin*

Tags The name given to clumps of wool encrusted with dung, which have to be discarded in *skirting*.

Tare The actual weight of the container, whether a woolpack, fadge, or bag, in which the wool is placed; this is deducted from the gross weight of the bale.

Tear The ratio of tops to noils after the combing process. *Tearing eight to one* means that out of 3.65kg (8lb) of scoured wool there would be 3.2kg (7lb) of tops to .45kg (1lb) of noil. See *Combing*

Teasel *Dipsacus sylvestris fullonum*, sometimes spelled *teazle* or *teasle*, is a tall thistle. In earlier times, and after careful selection, teasel heads were set into a square or rectangular wooden frame, called a *card* from the Latin *cardar* – tease, comb (or striker). This was used for nap raising. Teasels were also fitted later into the drums of a *gig-mill*, which was a nap-raising machine.

Teasel Crop British teasels, which are grown in Somerset, are considered the best although there are insufficient for the demand, and so teasels are imported from France and Spain. The French teasel tends to be favoured due to its hook formation. The wild teasel, which is a kind of scabious with a prickly head, is not to be confused with the cultivated variety which are known as 'fullers' teasel'; these have a burr (head) comprising of much stronger spines with hooked points. This natural form of raising the nap on woollens has been used for centuries and still has no mechanical competitor. The word *teaseler* can be traced back to 1607. A single mill may require 600,000 teasels in a year.

The seed is sown in April. The root structure of the young plants makes transplanting difficult; the upper portion is therefore cut off with a tool resembling a chisel and called a *teasel-spitter*. The plants are set out in October about 14,000 per acre. By the following spring

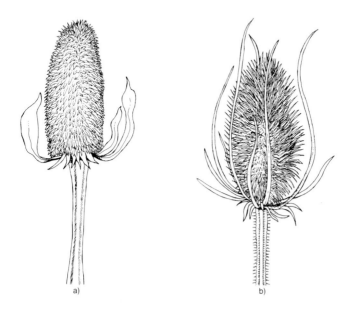

a)   b)

Fig 55 *TEASELS*: a) cultivated; b) wild, unsuitable for the textile trade

they are well established. The plant heads flower in July. When mature, they are cut by hand with a curved knife, the cutter wearing strong protective gloves. An average crop of 200,000 burrs to an acre will occupy one cutter for approximately ten days. The gathered heads are tied together in bundles of fifty and attached to long poles to be dried in the sun and wind. Wet or damp weather causes decay of the heads, therefore if weather is not suitable for outdoor drying, the teasels are brought inside and dried. The teasels are then despatched by road to the mills in packs of 20,000 burrs. The average yield per field is 12 to 17 packs, each of 20,000 burrs.

On reaching the mills, the burrs have their calyxes cut off with scissors, then they are fitted into long narrow frames called *rods*, which are clamped into the cylindrical drums of the *gig mill* assembled in the raising-room. These drums rotate at 120 rpm. The rolls of cloth are unwound and brought into contact with the drums by passing in one direction enabling the teasels to raise the surface of the cloth as they pass in the opposite direction. All UK teasels are graded by length from small, 2.5cm- (1in-) long heads to 10.3cm (4in) – large heads. The strength of the teasel increases with its size. When used on pure wool, cashmere and mohair the heads are neatly cut, drilled through the centre then slid onto spindles. The smaller teasels, which retain a small stem, are those packed tightly into metal rods. Twenty-four rods are fitted into a circular drum. When used on manmade fibres teasels require more frequent replacement.

Teasel Bat See *Teasel – Dipsacus sylvestris fullonum*

Teasel Gig Also spelled *teazle* is used when a rough surface is required on cloth. The cloth is passed between rollers fitted with teasel. This is called a teasel (or teazle) gig. A machine called a moser, which has wire covered rollers, is also used.

Teasing Also called *picking* involves separating the fibres in a lock of fleece. It is done before carding; the purpose is to part the fibres from one another so that when applied to the carders they form a light film.

METHOD: it is advisable to lay the fleece in a warm room or in the sun before teasing to soften the grease and make the fibres easier to separate. Teasing can be a messy task, so it is advisable to wear an apron and to cover the immediate floor area. This task is pleasant to do outdoors. Hold the locks lengthways in one hand and with the other gently pull apart and free the tips and roots into strands sideways (see Plate 52). As the fibres are parted, foreign matter eg lumps, vegetable matter, second cuts, which may not fall out naturally, should be removed. The amount of teasing depends on the quality and type of

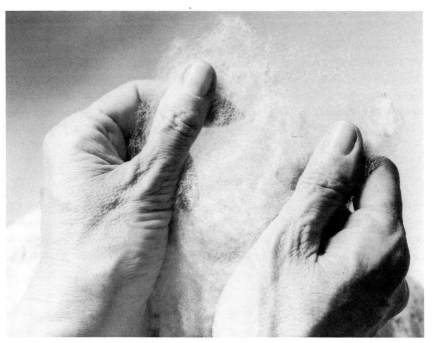

Plate 52 *TEASING*

fleece; some are straightforward to tease, others, the short stapled types, can be more clingy and difficult and require more teasing time spent on them. As teasing progresses, the fibre volume increases as more air is involved. Evenness will not result during this process; this will be produced later by carding. Once all the fibres are separated they are then ready to be carded. *Picking* is also the name given to a movement by students, while learning to spin, when they pull out small quantities of fibre from the rolag rather than using the required *drawing movement*.

Tegwool The fleece from the first clipping of a Down or Mountain yearling sheep (usually more than one and less than two years old).

Tender The term used to describe fleece that is lacking in strength for a variety of causes – lambing, sickness, shock, and lack of food. Whilst tender fleece has to be considered carefully, it is not necessary to discard all tender fleece.

Tension The most critical part of being able to spin well on a wheel is tension; this is the factor that will affect any yarn produced. It is advisable to test the wheel at all different strengths, and to carefully

255

study what happens at each stage and really become conversant with what a particular adjustment will produce. Tension on a wheel affects the traction and the wind-on rate. If the treadling becomes laborious, loosen the tension screw, thus bringing the mother-of-all nearer the wheel. In a spindle whorl with two grooves, the larger diameter is known as the weft groove, resulting in a softer yarn; the smaller diameter (nearest the bobbin) is called the warp groove for producing a yarn with a tighter twist. As the bobbin fills it is necessary to adjust the tension. The tension on the drive band must be increased to compensate for the reduction in the ratio differentials between the bobbin and whorl circumferences. The drive band should therefore be tightened as spinning progresses otherwise fewer tpi (twist per inch) will be inserted, and a softer yarn would result and the end product would lack uniformity.

Tension related to *shrinkage*. Fibres, when attenuated and being drawn into the yarn, still remain extended when winding onto the bobbin, therefore when they are eventually washed they relax, and become somewhat shorter, thereby returning to their original state. This is not true shrinkage; it is a relaxation, the degree varying according to the style of yarn.

Familiarity with the fibres to be spun, and with yarn design, are both closely related to tension. See *Twists Per Inch*.

Tensioning *Tension screw* also referred to as *adjustment screw* and *tension adjustment*: the *mother-of-all* on the spinning wheel, which comprises the maidens, bobbin and flyer, can be adjusted by means of the tension screw. Its purpose is to move the mother-of-all nearer to, or away from the wheel, thus altering the tension on the driving band so that the rate of winding on and the amount of twist in the yarn can be controlled. To draw the yarn in quickly, a tight band is required, which produces a softer twist. To slow down the rate of draw-on and to produce a greater amount of twist, reduce the tension on the driving band, which allows the bobbin to slip when held back by the spun yarn. Many wheels are designed for woollen spinning. If a worsted spin is required, and thus a greater twist, this can sometimes be obtained by altering the diameter of the pulley in relation to that of the flyer by winding yarn round it. Adjustment can also be made on some wheels, to suit a particular spinning requirement, by transferring the drive band onto the smaller diameter spindle whorl.

The placing of the tension screw varies according to the style of wheel. On a Saxony double band type, a wooden threaded screw enters the table at the left hand end and passes as far as the mother-of-all. From under the approximate centre of the mother-of-all, a second piece of wood goes through the table and it is into this that the tension screw passes. Turn the screw one way and the mother-of-all will move nearer the wheel and the tension on the drive band will lessen; turn the opposite way and it will move nearer the end of the table, resulting in a tightening of the drive band.

With an upright castle-type wheel the tension screw, or screws, are usually placed above the mother-of-all (some of these wheels have a double adjustment). On a great wheel the tensioning device will adjust the headpost to loosen or tighten the drive band. With a wheel having an accelerating head, the adjustment will put more or less tension on the second drive belt.

A brakeband added for tension control – single-band wheel, scotch tensioner or *friction band*: the scotch tension wheel has two tensioners. One moves the spinning unit closer to or further away from the driving wheel, and is a screw that opens or closes the hinged plates of the mother-of-all, which in turn tightens or loosens the main drive band. The second, a brakeband, passes round the bobbin groove to a special tension screw; when this screw is adjusted it advances or retards the wind-on rate of the bobbin (the mother-of-all is not moved). The first tension peg is set before spinning whilst the brakeband peg is adjusted when necessary during spinning. Without a brakeband on this style of wheel, the flyer and bobbin would revolve at the same pace and no wind-on of yarn would occur. A point to note about this type of tensioning: it is very sensitive and tension requirement is small; if too taut, both bobbin and flyer will remain stationary. As the bobbin fills, it will start to pull because of the increasing lengths of yarn on the momentarily stationary bobbin, then it becomes heavy and prevents the bobbin being driven faster than the flyer; this in turn makes feed-in of yarn difficult, therefore, increase the driving band tension and reduce tension on the brakeband.
See *Spinning Wheel; Tension*

Tertiary Colours The resulting colours produced by mixing primary and secondary colours.

Tex System See *Yarn Counts*

Textile Fibres These can be divided into several classes.

Class	Example	Elements
ANIMAL	Wool	carbon; hydrogen; oxygen; nitrogen; sulphur (the presence of nitrogen and sulphur adds to the complexity of a wool molecule)
	Silk	carbon; hydrogen; oxygen and nitrogen. Silk, unlike other natural fibres, is not made from growing cells.

VEGETABLE	Cotton	carbon; hydrogen; oxygen (atoms in the molecule of cellulose from which cotton is built up are relatively simple)
MINERAL	Asbestos	
MANMADE FIBRES	Nylon Regenerated fibres Chemically based synthetic fibres	Produced from liquid *polymers* made from *monomers*, simple molecules found in nature, ie air, water and coal. (The fibres are formed by forcing a liquid solution through small holes in a spinneret type nozzle.)

Textile Trade Evolution Until the seventeenth century, the guild system worked well. Spinners, dyers and weavers performed their craftwork within their own homes, using their own tools and materials and then selling their homemade items directly to the consumer. This arrangement was very like today's cottage industries. As happens, again in our time, middlemen spoiled the previous arrangement, and craftspeople sold to them. Not long after this, the middlemen started supplying the workers with materials, so they only used their own tools and skills. It is apparent, by reading the history of this period, that gradually the factory system developed so that eventually all that workers had to provide was their labour.
See *Wool Merchants*

Texture From the Latin *texere = to weave* and *textura = weaving*. A variety of textures can be produced both in the yarns created and in the subsequent knitting, crochet or weaving. Because millspun yarns are produced in such a wide range, many weavers use these, whereas in the past a spinner was required to supply all the weaver's needs. Today, with the renewed interest in natural articles, demand is increasing for the spinner to produce many different yarn types.

The Rising The term used in silk production when the silkworms climb up the straw placed in their trays and anchor themselves with the first thicker strands of silk, before starting to weave their surrounding cocoons. Other materials are also used for this purpose.
See *Sericulture*

Thread From the Anglo-Saxon *thraed*, meaning 'what is twisted'. The word thread is used in a general way to describe fibre types, for example silk, cotton and flax, which are spun and drawn out to various lengths; however, thread is really a cord consisting of two or more yarns or of simple spun threads firmly joined together by twisting.

Threading Hook A tool used with a spinning wheel. There are several designs, some have closed wires with the ends inserted into wooden handles; others have a single wire piece with a small hooked end and also have a handle. A bent piece of wire could be used, or a hairpin opened out with a hook made in the end. Whatever their design, they serve one purpose – to bring the leader (starter) thread out through the orifice. See *Leader*

Thread/Yarn Construction It is not difficult to form a thread. Once some students can do so, they are of the mistaken opinion that is all there is to the task. Thread construction is complex; variation in fleece types, the requirements of different yarn designs, the techniques involved all have to be learned and taken into consideration.
See *Draw-Long; Draw-Short; Fancy Yarn*

Throw A term related to the silk process to describe the twisting or folding, or both, of continuous filament yarns.

Thrown Silk Silk from the cocoons of cultivated silkworms. It is wound and twisted direct from the cocoons. The resulting thread is then sent to the mill with the gum still in it, this is called *hard silk*. The thread is woven in this state and the gum later removed during the finishing process. There are two kinds of thrown silk – *organzine* and *tram*. Organzine has a tight twist and is plied; this is used for the warp. Tram is only lightly twisted and is used for weft. The unit of thrown silk is the *denier*, the weight in grams of 9,000m or the weight in drams of 1,000yd. *Throwsters* is the name given to the people who double the threads to the required thickness.
See *Net Silk*

'Tick' Stained Wool which is badly discoloured by the excreta of sheep ticks or ked.

Tines Also called *broitches*. The teeth of the combs used in the woolcombing process.
See *Combing*

Tip The opposite end of the staple to the root, ie furthest away from the body of the sheep.

Tippy Wool The name given to a fault in the staple where the ends are excessively long and open. These 'ends' can be fragile and may have broken during weathering, or could break during spinning. The whole fleece has the appearance of excessive tips. The dyeing properties would vary considerably from the root portions.

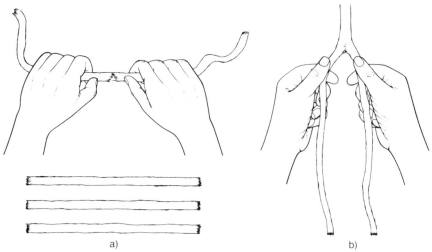

Fig 56 *TOP*: a) lengths of approximately 30.5cm (12in) are gently pulled apart and then spun out of the fold; b) alternatively the 'rope' can be divided lengthwise as many times as may be necessary until the required thickness is obtained. Very little attenuation will be required when spinning. Use a short draw; the resulting spin will be a worsted type

Top Also referred to as *wool top*. A continuous ropelike roving with the individual fibres lying parallel and of the same length; it is produced by the combing process which removes the short fibres (noils). May be produced by a spinner using the combing process or is available commercially prepared. Tops are sometimes a mixture of breeds, so it is not always possible to ascertain the content. There is no waste, as all impurities have been removed by scouring and combing; all that is required of the spinner is to split the tops into narrower portions (*fig 56*). Many fibre types are available as tops. In the preparation of yarn for commercial worsted spinning, the wool is combed, made into a long, continuous, ropelike form, and then wound into a large ball called *top*. When spinning top, the hand-spinner uses a technique called *spinning out of the fold*.
See *Combing; Noils; Topmakers*

Top Knot Wool from the crest or poll of the sheep.

Topmakers The name given to firms which produce only *tops*; the product is exported all over the world.

Topping The addition of colouring matter to produce the desired colour.

Tow Cards Coarser, heavier hand cards suitable for preparing flax, hemp and jute ready to spin; they can also be used for carding coarser hairs and wools. See *Flax; Irish Linen*

Tow Fork A distaff that has prongs to hold the tow flax during spinning. See *Flax*

Tow – Hackling Hackling, as with *scutching*, produces tow during the flax processing. The woody particles have already been removed by *scutching*. Mill processing of flax divides the hackling tow into two groups. The root ends are hackled first (called *root end tow*), and the tow collected. Then the opposite end, the leaf end (called *top end tow*) is hackled and collected separately; this is finer. See *Flax*

Tow-Line The longer fibres of flax separated from the flax tow during *hackling*. Usually arranged on a distaff for control during spinning. See *Distaff; Flax – Linum usitatissimum*

Tow-Manmade Produced in continuous filaments, then cut into staple lengths for spinning.

Tow Yarns Also referred to as *tow linen* is the name given to the yarns made from the broken tendrils of fibres from the main strands which have been broken during flax processing. Not as strong as line so it is advisable to ply. See *Flax*

Tram Silk Is silk that is often used for the weft in weaving; it is obtained from the best cocoons, comprising two or more single threads twisted together lightly. See *Sericulture*

Trash A term used in the cotton industry for all the foreign matter, ie seeds, dirt and leaves, which have to be freed from the tightly packed cotton before it can be blended and turned into *roving*.

Traverse The crisscross method used to wind yarn into a skein or onto a bobbin. It makes the finding of a broken end in unwinding much easier.

Treadle Bar See *Spinning – Learning to Spin*

Treadle Cord See *Spinning – Learning to Spin*

Treadle Rod See *Spinning – Learning to Spin*

Treadle Wheel A spinning wheel with a drive wheel and flyer assembly, worked by the spinner sitting on a chair or stool and operating a foot treadle, which causes the wheel to rotate. This, in turn, drives the flyer assembly by means of a driving band. There are many different styles and types.

Tree Cotton The term used to describe various plants of the *Gossypium* family growing in tropical habitats where they are perennials and reach a great size. In more temperate regions, where there are seasonal frosts, cotton is an annual.

True-to-Type A sheep that embodies the true characteristics peculiar to that particular breed.

Tsatlees Native reeled silks. These may have been carelessly reeled and therefore are faulty and will have to be re-reeled.
See *Cantons; Chinas*

Tuft A bunch of fibres.

Tupping The mating of ewe sheep. Traditionally tupping starts on November 5 each year.

Tupping Marks Marks left on the fleece of a ewe following mating. The underside of the ram is coloured so that the shepherd can see which ewes have been served. The colour is changed after a couple of weeks to indicate which ewes will lamb later. These coloured marks are sometimes difficult to remove.

Tup/Ram Male sheep. The wool on a male sheep is usually longer than that on the female sheep – the *ewe*.

Tussah *Tussar, tusser, tassar* or *tussore* is wild silk from *Antherea pernyi* in Asia, from *Tropoea luna* in the south of North America and from *Antherea mylitta* the giant Indian silkmoth. *Saturniidae* is the family of silkmoths found in many parts of the world. *Tussah*, the term most commonly used for all Asiatic wild silk, is coloured creamy-brown because of the tannin in the leaves on which the silkworm feeds. The cocoons are much larger than those of the domestic silkworm and more difficult to reel, due to the particular gum and construction of the cocoons. The individual filaments are flatter, coarser and stronger than those from *Bombyx mori* and do not join so easily. Boil-off is approximately 15 per cent, which is lower than in cultivated silks. A strong cloth from the fibre is called *tussore* sometimes spelt *tusseh*.
See *Silk Moth*

Tweed *Woollen count* = number of cuts containing 182.9m (200yd) required for 0.45kg (1lb).
For example, nine cut = 8.23m × 182.9m (9 × 200yd) per 0.45kg (1lb). Tweed yarns are always singles.

Twist Once fibres have been attenuated to the required thickness, twist is inserted to add strength and to form the fibres together. The twist can be inserted by a hand spindle, a great wheel or by using a spinning wheel. A clockwise twist is referred to as a Z-twist, and anti-clockwise as an S-Twist. When plying two or more singles together, they should be twisted together in the opposite direction to that used for the original spinning. Plying reduces some of the twist of the singles, therefore this must be compensated for in the initial singles spinning. The amount of twist inserted into a yarn is determined by the end requirement, eg knitting and crochet may require a soft yarn spun using a *long draw*. Weaving may require a high twisted yarn for a smooth cloth showing a clear weave. The yarn type is a result of careful choice of fleece and the spinning technique involved, whether woollen, semi-woollen, worsted or semi-worsted.
See *Draw-Long; Draw-Short; Plying; Twists Per Inch; S-Twist; Z-Twist*

Twisting-Over Usually caused by the hand controlling the fibre supply not working fast enough.

Twisting-Under Often caused by the front hand not controlling the twist build-up.
See *Tension; Tensioning*

Twist Silk Silk suitable for sewing.

Twists Per Inch = TPI. The number of twists imparted into one inch of yarn during a spinning process. As spinning progresses and the bobbin fills, the circumference increases, therefore more spun yarn is required to complete one turn of the bobbin; this results in fewer TPI and a yarn which would become softer; to compensate for this fact, and to maintain a constant twist, it is necessary to adjust the tension at regular intervals during spinning.
THPI = threads per inch
THPC = threads per centimetre

Two-Shear/Toothed The name given to denote the number of clippings, for example, the second clipping makes the ewe two-toothed.

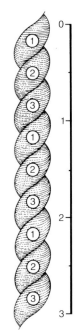

Fig 57 *TWISTS PER INCH* (TPI): enlarged twist showing three twists per inch, on a spun yarn the number of twists would be much greater

U-Flyer
'lyer · Ul
U-Flyer

rspin · Untwisted · Uprights · U-Flyer · Ultimates · U.
h · Untwisted · Uprights · U-Flyer · Ultimates · Under
rspin · Untwisted · Uprights · U-Flyer · Ultimates · U

U

U-Flyer Is sometimes referred to as *flyer*, also as *the guider*. The design of a bobbin and flyer made it possible for the twisting and winding-on to be completed as one operation, unlike the great wheel, which had two separate exercises, ie formation of yarn then feeding the yarn onto the spindle. The purpose of the flyer was to guide the yarn onto the bobbin. The flyer is horseshoe shaped and usually made of wood. The flyer arms should not be too close to the bobbin. The width between the open end of the flyer arms should be about the same measurement, or a little wider, than the length of the bobbin. Each side of the flyer arms are hooks (hecks) for the thread to pass under. Most modern wheels have metal hooks; occasionally one is encountered that has a moveable hook or peg. Sometimes a flyer design may have hooks only on one arm; therefore, as it is necessary for the flyer to be well balanced, the opposite hook free arm may be weighted or require weighting to adjust the balance.

When the hooks are inserted on the upper left hand side (the most usual placing) this indicates Z-twisting, ie the wheel is designed mainly to turn clockwise. When the hooks are found on the upper right hand side, this usually indicates that the wheel was designed to be mainly spun S-twisted, ie anticlockwise. The hooks are arranged so that one flyer arm fills a section of the bobbin, leaving gaps which the opposite arm fills. During spinning, the spinner moves the yarn from hook to hook starting from the hook farthest away, first on one flyer arm, then on the second flyer arm. The hooks should be carefully examined from time to time; wear may occur and then the hooks will require replacing.

The flyer assembly consists of a central metal spindle shaft, which is attached firmly to the centre curve of the flyer, this has a hole at one end (the *orifice*) and usually two holes (the *eyes*), each in line with a

Plate 53 Close-up of U-Flyer and its positioning: a) front maiden; b) back maiden; c) guide hooks; d) flyer; e) eye; f) leather bearing; g) orifice; h) spindle (through bobbin); i) bobbin; j) bobbin whorl; k) spindle whorl; l) tensioner (tension screw); m) mother-of-all; n) and o) drive band. If the drive band loops are almost together, this indicates very little difference in the diameter of the spindle and bobbin whorls, so the winding will be slow. A wider gap between same would indicate a better wind-on and evenly twisted yarn; p) wheel; q) table or bed

Plate 54 *U-FLYER*: a) orifice; b) collar; c) eye; d) flyer; e) hooks or hecks; f) spindle; g) screw thread; h) bobbin; i) bobbin whorl; j) spindle whorl; k) spacer

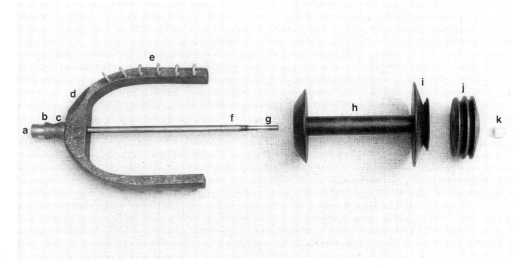

flyer arm. The bobbin, with a curved end that fits the curved shape of the flyer and a whorl attached to the opposite end, is placed onto the central spindle. The spindle whorl has a left hand thread so that the revolutions tighten it during spinning. The spindle whorl has a pulley, and a second pulley is placed on the bobbin whorl, which enables it to be rotated. The bobbin and flyer rotate and because of the differentials in the whorl diameter on the bobbin and spindle, wind-on of yarn takes place. The flyer assembly is usually inserted into leathers, between the front and back maidens. If the flyer does not revolve easily, adjustment may be required on the front maiden to produce alignment. On the Ashford wheel the whorl is part of the flyer.

Flyer-lead, also called *bobbin drag* (eg *scotch tensioner*): if the flyer rotates faster than the bobbin, it wraps the yarn around and onto the bobbin. To cause this to happen on this design of wheel, the bobbin is braked by a band over the bobbin pulley. If necessary to increase the winding-on, the friction on the bobbin should be increased.

Bobbin lead, also called *flyer drag* (eg *double band drive*): if the bobbin rotates faster than the flyer, then the bobbin winds yarn onto itself. The flyer may or may not be braked. The rotation of the flyer is produced by the drag of the yarn on the bobbin.

See *Leonardo da Vinci*

Ultimates Is a name used in relation to flax, jute, etc. The ultimates are the bundles of shorter fibres that are held together by a pectinous gum. The bundles are linked together by lateral fibres at varying places from root to tip, therefore there is often considerable contrast between each bundle of ultimates and the place of separation is not always clearly visible.

See *Flax – Linum usitatissimum*

Underspin The opposite of *overspin*, denotes too little twist inserted into the yarn when spinning. Each yarn should be designed with a purpose in mind, ie what strength is required and the yarn type; the yarn is underspun if it does not meet the design criteria.

Untwisted A term used relating to fibres and filaments from which part or all of the twist has been removed. Also relates to a plied yarn from which plying twist has been removed.

Uprights Also referred to as *bearers*.
See *Spinning – Learning to Spin*

Vat Dyes These are the 'fastest' dyes used. Can be purchased direct from the manufacturer in large quantities. They are insoluble in water. Many colour tones can be mixed by the spinner to whatever shades may be required.
See *Dyes and Dyeing*

Vegetable Fibres Sometimes referred to as *cellulose fibres* (unlike animal fibres, which are protein).
Vegetable fibres fall mainly into three categories:

1 *Bast* (stem) fibres eg flax
2 *Seed* fibres eg cotton
3 *Leaf* fibres eg sisal

Vegetable fibres are cool, strong and durable, but tend to be inelastic. Their high cellulose content resists decay. When spinning, moisture will assist in encouraging and retaining their twist eg *flax*.
See *Cotton; Flax; Hemp; Jute; Nettle; Ramie; Sisal*

Vicuna Sp *Lama Vicugna*: during the Peruvian Neolithic period, the vicuna and guanaco were domesticated. The Incas decreed that vicuna and guanaco should only be chased every four years. The vicuna is the smallest and wildest of the South American camels and is protected by law. It is an endangered species because it has been hunted almost to extinction. It lives in the High Andes in altitudes of 4,900 to 5,800m (16,000 to 19,000ft). Vicunas are small graceful animals, rich cinnamon brown in colour; the fibre is mostly down and is finer and softer than cashmere. The underside is lighter; it has light guard hairs on the chest. There are also llama-alpaca crosses called *huarizo* and *misti*; the llama is one of their descendants. Export is not permitted, it was halted by the Peruvian government in an attempt to build up the dwindling herds. The fibre should be spun as cashmere.
Note: The word vicuna is also used in the trade to describe a yarn made from a mixture of sheep wool and cotton. This has no connection with the animal of this name.

Virgin Wool New, unused raw wool spun for the first time and free from other fibres.

rp and W   *Water Pots · Webby · Whorl · Wiggins · Wild Silk · W*
nd Weft   *ter Pots · Webby · Whorl · Wiggins · Wild Silk · Wille*
rp and W   *Water Pots · Webby · Whorl · Wiggins · Wild Silk · W*

Warp and Weft Sometimes called *Woof*. In weaving, the warp threads are stretched firmly on a loom ready to receive the weft threads, which are then woven through the warp by the means of a shuttle, working in and out of the warp threads. Most Saxony type double band wheels have two flyer pulleys. Traditionally, the one with the smaller diameter was used for spinning the warp yarn, which must be strong, and the larger one was used for the weft yarn, which requires less twist.

WARP YARN SPINNING: the warp yarn should have a very firm twist and should be very even and smooth.

WEFT YARN SPINNING: the spinner can design the yarn suitable for the project without any restrictions.

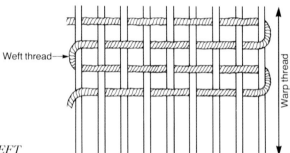

Fig 58 *WARP AND WEFT*

Washed Wool A term related to wool that has been rough washed on the sheep before shearing.

Washing See *Fleece – Scouring*

Wasty Wool A term used in industry to describe wool that is too tangled, weak and short to be spun.

Water Water is used in spinning in the following ways:

a) applied, often with oil, as an emulsion, as a means of controlling the fibres during spinning. A garden spray is a useful container.
b) to reduce static electricity, in particular during the combing process. Combers used to add water to their fibre to increase the weight and thereby their earnings.

See *Dyes and Dyeing; Felting*

Water Pots These were made in a variety of designs and types; their purpose was to hold water to moisten the flax as it was spun. Flax, spun dry, would become a spiky thread with the ends of the fibres protruding, therefore a source of moisture was necessary. In earlier times saliva was used; the thread was either drawn through the mouth or was moistened with the thumb and first finger of the spinning hand. From this practice evolved the use of small pots to contain the necessary water. There were numerous types, made from various materials; some were incorporated in the wheel designs in the table (bench or stock), others were hung by the mother-of-all. Other wheels had an arm with a pot, usually placed in a part of the wheel or the distaff within easy reach.
See *Flax*

Web The film of carded fibres on a handcard, during carding, before forming into a rolag. See *Carding*

Webby Wool that is lacking in strength, often starting to cott with little or no staple formations.

Wheel Alignment Adjustment Bars Some designs of Saxony wheels have wheel alignment adjustment bars, which are placed usually above the table of the wheel. Their purpose is to swivel the driving wheel very slightly, when necessary, to adjust the alignment with the bobbin and flyer groove; on other wheels adjustment is made by the front and back maidens to align the mother-of-all with the wheel.

Wheel Ratio The number of times the spindle or flyer turns, to one turn of the large wheel on a spinning wheel.

Whipped Cotton See *Bowing; Punis*

Whirrie See *Bobbin Holders*

White or Yellow Flax The very best Dutch flax, which is retted in running water and is capable of spinning a very fine yarn.

Whorl Sometimes called a *wharff, whirl* or *wharve*, is the spindle pulley on the spinning wheel. It may be also the weight at the base of a handspindle.

Wiggins The name given to the wool shorn from over the eyes of sheep to enable them to forage.
See *Merino*

Wild Plants Those specially protected by the Wildlife and Country-side Act 1981 (United Kingdom). See end of book for address of Nature Conservancy Council.

Wild Silk Filaments that have been taken from cocoons after the moth has emerged. The filaments are collected, slightly carded, and spun on a wheel or spindle. Cloth made from this has a dull surface. Types of wild silk include: *eri; Mongolian; muga; tussah*

Willeying Machine Wool is often blended. This is done by spreading by hand various parts of a particular mixture on top of one another. Then, oiled to assist the carding process, it is stacked and vertical sections removed as required. The resulting blend is passed through a willeying machine, which opens it out to ensure adequate and improved mixing.

Willow The name given to a machine used in woollen manufacture for opening and disentangling locks of wool, and cleansing them from sand and other loose impurities. The name comes from the willow tree, as this was the wood used in earlier models of the machine.

Willowing Also called *willeying*. Willow sticks were often used to beat the wool on a frame called a *felking board*, the object of the exercise was to open the wool and get rid of the dust.

Winding-On The process which wraps spun yarn onto a spindle (bobbin).

Wool The fibrous coat (covering) of the sheep.

Wool Blind A term used when the wool around a sheep's eyes is excessively long and interferes with its sight.

Wool Brokers Also called *wool broggers*. In early times any surplus of spun yarn or woven cloth could be sold to wool brokers; this aided the families financially. The broker sold the wool on behalf of the growers and bought the wool on behalf of the merchants. As with today, a commission was paid.

Wool Cards Hand cards that have fairly fine teeth suitable for carding wool.

Wool Classification This consists of:
a) bright
b) burry and seedy
c) choice
d) semi

Wool Classing A process requiring a great amount of skill, whereby the whole fleeces are separated into different classes before being baled and sold. This process assists the buyers to make a choice in line with their requirements.

Wool – Clean Wool that has been scoured and has had all the grease and dirt removed, and is sometimes referred to as *scoured wool*.

Woolcombers' Tools See *Combing*

Wool Fibres These belong to the family of proteins – the keratins. The protein keratin is itself composed of the most common chemical elements of carbon, oxygen, nitrogen, hydrogen and sulphur. The outer skin of the sheep, called the *epidermis*, protects the inner layer containing the important glands. The sweat glands open into the skin surface and the sebaceous glands open into the hair follicles. Opening into the follicles are two types of glands, one secretes *potassium salts* of certain fatty acids, and the other secretes fat, which lubricates the growing fibres, protecting them from rain and damage. The wool fibre grows by adding cells that gradually extend outwards. This growth can be retarded if the sheep has had ill-health or a poor diet.

Wool fibres grow from two different kinds of follicles, called primary and secondary. Those growing from the secondary follicles are much finer. The proportion of primary to secondary follicles in a fleece varies from one type of sheep to another. If secondary to primary are greater, eg 4 to 1, the fleece will be coarser; if 20 to 1, for example, then fineness will occur overall. A single wool fibre varies considerably in diameter. It can be as fine as 10 microns (1 micron = 1/25,000in) and as thick as 50 microns. It has been said that there could be from 5,000 to 50,000 wool fibres growing in a square inch of skin surface. When on the animal, wool contains a large quantity of grease that often exceeds the weight of the protein fibre itself. The diameter of sheep wool fibres are often elliptical rather than round.

A sheep's fleece grows coarser with age. Wool can become finer during the winter owing to seasonal and nutritional circumstances. Animal fibres are cellular structures comprising:

Cuticle the skin with overlapping serrations or imbrications pointing towards the tip that enables foreign matter to work its way out of the

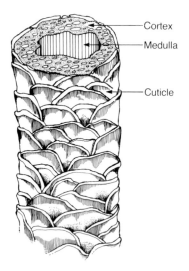

Cortex

Medulla

Cuticle

Fig 59 Enlarged diagram showing the structure of a medullated wool fibre. In a non-medullated fibre the cross section at the top of the diagram would be entirely cortex

fleece. The strength increases with the number of imbrications. Width and length also increases the strength.

Cortex the secondary layer which provides both strength and elasticity; this comprises long spindle-shaped cells forming a coil-like structure that can be stretched and returns to its original shape. In a finer fibre the cortex may form 90 per cent of the fibre mass.

Medulla or pith the central core of oval-shaped cells containing air. Some types may contain more medullar than others; they are not usual in wools finer than 50s quality and are more common below 46s. Kemp wool contains up to 15 per cent of medulla cells.

Medullation is mainly inherited, but can be affected by food and climate. Mountain wools often are medullated. The britch of a Romney fleece may be medullated; the rest of the fleece not.

AIR: air moving through woollen fibres becomes trapped and covers each surface with a thin layer of still air, which acts as an insulator. Air spaces exist because of the crimp in the fibres that prevents the fibres being close together; in these spaces the air becomes trapped.

CRIMP: fine wools often have more crimp; the quality of scales per inch relates to the thickness or thinness of the fibres. There is a greater number of crimps for the fine wools, ie the scales are smaller and overlap more closely, therefore they project more and result in a duller surface. When the scales are farther apart they are larger, the wool has a less crimped appearance and the surface looks smoother and more lustrous. A merino may have 27 to 30 crimps per 2.5cm (1in); a coarser wool only 5 to 7 crimps per 2.5cm (1in).

ELASTICITY: when stretched, wool will quickly recover its original shape. The overlapping scales permit wool to stretch up to 30 per cent when dry and 70 per cent when wet.

HEAT: wool is an insulator; it gives out heat, which warms the air passing through the fibres.

MOISTURE: wool can absorb moisture, in ordinary conditions 15 per cent of its weight. In damp air, however, it can absorb 30 to 50 per cent. Wool can absorb large quantities of moisture and not even feel damp.

STAPLE is sometimes referred to as *locks*. This is a group of fibres (can be thousands) which has grown together and is joined by dirt and natural grease, often at the tips. Staples vary in length and crimp according to the type.

WOOL QUALITY is referred to as its count. The count numbers vary from 28s to 100s to indicate the fibre diameter. The smaller the diameter of the fibre, ie the finer the wool, the greater the quantity of yarn that can be spun from a given weight.

Fine fibres in domestic sheep have an average diameter of 20 microns. Medium fibres on average equal 40 microns; hairy fibres start at approximately 80 microns (a micron is one thousandth of a mm).
See *Keratin; Loft; Lustre Wools; Plasticity; Quality; Strength; Style*

Wool Grease Also referred to as *woolfat* and *wool wax*. The natural off-white colour of the wool is made yellow by a greasy substance called *yolk*, deposited on the fibres. It is secreted from two tiny glands attached to the wool roots. The grease glands produce a wax secretion called *lanolin* and the sweat glands produce a watery solution called *suint*. The wax is comprised of a mixture of both types of secretions. The Fine wool breeds produce more wax from their sebaceous glands than the Longwool breeds; it is a lipid material and insoluble in water.

Wool – History Wool is part of Britain's history and heritage.
Relevant dates related to development
Wool was woven into cloth in England in the Bronze Age which began around 1900 BC.
In various places in the world, primitive man had domesticated sheep in 10,000 BC. Long before 10,000 BC, however, cloth was being spun and woven by the tribes in Northern Europe. Sheep were milked and this continues in various parts of the world today.
Finger spinning was practised at first; also weaving, which was done on a primitive upright loom comprising a weighted beam.
When the Romans landed in Britain in 55 BC, they found that the

Britons had developed a wool industry which the Roman masters encouraged them to continue.

The Saxon invasions of England that began in the fifth century nearly destroyed the industry.

When the Normans arrived in 1066, sheep breeding began to increase, and the industry expanded.

By the twelfth century, wool had become England's greatest national asset, the greatest wealth coming from the export of raw wool. Wool at this time mainly came from manors and abbey lands; monasteries also raised sheep. Main exporting of raw wool was to the German principalities, Italian states, and the Low Countries.

Guilds of weavers had existed for many years to guarantee work for experienced craftsmen. Due to the growing importance of the wool trade, a body was founded called *The Staple*, a depot to which, by law, raw wool for sale abroad had to be sent. The export tax levied by the king was collected there. The original Staple was located in Flanders, an important textile location, but later it was withdrawn to England where several ports became Staple towns.

The wool trade reached a peak of production in the thirteenth century then rapidly declined, due to the political situation.

In 1331, King Edward III encouraged Flemish master weavers to settle in Britain and the export trade of raw wool gradually recovered.

In 1590 knitting schools for children were started.

England's involvement and dependence on wool increased under Elizabeth (1558–1603); 80 per cent of exports at this time were wool goods.

1619 saw the start of worsted cloth making, with a subsidy obtained from the government by Edward Whalley of Norwich. From early days worsted had been made mainly in East Anglia, originally at Worstead, near Norwich, where it was commonly known as *Norwich stuffe*.

In the sixteenth century *Huguenot weavers*, much persecuted in France, came to England to seek refuge and brought their skills with them.

By 1770, cloth manufacture had spread to Leeds, Bradford, Halifax, Huddersfield and Wakefield.

The Industrial Revolution, 1750–1850, caused a great upheaval throughout Britain. Machines were invented by Arkwright, Compton, Hargreaves and Kay, probably stemming from the cotton industry in Lancashire; the object was to increase the output and processes of spinning and weaving. Some areas rebelled against mechanisation, others, such as Yorkshire, Scotland and the West Country, were more receptive.

See *Botany Wool; Flannel Act; Wool Brokers; Woolpack; Woolsack, The; Wool Staple*

Wool in the Grease Otherwise known as greasy wool is wool as it comes off the sheep's back, including dirt and foreign matter. The latter can constitute from 30 to 60 per cent.

Woollen Industry Wool is, without any doubt, the most amazing of all fibres. In British history, associations with the woollen textile industry date from the twelfth to the nineteenth century when it became somewhat overshadowed by the cotton industry. Research has not shown just how early woollen cloth was made in Britain; however, indications have been found dating back to the Iron Age.
The industry is divided into three separate divisions:
a) the fine woollen trade – using short staple fibres.
b) the low woollen trade – using waste.
c) the worsted trade – using the longer stapled fibres.

Woollen Spinning Wool is the easiest fibre for the beginner to use when learning to spin as it is crimped, scaly and rough, therefore it hooks together when twisted, unlike cotton and silk, ie smooth fibres that slide against one another. In woollen spinning the fibres are carded, not combed, therefore the fibres are not straight and aligned, but have a high proportion of air in the wool; the resulting yarn is soft and bulky. The cloth manufactured from it is warm and has an ill-defined weave, often with a hairy surface. The wool length is often of secondary importance to fineness, eg in worsted spinning, on the whole a finer wool can be spun into a finer yarn even if it may be shorter than some others. See *Draw-Long*

Woollen Yarn Yarns spun from fibres that are not parallel.

Woolmark The woolmark is the International Wool Secretariat's symbol for products made from pure new wool produced to its quality specifications, Woolmark products have to be made from new (virgin) wool, although five per cent of other fibres may be added for decoration.

Wool Merchants Also called *clothiers*. Before the Industrial Revolution, spinning was done at home and the yarn was then collected by the wool merchants. Eventually factories developed for the spinners to work in. Not all parts of the country were affected, only those that relied on the wool merchants to supply them with the wool. Farmers in various parts of the country who had sheep for their raw materials retained their independence for longer. However, finally they too banded together and were, in fact, the start of the wealthy woollen merchants of Bradford. At this stage machinery was not used, simply a large number of great wheels in factories.
See *Textile Trade Evolution*

Wool – New Also called *pure wool*: wool yarn with this label means it has been made from fibres that have come straight from the sheep.

Woolpack In earlier times people who worked with wool in Britain obtained their material in the following ways:

a) from the manufacturers who bought direct from the larger farmer
b) from the staplers who purchased the wool by travelling around from farm to farm
c) direct from the farmer
d) in the market place

A woolpack weighed 108.86kg (240lb). Today a woolpack is the jute container for wool measuring 1.37m × 0.69m (4ft 6in × 2ft 3in).

Wool – Poor *Terms used in industry:*
Cotty   – matted
Frowsy   – dull in appearance
Kempy   – thick fibres (kemp), which do not take dye well and can be white, red and brown in colour
Tender   – breaks easily
Tippy   – has brittle dry tips
Wasty   – weak, short, tangled wool that cannot be used.

Wool – Pulled Taken from a dead animal; it will have roots on the fibres so is best avoided.

Wool – Raw Is called *fleece in the grease*. It has simply been shorn from the sheep.

Woolsack, The In earlier times, in cases when laws regulating the export of sheep and wool were broken, the culprit was tried by a judge seated on a woolsack, just as today the Lord Chancellor sits on the Woolsack in the House of Lords.

Wool Slip The name given to a wool break in the fleece of a sheep in winter.

Wool Sorter It is the wool sorter's job, after classing, to avoid any variation in each single fleece where possible.

Wool Sorting The grading of fleeces into lots, each containing only one quality. Usually carried out by the wool user.

Wool Staple A town, during the Middle Ages, where, by law, the raw wool was sent for export and where the sales took place. Export tax was also collected there.

Wool Stapler The name given to a wool supplier.

Wool Terminology

CLEAN AND OPEN	a clean, unclotted, non-matted fleece, having no stains or vegetable matter
COLOUR	any discoloration in a white fleece. Normal dirt and grease will wash out. Deep stains may occur because of tupping marks, dip stains, etc, which can be difficult, or impossible, to remove.
COLOURED FLEECES	any fleece, other than white, eg black, brown, grey and colour mixtures
CRIMP	the wavy lines in the staple; they are variable according to type
COUNT	the quality range; the higher the numbering, the finer the wool. The count refers to the number of 560yd hanks available from 1lb of wool.
LENGTH	refers to the staple length, which is measured from root to tip when unstretched
SOUNDNESS	overall quality with little waste.

Wool Wheel See *Great Wheel*

Wool Winding The term used during shearing of sheep when the fleece are folded in a particular form. See *Swifts*

Worsted Count The number of 560yd that weigh 1lb. The International Organisation for Standardisation has recommended the use of the tex system for describing the linear density of all textile yarns. The tex unit is the weight in grams of 1km of yarn thus,

$$\text{tex} = \frac{885.8}{\text{worsted count.}}$$

If the spinner has to spin from skeins each of 560yd length to equal 0.45kg (1lb) weight, then the size or count is 4s. If the yarn is fine it will naturally weigh less and more skeins will result, therefore six skeins would be written as 6s, ie six skeins weighing in total 0.45kg (1lb). If the six skeins are then plied as 2-ply (which will result in three skeins of 2-ply) it will still weigh the original 0.45kg (1lb) even though it is now half the original yardage. The ply will be given in the count, usually in front of the size number of the singles, so this yarn will now be described as 2/6s, occasionally reversed as 6s/2.

A combing is classified according to its quality number, which is intended to indicate the highest count to which it can be spun; wool-classers tend to relate this to the degree of fineness of the fibre.

Worsteds Fabrics made from yarns in which the long wool fibres lie parallel.

Worsted Spinning Prepare the fibres by combing. True worsted requires processed tops prepared by using woolcombs, pad and diz. Semi-worsted is spun with combed aligned locks, using a short drafting action. With worsted spinning there is no twist between the hands.

METHOD: reversed hands may be used, if more comfortable to the spinner.

If using a spinning wheel, attach the fibre supply by holding the leader yarn, which is joined to the bobbin in the usual way, alongside the staple and catch a few fibres to join. Using the right hand, grip the

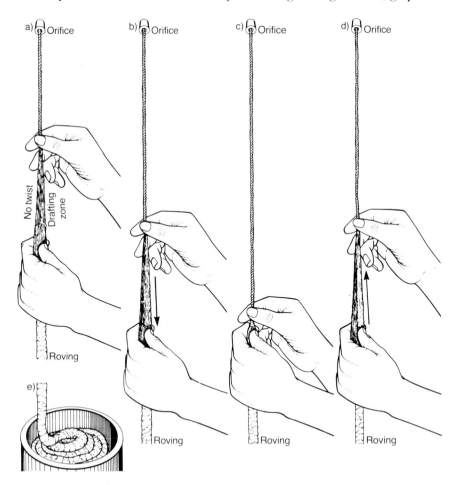

Fig 60 True *WORSTED SPINNING*

yarn with the thumb and index finger, never permitting the twist to move to the drafting area; the left hand should be placed firmly about 5cm (2in) up the roving (*fig 60a*). With the left hand, draft the fibres away from the right hand (some spinners prefer to draft with the right hand away from the left) – only a short distance – or they will part from one another because there is no twist at this stage to hold them together. They can only be drafted to their length and the drafting triangle will be small. Move the right fingers with a sliding action towards the left hand; this not only smooths the yarn but, by doing so, increases the lustre of the yarn. The twist follows behind the right hand, which does not leave the yarn being formed. No twist should be permitted to enter the drafting zone (*fig 60b*). When the right hand reaches the left hand (*fig 60c*), relieve pressure with the left hand on the fibre supply and draft forward with the right hand (*fig 60d*), then repeat (b) and (c). Be constant in the amount of fibre drafted each time and in the drafting zone and the twists per inch. Continue in this way, holding the twist back with the right hand, and when the fibres are drafted impart twist. Throughout, the treadling should be slow and at an even pace. Due to their relatively high twist, worsted singles can be rather unstable; worsted yarns are nearly always plied, which re-aligns them into their parallel state showing their lustre to the best advantage. The fibre supply (roving) hangs down and is coiled into a container (*fig 60e*).

Worsted Yarn Also called *comb yarn* (and *combing wools* to distinguish them from *clothing wools*, which are those used for woollens). The name derived from Worstead in Norfolk, England, where it was first manufactured. Fibres that are considered the best for worsted yarn have comparatively straight fibres, are regular in staple, long in relation to fineness, with a good lustre, sound and of good colour.

Worsted yarn is spun from wool fibres which have been combed not carded, to remove the long fibres from the short ones. The combed fibres are of uniform length and parallel to one another. They are made into a sliver then wound into a ball called *top*. The resulting spun yarn is strong, smooth, cool and with a good lustre. Unlike woollen yarn, it is almost non-elastic. The woven material made from the worsted yarn has a well defined close weave with a smooth surface, and is lightweight.

Not all worsted yarns are prepared by the combing process; many carpet yarns are carded only.

The short fibres remaining after combing are sometimes carded for a woollen yarn.

See *Combing; Worsted Count; Worsted Spinning*

Yarn · Y
n · Yiel
Yarn · Y

Yucatan Sisal · Yucca · Z-Twist · Zuni and Hopi · Yak
catan Sisal · Yucca · Z-Twist · Zuni and Hopi · Yak · Y
Yucatan Sisal · Yucca · Z-Twist · Zuni and Hopi · Yak

YZ

Yak *Poephagus* or *Bos grunniens* is native to Central Asia. The wild Tibetan yak has long curved horns and long black or brownish/black hair on the chest, legs, flank and tail, growing in a wave function to the ground. The animals are large and heavy. The domestic yak is similar to the wild yak apart from its colouring, which varies from white and grey to shades of brown, black and occasionally red. There is an undercoat of down/wool fibres amidst the hair. The down is nearly as fine as cashmere, and the wool content is comparable to a coarse sheep's wool.

To spin hair: dampen with oil before spinning. The hair is bristly, so put in sufficient twist; it is overtwisted if it starts to kink. Spin the down as cashmere. Unspun yak hair is attractive when used as a weft for weaving. Yak hair is made into rope and some is woven into cloth.

Yarn A collective noun relating to a continuous length of fibres, usually singles, which have been joined by twisting together as a result of a spinning process.

Yarn Counts Are also referred to as *count of yarn, yarn number, yarn linear density*. Yarns, produced to a definite yardage and to a given weight, have figures to denote this; they are called the yarn counts. In industry, introduction of the *tex* system that uses the same calculations for all systems has proved far simpler than previous methods; however, the hand textile trade still uses the following in many cases:

COTTON	The number of hanks or skeins each containing 840yd that equal 1lb.
SILK-DENIER SYSTEM	Used to determine the silk count and also manmade extruded yarns. Based on a fixed yarn length to a variable weight. Denier count, the weight in grams per 9,000m.
LINEN	The count in number of *leas* (*hank*) containing 300yd in 1lb.
RAW SILK	The count in the number of hanks or skeins each 1,000yd long in 1oz.
SPUN SILK	The single yarn count is based on that for *cotton*. For plied spun silk, the number of threads is written after the actual yarn count eg 60/2s = 60 counts ie 60 hanks to 1lb weight, the yarn comprised of two finer count single threads.
THROWN SILK	A number is used to denote how many singles have been used to produce the thread, ie 2-thread, 3-thread, etc.

arn · Yield · Yogis · Yolk · Yucatan Sisal · Yucca · Z-Twist · Zuni and Hopi · Yak · Y
· Yield · Yogis · Yolk · Yucatan Sisal · Yucca · Z-Twist · Zuni and Hopi · Yak · Ya
arn · Yield · Yogis · Yolk · Yucatan Sisal · Yucca · Z-Twist · Zuni and Hopi · Yak · Y

WOOL – WORSTED	The number of 560yd hanks in 1lb.
WOOLLEN YARN	Varies according to the different parts of the British Isles, viz:
	Galashiels: the number of 300yd cuts (or hanks) in 24oz.
	Sutherland: the number of 200yd hanks per lb.
	West of England: the number of 320yd *snaps* (or hanks) per lb.
	Yorkshire: the number of 256yd hanks per lb.
TEX	An international system to indicate the weight in grams of 1km (1,000m) of yarn; the higher the number, the thicker the yarn. With earlier systems the indication was the reverse, ie the higher the number, the finer the yarn. In the *tex* system a yarn numbered 11 *tex* means that it measures 1km and weighs 11g, the yarn count is followed by the word 'tex'. The word 'plied' is not used in this system, it is referred to as 'folded'.
	In the information, the direction of the twist is also given on the labelled yarns.

Yarn Design Planning, preparation and practicabilities are all involved in yarn design.

A spinner, to be really proficient, should be able to meet almost any demands made for a particular design. Vast ranges of fibres, both natural and manmade, are available to today's spinners, who also have techniques and methods to fulfil their design needs. The need to be conversant with all fibre types and preparation methods is, in itself, a stimulating element to yarn design. The ability to produce a yarn to a particular requirement demands that the spinner should choose the right fibre, prepare it correctly (for example, blending of colours) and then spin the required design. True yarn design must be controlled throughout. To arrive at a product by chance is not yarn design, as it is unlikely that the same design could be produced again.

Possibly learner spinners start on yarn design unknowingly, before they can even spin correctly. Early spinning mistakes may be comparable, in some cases, to the techniques of producing novelty yarns (for example, the forming of slubs).

There are many types of novelty yarns, for example: *boucle; corkscrew; flake; flocked; loop* or *curl; knop* or *knot; ratine; seed* or *splash; slub; snarl*, and others.

See *Yarn – Size*

Yarns – Fancy Plied A variety of yarn designs can be created by plying singles using different types of twist; for example, an S-twisted yarn plus a Z-twisted yarn plus S-twisted – the differences that occur with looseness or tightness can produce an interesting yarn. In plying, the characteristics alter one to another, which can produce an attractive yarn. When plying yarns of differing types make sure that they have a) the same shrinkage rate and b) comparable elasticity and durability. Plying different colours together can look very effective. If the spinner intends to design many yarns and ply them, it is a good practice to keep a notebook to record all details of the fibre, spinning techniques used, etc, to produce a particular yarn, and keep a small sample also in the notebook. This will enable any successful designs to be repeated.

Yarn – Size To produce a yarn to a particular size often requires experimentation, taking into consideration fleece type, preparation and spinning methods. When the desired size is obtained, tape a piece to the wheel table or where it can easily be seen. If the yarn is to be eventually plied, test for this by allowing a piece to double back on itself. Allow for the loss of twist that will occur in each single during plying (which can be as much as half in some cases); compensate for this loss in the original spinning. Washing can alter a yarn by increasing the bulk.
YARN – FINE: as with yarn size, test first with a trial piece. Carefully choose the fleece and type of spin.
YARN – THICK: a great wheel can be used, or a spinning wheel which has a large orifice. A firm twist will be required to produce a good clear yarn.

Yield After the removal of vegetation and natural grease by scouring, the wool fibre remaining is referred to as the yield. The non-wool content of the fleece may be high, accounting possibly for the bulk of the total weight, and therefore its poor value; in some cases the wool content may be as low as 25 per cent. The yields vary from season to season. A low yield may also indicate that the fleece could be a problem to handle. Before scouring, the yield throughout a fleece is considerable due to the content of wax, suint and dirt varying; the yield at the shoulder is higher than the side for example.

Yogis In India these ascetics attributed to a person reasons for spinning, to his/her level of awareness.
a) the lowest level was spinning yarn to raise money by selling it
b) the next level, spin to weave
c) the level following b) to spin to give away their yarn to the poor
d) the highest level of all was spinning as meditation.

Yolk The sebaceous glands (two tiny glands attached to the wool roots) of the sheep open into the hair follicles and secrete the wool grease (which is actually wax) which combines with *suint* from the sweat glands. The resulting combination is called *yolk*. The quantity of yolk in a fleece may vary from approximately 15 to 50 per cent of the greasy waste; this helps to keep the fleece in good condition. The grease is insoluble in water, so must be removed by extraction or emulsification. The suint is soluble in water, as it consists mainly of potassium salts of various fatty acids. The wax, grease or fat, a byproduct of the scouring, is used in the manufacture of various pharmaceutical preparations including lanolin, ointments, also soap, etc. It is, however, unusual in Great Britain to recover potassium salts as a byproduct. The suint is used as a scouring agent. Due to its natural cleansing properties it is capable of cutting down the quantities used, or of removing the need to use soap that would otherwise have been necessary.

Yolk Stain Stain in the fleece caused by pigment from the yolk.

Yucatan Sisal A product of agave fibres. The fibre is scraped from the inside of the leaves and is golden in colour. Also referred to as *sisal*.

Yucca *Yucca filamentosa*: a form of sisal. The 6.1m (20ft) stem is known as *Adam's needle* and the fibre-bearing fronds as *Eve's thread*.

Yucca *Yucca baccata*: the soapweed commonly seen in the South West of America. The Navajo Indians used to wash their yarn in yucca suds made from the yucca root; it was an excellent cleanser. Today it is found in the warmer areas of the USA and is excellent for washing hair and wool.

Z-Twist Yarns spun clockwise.

Zuni and Hopi Are American Indians who have pursued fibre art for untold generations. The *Hopi* are very old, archaeologically speaking; a peaceful clannish group who chose to withdraw rather than war with invaders. They are marvellous weavers. The Navajo were latecomers, more aggressive and warlike, but greater artists.

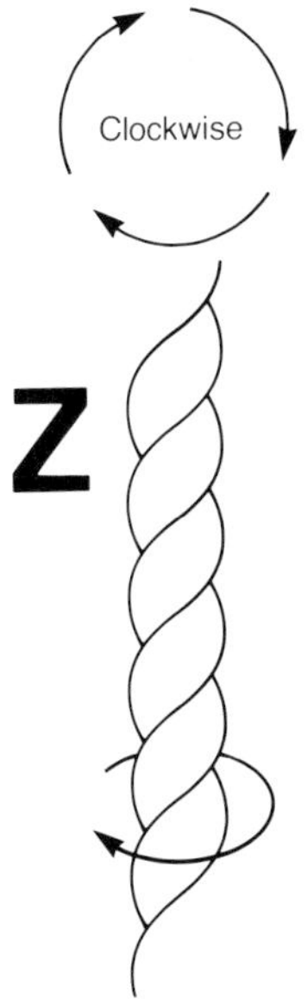

Fig 61 Single Z-spun yarn

Alexander, Peter and Hudson, Robert F. (Second Edition by Earand Christopher), *Wool, its Chemistry and Physics* (Chapman & Hall Ltd, 1954)

Amos, Alden and Druding, Susan, *A Hundred and One Questions for Spinners* (Straw Into Gold Editions, 1978)

Aspin, Chris, *The Cotton Industry: Shire Album 63* (Shire Publications Ltd, 1981)

Aspin, Chris, *The Woollen Industry: Shire Album 81* (Shire Publications Ltd, 1982)

Baines, Patricia, *Spinning Wheels, Spinners & Spinning* (B. T. Batsford Ltd, 1977)

Bowen, Godfrey, *Wool Away* (Whitcombe & Tombs Ltd, 1955; Reprint Van Nostrand Reinhold Co, 1974)

British Wool Marketing Board, *British Sheep Breeds*

British Wool Marketing Board, *Wool Grade Specifications*

Brown, Rachel, *The Weaving, Spinning & Dyeing Book* (Routledge & Kegan Paul Ltd, 1979)

Burrill, Jo, *Spinning on the Wheel*, Dryad Leaflet 532 (Dryad Press, 1981)

Chadwick, Eileen, *The Craft of Handspinning* (B. T. Batsford Ltd, 1980)

Crockett, Candace, *The Complete Spinning Book* (Watson-Guptill Publications, 1977)

Crowfoot, M. Grace, *Methods of Handspinning in Egypt and Sudan* (Bankfield Museum; Produced by Ruth Bean, Bedford, 1974)

Dalby, Gill and Christmas, Liz, *Spinning and Dyeing* (David & Charles, 1984)

Davenport, G. Elsie, *Your Handspinning* (Select Books, 1953)

Davenport, G. Elsie, *Your Yarn Dyeing* (Select Books, 1953)

Dixon, Margaret, *The Wool Book* (Hamlyn, 1979); *Wool Spinning*, Dryad Leaflet 526 (Dryad Press, 1978)

Dyer, Anne, *Dyes from Natural Sources* (G. Bell & Sons Ltd, 1976)

Fannin, A., *Handspinning* (Van Nostrand Reinhold, 1981)

Farnfield, C. A. and Alvey, P. J., eds, *Textile, Terms & Definitions* (The Textile Institute, 1975, 7th Edn)

Gaddum, H. T., *Silk* (H. T. Gaddum & Co. Ltd, 1948)

Grasett, K., *Complete Guide to Hand Spinning*, Vols 1, 2 and 3 (London School of Weaving, 1930)

Hills, R. L., *Cotton Spinning* (The North Western Museum of Science & Industry, 1981 Edn)

Hochberg, Bette, *Fibre Facts* (Bette Hochberg, USA, 1981)

—— *Handspindles* (Bette & Bernard Hochberg, USA, 1977)

—— *Handspinners Handbook* (Bette & Bernard Hochberg, USA, 1976)

—— *Spin Span Spun* (Bette Hochberg, USA, 1979)

BIBLIOGRAPHY

Jackson, Constance and Plowman, Judith, *The Woolcraft Book* (Collins 1980)

Kilbride, Thomas, *Spinning and Weaving at Home* (Thorsons Publishers, 1980)

Kolander, Cheryl, *A Silk Worker's Notebook* (Interweave Press, Inc, 1979)

Kroll, Carol, *The Whole Craft of Spinning* (Dover Publications, 1981)

Leadbeater, Eliza, *Handspinning* (Cassell Ltd, 1976)

Leadbeater, Eliza, *Spinning and Spinning Wheels: Shire Album 43* (Shire Publications Ltd, 1979)

Mercer, John, *The Spinners Workshop* (Prism Press, 1978)

Morton, W. E. and Wray, G. R., *An Introduction to the Study of Spinning* (Longmans Green & Co. Ltd, 1962 Edn)

Onions, W. J., *Wool* (Ernest Benn, 1962)

Pauli, Karen, *The Care and Feeding of Spinning Wheels* (Interweave Press, 1981)

Reichard, Gladys A., *Navajo Shepherd and Weaver* (J. J. Augustin, New York City, 1936)

Rippengal, Joan, *How to Dye in Your Kitchen* (Joan Rippengal, 1980)

Ross, Mabel, *The Essentials of Handspinning* (Mabel Ross, 1980)

Ross, Mabel, *The Essentials of Yarn Design for Handspinners* (Mabel Ross, 1983)

Ryder, Michael, *Sheep and Wool* (White Rose II, 23 Swanston Place, Edinburgh, 1978)

Stepp, Ann, *A Silkworm is Born* (Sterling Publishing Co., New York, 1972)

Sutton, Ann, Collinwood, Peter and Hubbard St. Aubyn, Geraldine, *The Craft of the Weaver* (British Broadcasting Corporation, 1982)

Teal, Peter, *Hand Woolcombing & Spinning* (Blandford Press, 1976)

Turner, Katy, *The Legacy of the Great Wheel* (Select Books, 1980)

Vale, E., *The World of Cotton* (R. Hale, 1951)

Wickens, M. Hetty, *Vegetable or Natural Dyeing in Wool*, Dryad Leaflet 525 (Dryad Press, 1978)

The Book of Wool, Issued by The Department of Education, International Wool Secretariat

· ACKNOWLEDGEMENTS ·

My sincere thanks and appreciation to the following:

Margaret Annand of Mea Crafts for teaching me the craft of spinning;

Richard and Elizabeth Ashford of Ashford Handicrafts for all their advice and support and for permitting use of material from their spinning booklet.

Paul Baldesare – *photographer* for permission to use the photographs of the disabled and spinning; Ray Banks, *photographer* who did the photography for this book other than those specially acknowledged.

Fran Benton who showed me how to spin mawata.

Ernest Benn Ltd, the original publishers of *Wool* by W. J. Onions, used as a reference for fellmongering details and terms related to rags and shoddies.

British Man-Made Fibres Federation for all their information; British Wool Marketing Board for the useful literature, advice and information especially relating to terms used in the woollen and worsted trades.

Jean R. Case for all her advice, literature and samples of silk; City of Bradford Metropolitan Council, Mr R. K. McHugh, Industrial Museum for his help in connection with the Woolcombing entry and permission to use photographs on pages 47–9 and 196, Gillian Cole for designing the spinning clothes (other than in the great wheel photograph) and Betty Edwards for making them.

The Late Peter Gaddum for his advice on silk; Robert Gooden of the Lullington Silk Farm for his advice.

Gregory, Prentis & Green Ltd for all their help.

Nigel C. Herring of Bankfield Museum for permission to reproduce two illustrations from Ling Roth's *Hand Woolcombing* on pages 44–5.

Chris Hughes for sharing her spinning skills, and for proofreading the manuscript.

Photographer Joan Jones for providing the group project photograph on page 144; J. B. Kinnear of The Textile Institute for granting permission to reproduce the Table Classification of Textile Fibres on page 40). Joan Lawley, Tynsell Handspinners, for supplying the photographs on pages 51 and 117 and for her advice and help; Bette and John Ransome for designing the *Capella* great wheel on page 142, hand distaff page 73 and niddy noddy page 175 and Bette, for supplying information; Dr M. L. Ryder for his advice and books, especially *Sheep and Wool for Handicraft Workers*, used in the research of this book; Paula Simmons on behalf of Patrick Green Carders for permission to use their drawing of a carding machine.

Tina Stubbs and Vera Meadows for typing the manuscript; The Irish Linen Guild for permission to use material from the guild leaflets, and for all their help; Trustees of The Science Museum (London) for permission to use the photographs on pages 36, 37, 57, 160, 216, 221, 222, 234; Katy Turner who supplied me with valuable information and also granted permission to draw The Bat Head from her photograph; Westbrook Lanolin Co. for information relating to the extraction and manufacture of lanolin.

A special mention to the following authors whose books on the subject of spinning taught me so much in my earlier days: Patrica Baines; Eileen Chadwick; Candace Crockett; Bette Hochberg; Eliza Leadbeater; Peter Teal; Katy Turner.

SPINNING WHEELS AND EQUIPMENT

Australia: The Craft Warehouse, 30 Guess Avenue, Arncliffe, NSW 2205

Austria: Web Wollzentrum, A – 1010 Wien, Habsburgergasse 9

Belgium: Artisans, M. Foucart, Boul. Paul Janson 11 – 13, 6000 Charleroi

Canada: Treenway Crafts, 3841 Duke Road, RR1, Victoria, BC, V8X 3W9

Denmark: Spindegrej Struer, Venogade 3, DK 7600 Struer

Falkland Islands: Spinning and Weaving Guild, PO Box 1255, Stanley

Finland: Finn Aimo, 5470 Volizoki, Kaulis

France: Celle Bernheim et Fils, 33 Rue des Jeuneurs, Paris

West Germany: Friedrich Traub KG, D-7065 Winterbach, Schorndorfer Str BE 18

Greenland: Lief Ipsen, PO Box 243, DK 3911 Holsteinsborg

Hong Kong: Mr David Epstein, 11th Floor Sincere Insurance Building, 4–6 Hennessy Road, Hong Kong

Ireland: Craftspun Yarns Ltd, Johnston, Naas, County Kildare

Japan: Ananda Co. Ltd, 80 Jyomyo-Ji, Kamakura City, Japan 248

Republic of Korea: Haelim Sangsa, CPO Box 9716, Seoul

Netherlands: M and M Nederland, G Borgesiusstraat 27, 7391 V.A. Twello

New Zealand: Ashford Handicrafts, PO Box 474, Ashburton, Canterbury, South Island

Norway: Spinninger, Boks 36, 1362 Billingstad

Papua New Guinea: Eastern Highland Cultural Centre, c/o Ms Anne Montgomery, PO Box 37, Kainantu

South Africa: R. A. Campbell Marketing, Rolfes House, 6 Dorman Street, PO Box 6919, Gardens 8001, Cape Town

Spain: Indigo Estudio Textil Churruca, 19–1 Est Izoda, Madrid 4

Sweden: Bellis Hemslojd, PO Box 4046, 5–250–04 Helsingborg

Switzerland: Spinnstube, Schimied en Gasse 6, 2502 Biel

United Kingdom: Fibrecrafts, Style Cottage, Lower Eashing, Nr Godalming, Surrey, GU7 2QD
All requirements for spinning

Haldane & Co (Woodturners) Ltd, Gateside, Cupar, Fyfe KY14 7ST, Scotland
Spinning wheel makers and stockists of spinning equipment

Little London Spinners, Unit 8, Home Farm Rural Industries, East Tytherley Road, Lockerley, Romsey, Hampshire, SO5 51 0JT
All requirements for spinning

STOCKISTS

Spinning Wood, 'Hazeldene', 77 Comptons Lane, Horsham, West Sussex RH13 5NS
Wood turner specialising in spinning wheels and accessories

Suffolk Herbs, John and Caroline Stevens, Sawyers Farm, Little Cornard, Sudbury, Suffolk
Seed specialists, sae for catalogue

The Textile Bookshop, Tynwald Mills, St John's, Isle of Man

Tynsell Handspinners, 3 Chapel Brow, Tintwistle, Hyde, Cheshire SK4 7LB
All requirements for spinning, including books, wool hackles and combs and flax tools

United States of America: Textile Artists Supply, 3006 San Pablo Avenue, Berkeley, CA 94702

Fallbrook House, RD 2, Box 17, Troy, PA 16947
Silk Fibres

United Kingdom
British Wool Marketing Board, Oak Mills, Station Road, Clayton, Bradford, West Yorkshire, BD14 6JD

Dylon International Ltd, Worsley Bridge Road, Lower Sydenham, London, SE26 5HD

International Wool Secretariat, 6, Carlton Gardens, London, SW1

Kemtex Services Ltd, Textile Consultants, Dyestuffs & Chemicals Supplier, Victoria Works, Wilton Street, Denton, Manchester, M34 3ND

Nature Conservancy Council, Northminster House, Peterborough, Cambridgeshire, PE1 1UA

The Rare Breeds Survival Trust Ltd, 4th Street, National Agricultural Centre, Kenilworth, Warwickshire, CV8 2L6